U0095147

品鉴英语句子之美

——学地道英语　译华夏文章

刘士聪　编著

南开大学出版社

天　津

图书在版编目(CIP)数据

品鉴英语句子之美 ：学地道英语，译华夏文章 / 刘
士聪编著. —天津 ：南开大学出版社，2024.4
ISBN 978-7-310-06557-8

Ⅰ.①品… Ⅱ.①刘… Ⅲ.①英语－句法－翻译－研
究 Ⅳ.①H314.3

中国国家版本馆 CIP 数据核字(2024)第 000613 号

品鉴英语句子之美——学地道英语 译华夏文章
PINJIAN YINGYU JUZI ZHI MEI
——XUE DIDAO YINGYU YI HUAXIA WENZHANG

南开大学出版社出版发行
出版人：刘文华
地址：天津市南开区卫津路 94 号　　邮政编码：300071
营销部电话：(022)23508339　营销部传真：(022)23508542
https://nkup.nankai.edu.cn

天津创先河普业印刷有限公司印刷　全国各地新华书店经销
2024 年 4 月第 1 版　　2024 年 4 月第 1 次印刷
230×165 毫米　16 开本　16.75 印张　2 插页　230 千字
定价:88.00 元

如遇图书印装质量问题,请与本社营销部联系调换,电话:(022)23508339

　　这本小书实为读书笔记，读书时积累的句子，结集在一起，附上一点感想，属经验、感悟之谈。

　　每当谈到英语学习时，我总有两个信念：

　　一、在非英语环境里学英语主要是通过读书，我甚至认为，即使在英语环境里，英语水平的提高也主要靠读书；

　　二、成就好作品，比如一首诗、一篇文章或一部书，有多个因素，但好句子是成就好作品的一个重要因素，英语、汉语莫不如此。因此，学习写英语句子、译英语句子是永远的基本功，而写好英语句子、译好英语句子，对于我们操汉语的人来说，是一生的追求。

　　有人说写句子是艺术。

　　美国 NBA 有一个球星名叫 McGrady，中国球迷称之为麦迪，麦迪曾与姚明一起在休斯敦火箭队打球。他的球技之好可谓出神入化，一位记者这样评价他在球场上的表现：

　　Indeed, McGrady's body control, his energy, his shooting—watching these are (is) like watching an artist at work, blending colors, constructing sentences, or playing music.

　　这位记者把写句子与绘画和音乐一起送进艺术殿堂。

　　好诗文必有好句子，好句子在诗文中的重要性几乎到了"文以句传"的地步。

　　比如王维的《九月九日忆山东兄弟》，这首诗人们未必都知道，但其中"每逢佳节倍思亲"诗句知道的人就多了，而且经常引用，每逢传统节日，人们在想念远方的亲朋好友时就想起这句诗。

　　司马迁在《报任安书》中所说"穷天人之际，通古今之变，成一家之言"，也已成了千古名句，史学家、文学家无人不知，无人不晓。

　　在英语里也有类似情况，比如美国作家 E. B. 怀特特别推崇的一个句子：

These are the times that try men's souls.

　　这是美国独立战争时期英裔宣传鼓动家托马斯·潘恩（Thomas Paine）写的小册子《美国危机》（*The American Crisis*）开头的一句话。怀特说，由几个简单的小词构成的这句话，人们已经引用了二百多年，还将继续引用下去。他说，这句话的意思可用别的说法表达，但怎么说都不行，人们很快就会忘记，可见好句子的艺术魅力。

　　英国作家毛姆（William Somerset Maugham）在他的文章《清晰，简洁，和谐》（"Lucidity，Simplicity，Euphony"）里说，"Words have weight, sound and appearance; it is only by considering these that you can write a sentence that is good to look at and good to listen to"。他说写句子既要好看又要好听。

　　观之好看，读之好听，这是毛姆对英语句子的感悟，由此可见，他也把写句子看作艺术。

　　所谓"好看"指它的结构，"好听"指它的声响和乐感，可以说，句子是综合艺术，是结构和声响的综合，具有建筑和音乐的艺术特征。

　　什么样的句子才算"观之好看，读之好听"呢？

　　司马迁的"穷天人之际，通古今之变，成一家之言"当之无愧。这是一个由三个小句组成的排比句，各有一个动词为小句开头，分别是"穷""通""成"，句尾是三个"之"字结构，"之际""之变""之言"，构建了一个结构平衡的句子，属"观之好看"；读的时候可以明显感觉到句子的节奏，这属"读之好听"。

　　《浮生六记》里有一段描写芸娘在新婚之夜读书的文字，有一句是这样说的：

"高烧银烛，低垂粉颈，不知观何书而出神若此……"

这也是一个颇具美感的句子，甚至连它的构词都是"观之好看，读之好听"，"银烛""高烧"，"粉颈""低垂"，芸娘埋头读书的美好形象跃然纸上。

英国译者雪莉·布莱克（Shirley M. Black）这样翻译这个句子：

"She was sitting, in the light from a pair of tall silver candles, with her delicate white neck bent over a book, so completely absorbed in her reading..."

译文中有两个介词短语构成的状语，"in the light from a pair of tall silver candles"和"with her delicate white neck bent over a book"，这两个短语不仅词的数目相差无几，就连重读的音节数目也是相等，实属"观之好看，读之好听"。

此句原文和译文的"好看"，不仅表现在文字上，也表现在文字所创造的人物形象上。

好句子是诗文的点睛之笔。

诗文中的名句毕竟有限，但如果我们细心观察、细心体会，就会发现，具有美感（beauty）和力量（power）的好句子不在少数。

句子的美感主要表现在三个方面：第一，动词的运用，包括动词与宾语和动词与状语的搭配；第二，短语，即不同词汇的搭配；第三，句子的组织。其中，句子的组织尤其重要。

中国留美先驱容闳回忆他在美国学习英语的经历时说，他的老师特别强调英语句子之美和英语句子结构：

"... he laid a greater stress on pointing out the beauties of a sentence and its construction, than he did on grammatical rules, moods and tenses."

这位美国老师强调句子之美和句子结构，这对我们很有启发，因为汉英两种语言在句子结构上的差异太大了，对于我们，学习英语句子结构更显重要。而且，这位老师把英语学习上升到语言审美层次、审美修养的一部分。

　　动词、短语和句子，这三者是有机的整体，不是孤立的。好句子除结构好之外，必有好动词或好短语，可谓"好中有好"。

　　对于翻译工作者，"翻译中国""讲好中国故事"是光荣的历史使命，为了不辱使命，要培养"写好英语句子，作好英语文章"的能力。取得这个能力的有效途径是读书，有心从事汉英翻译的人们要立志阅读英语原著，在读书上肯花时间，肯下真功，"书痴者文必工"。

　　写句子是艺术，是创作艺术。读句子也是艺术，是欣赏艺术。像音乐家欣赏音乐那样，像画家欣赏绘画那样，欣赏句子，在句子这个微观世界里寻找无限美感，这为读者和译者所独享，不论科技发展到何等地步也代替不了。

　　这本小书所列内容都是独立的句子，以句子为单位编排，之间没有联系，没有系统。读者所面对的是单个的句子和围绕句子所做的讨论，随意翻到某页都可作为阅读的开始，所需关注的是句中的动词、短语和结构，体味其美，体味其妙。这就是这本小书的初衷。

　　书中所举例句及所做分析难免有不妥之处，欢迎读者批评指正。

刘士聪

2023 年 10 月于南开园

目 录

雪莉·布莱克（Shirley M. Black）翻译《浮生六记》: *Chapters from A Floating Life*

简 介

《浮生六记》为清代乾、嘉时期文人沈复所写自传，记叙作者和妻子陈芸（芸娘）婚后的"实情实事"，夫妻举案齐眉、相濡以沫的一段美满生活以及后来因家庭变故而遭遇的悲剧；绘制了两百多年前一个普通文人家庭和南方百姓生活的真实图画。

《浮生六记》以文言文书写，文字简洁流畅、极富美感，读来难以释手。据专家统计，《浮生六记》到目前为止已有 160 余种版本问世，可见其流传之广，读者喜爱之甚。其英译文也已有四个版本：

1. 林语堂译本：*Six Chapters of A Floating Life*（1935）；

2. 英国人雪莉·布莱克（Shirley M. Black）译本：*Chapters from A Floating Life*（1960）；

3. 白伦（Leonard Pratt）和江素惠合译本：*Six Records of a Floating Life*（2006）；

4. 格雷厄姆·桑德斯（Graham Sanders）译本：*Records of a Life Adrift*（2011）。

现从雪莉·布莱克的译文中撷取一些译例，领略她的译文风格，学习她的翻译技巧。译例中所引用的原文皆取自淮茗注释的《浮生六记》（郑州：中州古籍出版社，2010）。

布莱克在其译文的前言里这样说明她的翻译原则：

第一，tried... to recreate the subtle emotional atmosphere；

第二，tried to be as meticulous as I could in expressing the exact meaning of the Chinese words；

第三，trying to approximate the feeling of the author's own way of expressing himself。

在她的译文里，布莱克往往不是词、句对译，而是对语义浓缩的汉语文言进行解读，然后用英语将其内在含义说透，且行文自然流畅，少有翻译腔。她的这种解释性的翻译策略主要是考虑了译文读者的接受效果。

美国汉学家宇文所安（Stephen Owen）在谈到中国文论和中国古典哲学著作中的术语翻译时说："……其实没有什么最佳的翻译，只有好的解说。任何翻译都对原文有所改变，而且，任何一种传统的核心概念和术语的翻译都存在这个问题……"（《中国文论》，导言）

中国古典文学作品和现当代文学作品中叙述和描写的语汇，不同于学术著作中的"术语"，但对它们的翻译，宇文所安所说的"解说"也适用。在布莱克的《浮生六记》译文里，这种情况屡见不鲜。

如，书中描写陈芸时有这样的文字：

"其形削肩长颈，瘦不露骨，眉弯目秀，顾盼神飞，唯两齿微露，似非佳相。一种缠绵之态，令人之意也消。"

句中的"顾盼神飞"，布莱克是这样翻译的：

Her glance sparkled with intelligence and humour...

《红楼梦》第三回描写探春时也用了这个词：

"第二个削肩细腰，长挑身材，鸭蛋脸儿，俊眼修眉，顾盼神飞，文彩精华，见之忘欲。"

句中的"顾盼神飞"，霍克斯是这样翻译的：

She had an oval face under whose well-formed brows large, expressive eyes shot out glances that sparkled with animation.

布莱克和霍克斯的译法都很传神，他们都用了名词"glance(s)"和动词短语"sparkled with"，基本上都是采用了解释性翻译，也就是我们常说的"意译"。

此类汉语词语在英语里很难找到对应词，只好对其进行解释，解释好了可以成就好的译文。

布莱克的《浮生六记》译文对原文有删减，对情节有编排；细观全文，偶尔有误解和误译，翻译中国古代的文言文作品，这种现象难以避免。

下面我们举些实例观察、研究布莱克的翻译技巧。

译例 1

▶ **原文** 生而颖慧，学语时，口授《琵琶行》，即能成诵。

▶ **译文** Even as a baby Yuen had shown signs of unusual intelligence and understanding. Not long after she had learned to talk her parents taught her to recite Po Chu-I's long narrative poem "The Song of the Lute". After hearing it once or twice, the child could repeat the whole poem from beginning to end, word for word, without making a single mistake.（p. 3）

这句话原文只有十几个字，译者用英语写了一大篇，其中有值得揣摩之处。

1. ［原文］生而颖慧……

［译文］Even as a baby Yuen had shown signs of unusual intelligence and understanding.

［说明］这里的"生"，汉语有"天生"的意思，但译文没有说"When she was born..."，而是译作"Even as a baby"，指芸小时候，这样理解、这样翻译合适；"颖慧"，译作"... of unusual intelligence and understanding"，

指智力好、理解能力强，译文的意思确切。

这句话原文里没有动词，译文选择使用动词"had shown..."，很好的选词。

2.〔原文〕学语时，口授《琵琶行》，即能成诵。

〔译文〕Not long after she had learned to talk her parents taught her to recite Po Chu-I's long narrative poem "The Song of the Lute". After hearing it once or twice, the child could repeat the whole poem from beginning to end, word for word, without making a single mistake.

〔说明〕"学语时"，译文指陈芸开始学说话时，所确定的时间清楚，合乎逻辑；"即能成诵"，此处的"即"，意为"很快"，译文的"once or twice"，听了一两遍，也可以理解为"很快"；译文在"repeat the whole poem from beginning to end"之后，又加了两个状语短语，"word for word"和"without making a single mistake"，译者要把"成诵"的含义说透彻。

译例 2

▶ 原文　一日，于书簏中得《琵琶行》，挨字而认，始识字。

▶ 译文　One day, in a waste-paper basket, Yuen found a copy of "The Song of the Lute". From the tattered pages of the discarded book, with her memory of the words of the poem to guide her, she learned to recognize the characters and in this way taught herself to read.（p. 4）

💡 说明　"挨字而认"，即，对照她当初背诵的《琵琶行》诗句，逐一认字；特别是"挨字"，"with her memory of the words of the poem to guide her"有点睛之妙；原文两个字，译文用了 12 个词，但此时字数多少已不重要，我们只顾赞叹其独到之妙，非常人之所及也。

两点补充说明：

1. 关于"书籦"，《现代汉语词典》有两个解释，一为盛书的竹箱，二为字纸篓，译者选择后者，译作"a waste-paper basket"是可以的，若按前者译似乎更好。

2. 若按"书箱"译，译文中的"From the tattered pages of the discarded book"就不必要了。

译例3

▶ **原文**　……时但见满室鲜衣，芸独通体素淡，仅新其鞋而已。见其绣制精巧，询为己作，始知其慧心不仅在笔墨也。

💡 **说明**　乾隆乙未（1775）冬，陈芸"堂姐出阁，余又随母往"，作者见到芸时对她的装束做如上描述。

▶ **译文**　The house was gay, on this ceremonious occasion, with the rainbow-hued new robes of the family and the wedding guests. Yuen alone, looked her quiet, simple self, having added nothing to her everyday dress but a pair of bright new shoes. When I had admired the artistry of their embroidery and learned that she had made the shoes herself, I began to understand that Yuen was extremely capable and practical; that reading, writing, and composing poetry were only a few of her many accomplishments.（p. 5）

1.［原文］……时但见满室鲜衣……

［译文］The house was gay, on this ceremonious occasion, with the rainbow-hued new robes of the family and the wedding guests.

［说明］译者运用想象，将"满室鲜衣"译作家人和客人色彩鲜艳的新衣，"on this ceremonious occasion"这个插入成分是译者补充的文字，从原文角度看可以接受，从译文读者角度看，似乎必要。

2. ［原文］芸独通体素淡，仅新其鞋而已。

［译文］Yuen alone, looked her quiet, simple self, having added nothing to her everyday dress but a pair of bright new shoes.

［说明］译者用了"quiet""simple"两个形容词，不仅指芸的穿着素淡，也让读者体会到芸的沉静的性格以及她的以"素淡"为美，这也是对人物的进一步阐释。

3. ［原文］见其绣制精巧，询为己作，始知其慧心不仅在笔墨也。

［译文］When I had admired the artistry of their embroidery and learned that she had made the shoes herself, I began to understand that Yuen was extremely capable and practical; that reading, writing, and composing poetry were only a few of her many accomplishments.

［说明］"见其绣制精巧"，译为"When I had admired the artistry of their embroidery"，原文有"精巧"二字，含有"令人羡慕"之意，译文中的"admired"由此而来；将"笔墨"译作"reading, writing, and composing poetry"，这里的"笔墨"具体指芸的文字及诗文能力，译文符合原文所指，且具体、确切，译文读者理解起来没有障碍；"始知其慧心不仅在笔墨也"，芸不仅诗文能力强，而且做得一手好针线，由此便有了译文中的"Yuen was extremely capable and practical"。

译者努力挖掘原文内涵，所做的"解说"和"补偿"皆符合原意，译文不浅不薄，有血有肉有味道。

译例4

▶ **原文**　其形削肩长项，瘦不露骨，眉弯目秀，顾盼神飞……一种缠绵之态，令人之意也消。

▶ **译文**　The simplicity of her robe seemed to accentuate her fragile beauty and the slenderness of her graceful figure, with its sloping shoulders and long, delicate neck. Her eyes looked very dark beneath the curving wings of her brows. Her glance sparkled with intelligence and humour... Above all else, a clinging softness in her manner, an indefinable air of tenderness and vulnerability about her, touched my heart deeply, making me wish to stay forever by her side.（p. 5）

1.［原文］其形削肩长项，瘦不露骨……

［译文］The simplicity of her robe seemed to accentuate her fragile beauty and the slenderness of her graceful figure, with its sloping shoulders and long, delicate neck.

［说明］译文重点放在翻译芸的"瘦不露骨"上，译文用"her fragile beauty and the slenderness of her graceful figure"来表示，"The simplicity of her robe"源自前文的"her quiet, simple self"，动词"accentuate"用得好，"to emphasize"，即"突显"的意思，勾画出一个古代女子的美好形象。

2.［原文］眉弯目秀，顾盼神飞……

［译文］Her eyes looked very dark beneath the curving wings of her brows. Her glance sparkled with intelligence and humour...

［说明］这个句子的译文前面已经讨论过，这里不再重复。

3.［原文］一种缠绵之态，令人之意也消。

［译文］Above all else, a clinging softness in her manner, an indefinable air of tenderness and vulnerability about her, touched my heart deeply, making me wish to stay forever by her side.

［说明］"缠绵之态"，意为"婉转动人"，可以说"歌声柔和缠绵"；但用来描写人的仪态或举止时，"缠绵"是什么样子？怎么翻译为好？译者根据她的理解和想象将其译作"a clinging softness in her manner, an indefinable air of tenderness and vulnerability about her", 其中"a clinging softness"指"情感上的依恋", 从作者和芸之间的感情看, 传译了"缠绵"的内涵, 加之"an indefinable air of tenderness", 使"缠绵"的含义更加具体、充实; 关于"vulnerability", 译者可能由"缠绵"而想到情感上的"脆弱", 或易受伤害等因素, 若是出于这种考虑, 也说明译者思维的缜密, 其实, 即便不补充这个部分, 译文也已很好了。

关于"令人之意也消", 淮茗在其《浮生六记》注释本中有解释: "让人萌生爱恋之意, 难以割舍", 即放不下、忘不掉。译文"making me wish to stay forever by her side"有"难以割舍"之意, 很符合原意。

译例 5

▶ **原文** ……悄然入室, 伴妪盹于床下, 芸卸妆尚未卧, 高烧银烛, 低垂粉颈, 不知观何书而出神若此……

▶ **译文** Quietly I entered my bridal chamber, where the bride's attendant lay dozing on the floor. Yuen, who had taken off her wedding finery, was not yet in bed. She was sitting, in the light from a pair of tall silver candles, with her delicate white neck bent over a book, so completely absorbed in her reading that she was unaware that I had come into the room. (p. 8)

💡 **说明** 婚庆之夜, 沈复送走客人, 回到洞房时发现芸在聚精会神埋头读书, 译文与原文有异曲同工之妙, 尤其是将"高烧银烛"译作"in the light from a pair of tall silver candles"(在烛光之下), 将"低垂粉颈"译作"with her delicate white neck bent over a book", 不但译了"粉颈", 也译了芸埋头读书的状态。在句中这两个成分作为状语, 刻画了一个古代淑女优雅的形象, 成功再现了原文审美效果, 属经典译句。

好的作家和译家都追求文字之美。有人说, 写句子是艺术, 很有道理。英国作家毛姆(William Somerset Maugham)说过:

"Words have weight, sound and appearance; it is only by considering these that you can write a sentence that is good to look at and good to listen to."

他要求写句子既要好听又要好看。这是他对英语句子的感悟。

布莱克的这个译句不仅好听、好看，意境也好。

译例 6

▶ **原文**　余性爽直，落拓不羁；芸若腐儒，迂拘多礼。

▶ **译文**　I am naturally straightforward and easy-going, unhampered by convention; but Yuen, like a pedantic old Confucian scholar, firmly believed in propriety and ceremony, and insisted on observing many old-fashioned formalities in our daily life.（pp. 14-15）

1. ［原文］余性爽直，落拓不羁……

［译文］I am naturally straightforward and easy-going, unhampered by convention...

［说明］"爽直"，译作"straightforward"，表示人的品性，意为"honest and frank"；"落拓"，即"落拓不羁"，译文用了"easy-going"和"unhampered by convention"，"easy-going"有"relaxed and tolerant in approach and manner"之意，也是一种潇洒的表现，译文准确表达了原文意思。

2. ［原文］……芸若腐儒，迂拘多礼。

［译文］... but Yuen, like a pedantic old Confucian scholar, firmly believed in propriety and ceremony, and insisted on observing many old-fashioned formalities in our daily life.

［说明］"迂拘多礼"的译文从两个方面做解释："firmly believed in

propriety and ceremony", 相信得体的举止和礼仪; "insisted on observing many old-fashioned formalities in our daily life", 坚持遵守生活中的老规矩。

　　用今日英语翻译汉语文言文时, 译文难以做到与原文叙述风格保持一致。文言文言简意赅, 信息量大, 与英语在句法结构上有很大差别; 英译文一方面要扩充信息, 另一方面要以完整的英语句式重写原文, 再加之思维方式的因素, 叙事风格难以趋同。但重要的是在兼顾达意的同时, 尽量在表达方式上体现一种简洁的行文风格。

译例 7

　　▶ **原文**　居三月, 如十年之隔。每当风生竹院, 月上蕉窗, 对景怀人, 梦魂颠倒。

　　▶ **译文**　The next three months, as I dragged my way through them, felt like ten years of unendurable separation. Every time the wind rustled the bamboos in my courtyard or the moon silvered the leaves of the banana trees beside my window, I remembered other moons and other nights until my soul became entranced with an unreal world of dreams and fancies.（pp. 10-11）

　　📍 **说明**　此段文字描写沈复尊父亲意志, 离开新婚妻子赴杭州赵省斋先生门下学习期间感到孤独的情景。

　　1.〔原文〕居三月, 如十年之隔。

　　〔译文〕The next three months, as I dragged my way through them, felt like ten years of unendurable separation.

　　〔说明〕这个说法在汉语里用得比较多, 不同译者会有不同译法。这里译文增加了 "as I dragged my way through them", 突出作者度日如年的感觉, 把原文意思译出来了, 颇觉厚重。

2.［原文］每当风生竹院，月上蕉窗，对景怀人，梦魂颠倒。

［译文］Every time the wind rustled the bamboos in my courtyard or the moon silvered the leaves of the banana trees beside my window, I remembered other moons and other nights until my soul became entranced with an unreal world of dreams and fancies.

［说明］"风生竹院，月上蕉窗"，诗一般的语言。首先是"竹院"和"蕉窗"，怎么翻译？如何落笔？译者将"竹院"写作"the bamboos in my courtyard"——院里的竹子，将"蕉窗"写作"the banana trees beside my window"——窗旁的蕉树，这样理解是合理的，用英语这样处理，意思清楚，行文也自然。"rustled"和"silvered"两个动词用得好，前者让我们看见竹枝摇曳，听见竹叶窸窣；后者让我们看见蕉叶上的斑驳月光。译文成功描绘了院中的景色，让只身在外的作者越发思念家中的爱妻。

"对景怀人，梦魂颠倒"的翻译值得揣摩，"I remembered other moons and other nights until my soul became entranced with an unreal world of dreams and fancies"，此情此景不禁让沈复想起在家与爱妻一起度过的夜晚，思绪万千，沉坠于梦幻之中。

这段译文里有一点似可再作斟酌，即"月上蕉窗"中的宾语（作为动宾或介宾）应该是"窗"而不是"蕉"，此句似可换一个方式表达：

"Every time the wind rustled the bamboos in my courtyard and the moon cast its light on my window through the dancing leaves of the banana trees..."

译例 8

▶ 原文　……但见隔岸萤光，明灭万点，梳织于柳堤蓼渚间。

💡 说明　原文上文：七月望，俗谓之鬼节，芸备小酌，拟邀月畅饮。夜忽阴云如晦，芸愀然曰："妾能与君白头偕老，月轮当出。"余亦索然。

▶ **译文**　... I, too, felt depressed and apprehensive, looking across the water to the darkness of the opposite shore, where will-o'-the-wisps, shining in the blackness like thousands of tiny, bright lanterns, wove in and out among the tangled willows. (p. 21)

💡 **说明**　原文诗一般的语言创造了诗一般的意境。译文简单的用词、自然的搭配、紧凑的衔接、优雅的句子，也创造了一个神秘的和诗一般的意境。英语和汉语都具有神奇的表现力。

译文是一个编织严密的英语句子，主句里有一个分词短语用来修饰主语，"where"引起的从句里也有一个分词短语，用来修饰"will-o'-the-wisps"，"wove in and out among the tangled willows"形象地再现了隔岸萤火虫"梳织于柳堤蓼渚间"的夜景。

另外，这里将"萤光"译作"will-o'-the-wisps"（鬼火），也许因为是鬼节，"夜忽阴云如晦，芸怃然……余亦索然"，结合上下文，译者或以此有意创造一种神秘气氛。

译例9

▶ **原文**　余与芸联句以遣闷怀，而两韵之后，逾联逾纵，想入非夷，随口乱道。

▶ **译文**　To dispel our fears and depression we began composing poetry, one of us starting a verse, the other finishing it; each composing a couplet in turn. Rhyming back and forth, we began to let our imagination run wild; indulging our most foolish fancies until we found ourselves laughing hysterically at the most ridiculous nonsense verses. (p. 21)

1. [原文] 余与芸联句以遣闷怀……

[译文] To dispel our fears and depression we began composing poetry, one of us starting a verse, the other finishing it; each composing a couplet in turn.

［说明］译文译出了句子的基本意思，依据上下文将"联句"译作"composing poetry"，将"闷怀"译作"our fears and depression"。此外，还补充三个独立主格结构解释什么是"联句"，这个补充很必要，解释也很清楚，既符合原文意思，也满足译文读者需要。

2.［原文］而两韵之后，逾联逾纵，想入非夷，随口乱道。

［译文］Rhyming back and forth, we began to let our imagination run wild; indulging our most foolish fancies until we found ourselves laughing hysterically at the most ridiculous nonsense verses.

［说明］"而两韵之后"译作"Rhyming back and forth"，这个处理相当于汉语的"联着联着"，或"联来联去"，意思和口气都与原文相符，也很贴切；"逾联逾纵"译作"let our imagination run wild"，符合汉语"纵"的含义；"想入非夷，随口乱道"，"非夷"译作"indulging our most foolish fancies"，"乱道"译作"the most ridiculous nonsense verses"，斟酌有分寸，表达很确切。

译例10

▶ **原文**　循级至亭心，周望极目可数里，炊烟四起，晚霞灿然。

📍 **说明**　原文上文：过石桥，进门折东，曲径而入。叠石成山，林木葱翠，亭在土山之巅。

▶ **译文**　From this elevation, as far as the eye could see, the land fell away to the horizon in every direction. Smoke was rising from the cooking fires of the houses far below, curling upward against a background of brilliantly-coloured sunset clouds.（p. 23）

1. [原文] 循级至亭心，周望极目可数里……

[译文] From this elevation, as far as the eye could see, the land fell away to the horizon in every direction.

[说明] 其中的"极目"译作"as far as the eye could see"，"可数里"译作"the land fell away to the horizon"，可以想象，亭子下面的土地绵延开去直至天际，而"周望"则用一个介词短语"in every direction"顺便表达出来。

2. [原文] 炊烟四起，晚霞灿然。

[译文] Smoke was rising from the cooking fires of the houses far below, curling upward against a background of brilliantly-coloured sunset clouds.

[说明] 映着晚霞，炊烟袅袅，一派田园风光。译文在"rising from the cooking fires"之后又用一个分词短语"curling upward against a background of brilliantly-coloured sunset clouds"将晚霞的灿烂色彩译了出来，译者没有拘泥原文形式，而是根据原文的描述运用自己的想象，用英语描画了乡村傍晚的景象，一幅富有诗意的田园景色，自然而无雕琢之嫌。

译者对这几个短句的处理方式是翻译加创作。译者为译好《浮生六记》，在运用今日英语表达汉语文言文方面下了功夫，其译文不追求字面和句式对应，而追求在语义和审美层面与原文保持一致。在译者看来，这似乎更为重要，在我们读来，也感觉这种译法的审美效果好。她所探索的翻译途径，对汉语文学作品的英译有启发。

译例 11

▶ 原文　陈芸答曰："杜诗锤炼精纯，李诗潇洒落拓，与其学杜之森严，不如学李之活泼。"

▶ 译文　"Tu Fu, I think, is first of all a master of style," she answered. "His work is admired as much for its refinement of form as for its grandeur of conception.

Li's poems, on the other hand, are free and unconventional, filled with freshness and vigour. I admire the dignity and majesty of Master Tu," she smiled, "but I prefer the freedom and liveliness of Master Li."

📍 **说明** 沈复夫妇常在家里讨论诗文。有一回，沈复问陈芸："唐以诗取士，而诗之宗匠，必推李杜，卿爱宗何人？"

1. ［原文］杜诗锤炼精纯……

［译文］"Tu Fu, I think, is first of all a master of style," she answered. "His work is admired as much for its refinement of form as for its grandeur of conception."（p.12）

［说明］"锤炼精纯"高度概括了杜诗特征，译文首先说杜甫是风格大师，"a master of style"，再从"形式"与"构思"两个方面将其具体化："its refinement of form"和"its grandeur of conception"，二者都是"锤炼"的结果，表达了"锤炼精纯"的实质内容。

2. ［原文］李诗潇洒落拓……

［译文］"Li's poems, on the other hand, are free and unconventional, filled with freshness and vigour."（p.12）

［说明］其实，"free and unconventional"已经很好地表达了"潇洒落拓"的含意，为了让译文更充实、更有张力，译者又补充了"filled with freshness and vigour"，效果是好的。

3. ［原文］与其学杜之森严，不如学李之活泼。

［译文］"I admire the dignity and majesty of Master Tu," she smiled, "but I prefer the freedom and liveliness of Master Li."（p.12）

［说明］"森严"一词，《现代汉语词典》解释为"整齐严肃"，译者用"dignity and majesty"表达了原文的内涵。

译例 12

▶ **原文** 芸曰："格律谨严，词旨老当，诚杜所独擅。但李诗宛如姑射仙子，有一种落花流水之趣，令人可爱。"

▶ **译文** "For perfection of form, beauty of phrase, and nobility of thought Tu's poems are certainly unequaled," Yuen admitted; "but Li's poems have the lyric charm of fairy maidens. He seems to write as naturally as petals fall and waters flow. That is why I love him."（p.13）

1. ［原文］芸曰："格律谨严，词旨老当，诚杜所独擅……

［译文］"For perfection of form, beauty of phrase, and nobility of thought Tu's poems are certainly unequaled," Yuen admitted...

［说明］译者采取将原文词汇拆解开来的方法进行解释，将"格律谨严"理解为形式的完美，译作"perfection of form"，将"词旨"分别译作"beauty of phrase"和"nobility of thought"，将"独擅"译作"unequaled"，这样的处理方式对原文做了很好的解读，译文读者理解起来也没有困难，是好译文。

2. ［原文］但李诗宛如姑射仙子……

［译文］but Li's poems have the lyric charm of fairy maidens...

［说明］"姑射仙子"为《庄子》中所描写的女神形象，译文用直叙方法表达了这个典故的意思。

3. ［原文］有一种落花流水之趣，令人可爱。

［译文］He seems to write as naturally as petals fall and waters flow. That is why I love him.

［说明］这句话的译文不但意境好，节奏也好，尤其是对"落花流水"

的处理，和原文一样轻松而自然，再现了原文的美感。

汉语里有很多意义朦胧但又十分概括的词语，特别是在论述中国各门类艺术时，如文学、诗歌、戏剧、音乐、书法、绘画等，经常会碰见一些约定俗成的表达方式，这些表达方式不用说翻译成英语，就是用汉语解释有时也很难说清楚，比如文中的"锤炼精纯""潇洒落拓""森严""落花流水"等。

对这类词汇进行翻译时，重要的一环是理解好，在正确理解的基础上进行解释，布莱克的翻译为我们做了示范。

她所翻译的《浮生六记》有与众不同之处。她的翻译有明确指导思想：第一，再现原文微妙的情感氛围。第二，超出了语言层面的形式"对应"，她的做法实际上是"翻译"加"创作"。所谓"翻译"，指她以原文内容为依据，这是生产译文的基础；所谓"创作"，因为她要把原文"微妙的情感氛围"和"汉字的确切意思"译出来，就须摆脱原文句法和行文方式的束缚，进行增译和变通。在一定程度上，这是遵从英语表达习惯和行文方式进行创作。

附：笔者为中译出版社于 2022 年重印 *Chapters from A Floating Life* 所写序言

中译出版社要出英国人雪莉·布莱克（Shirley M. Black）翻译的《浮生六记》译本，*Chapters from A Floating Life*，嘱我写序。这个译本我很喜欢，也很爱读。借此机会，谈谈对这个译本的感觉和认识。

清乾隆、嘉庆年间苏州人沈复，他写了一本《浮生六记》，记叙他与妻子陈芸短暂一生的故事。这个真实故事让我们了解二百多年前一个普通的小知识分子的家庭生活及当时的社会风情。书中特别细致地记录了沈复与妻子婚后和谐的夫妻生活、文化情趣，以及后来因其家庭变故和疾病所造成的困顿，母子诀别，夫妻颠沛流离，直至陈芸病入膏肓，因无钱就医而客死他乡。二十几年的短暂婚姻，让他们享受了夫妻生活的快乐与情趣，也经历了旧时封建礼俗的磨难。半生潦倒，余生坎坷，悲哉，悲哉，读之凄然，为之惋惜。

沈复不是当今意义上的作家，但他却有很高的文学修养和语言天赋，他以朴素而富有文采的文字所记载的感人故事成就了中国文学史上一部优秀作品，感动了万千读者，流传至今，也必将传之后世。

一部文学作品，能够流传，取决于两个因素：一要故事感人，二要文字讲究，二者不可缺一。《浮生六记》正是因为在这两个方面的成功，不仅吸引了众多读者，也吸引了不同时期的翻译家。他们立志并倾注了很高的热情将这本书翻译成英语。目前见到的有四个译本：

1. *Six Chapters of A Floating Life*，林语堂译，1935 年以双语形式刊登于上海英文杂志《天下月刊》和《西风月刊》；

2. *Chapters from A Floating Life*，雪莉·布莱克译，1960 年在伦敦出版；

3. *Six Records of a Floating Life*，白伦（Leonard Pratt）、江素惠（Chiang Su-hui）合译，以双语形式由译林出版社出版，2006 年；

4. 格雷厄姆·桑德斯（Graham Sanders）译本：*Records of a Life Adrift*，2011 年。

《浮生六记》原文分六卷，前三位译者都只翻译了前四卷，因为后两卷，即第五卷《中山记历》和第六卷《养生记道》，据考证，不是沈复原作，所以，这两卷都未翻译，只有桑德斯译了全部六卷，是全译本。

在四个译文里，林译本、白/江译本和桑德斯译本都是依照原文的情节翻译，未做增删，未做改动。

雪莉·布莱克译本是另一种情况，她删除了原文中相当一部分文字，并在译文中对原文做了重新编排，理由是：

I have omitted many episodes from the fourth part, concerned with visits to temples and scenic places, which are rather alike and would not mean much to the reader unacquainted with the actual places described. Some sections of literary criticism, gardening and botany I have also left out, as I felt they were of too specialized a nature to be of general interest. Other episodes I have rearranged into a less confusing chronological order.

此外，她的译文还插入了原文所没有的清代画家的十来幅画作，她认为：

The illustrations used in the book are reproductions of paintings by some of the best of the individualist painters of the Ch'ing dynasty—paintings which Shen Fu, Yuen and their friends might have chosen, and in styles in which they might well have painted.

译文中有几个地方，为了解释原文中的典故，增添了一些文字。

经过译者的一番整理，译文比原文在篇幅上有压缩，面目有区别。

关于对原文的增与删，以及所做的重新编排，译者说得很清楚，故这里对其是与非、利与弊等，暂不做讨论。我们集中讨论她所翻译的部分，主要围绕译者所写的前言中谈及她所设定的几个翻译原则进行讨论，对我们研究她的译文有启发。

一般情况下，译者在动笔翻译之前都有一个大略的或清晰的指导思想和翻译策略，因而译出来的文字也各有自己的特色。布莱克给自己提了三个原则，她说：

In translating the memoirs I have tried first of all to recreate the subtle emotional atmosphere, at once tragic, passionate and gay, which is, in my opinion, the outstanding characteristic of Shen Fu's original. I have also tried to be as meticulous as I could in expressing the exact meaning of the Chinese words, at the same time trying to approximate the feeling of the author's own way of expressing himself.

她的这个声明，一方面表示了她的信心，一方面表明了她对汉英翻译之难的认识，正如她自己所说，"This is a rather difficult job with languages as different from one another as Chinese and English and I do not know that I have even partially succeeded"。同时，这个声明也表明了她的高度责任感。

后来翻译《红楼梦》的霍克斯（David Hawkes）在他为译文写的序言里，也有类似的表示，他说：

My one abiding principle has been to translate *everything*—even puns... I cannot pretend always to have done so successfully, but if I can convey to the reader even a fraction of the pleasure this Chinese novel has given me, I shall not have lived in vain.

"把所有的东西都译出来——甚至双关语"。他把译好《红楼梦》作为自己的终身事业，为能译好这本书而感觉光荣，感觉不虚此生。这是多么好的声明，多么大的雄心壮志，多么高的责任感。

在汉英翻译历史上，有布莱克和霍克斯这样的翻译家，是很难得的现象，也是很令人鼓舞的榜样，值得译家们学习。

布莱克的这段声明概括起来，第一，"to recreate the subtle emotional atmosphere"；第二，"to be as meticulous as I could in expressing the exact meaning of the Chinese words"；第三，"to approximate the feeling of the author's own way of expressing himself"。

她的这个声明对我们阅读和理解她的译文很重要。为了讨论方便，不妨将这三点分开来谈，但它们又不是孤立的，在译文中往往交织在一起。

由于译者遵循着这几条声明，我们在她的译文里经常发现，她不是严格地依据原文做词与句的对译，而是对语义浓缩的文言文用英语进行解释，将其丰富的内涵挖掘出来，展示其语言的审美特征；有时也对原文里的文化或典故进行阐释，而且译文行文自然、流畅，少有翻译腔。这是因为译者考虑了译文读者的接受心理和审美需求，而努力译出这样的文字，实属难得。而且，这种译法并不违背原文意旨。因此，我们说，她的译文带有"释义"的性质，也带有"创作"的痕迹。

第一，所谓"emotional atmosphere"，指"思想情绪"，或"情绪氛围"，常常与环境相关。在原文，成功描写这种情绪者并不鲜见，在译文，特别是在文言文的英译文里，成功孕育这种情绪，并运用具有美感的文字将其表达出来，使其具有感染力，十分可贵。

我们看陈芸在新婚之夜忘情读书的情景：

［原文］……悄然入室，伴妪盹于床下，芸卸妆尚未卧，高烧银烛，低垂粉颈，不知观何书而出神若此……

［译文］Quietly I entered my bridal chamber, where the bride's attendant lay dozing on the floor. Yuen, who had taken off her wedding finery, was not yet in bed. She was sitting, in the light from a pair of tall silver candles, with her delicate white neck bent over a book, so completely absorbed in her reading that she was unaware that I had come into the room.（p. 8）

这段译文与原文有异曲同工之妙，尤其是将"高烧银烛"译作"in the light from a pair of tall silver candles"；将"低垂粉颈"译作"with her delicate white neck bent over a book"，将二者作为"She was sitting..."的状语，刻画了芸在烛光之下读书的优雅姿态。当沈复问道："姊连日辛苦，何犹孜孜不倦耶？"芸答曰："顷正欲卧，开橱得此书，不觉阅之忘倦。"她得到的这本书正是《西厢记》，这本书让她忘记了新婚之欢，而沉浸在另外一个世界里，这何尝不是一种"情绪氛围"，或"精神境界"？译文语言之优美，形象之鲜明，堪比原文，属经典译句。

译文中的"with... bent over a book"，值得特别留意，描绘的是一种状态，一个美人读书的优美状态；若将其写成"was bending her neck..."，则是一个进行中的动作，那就无美可言了。

顺便提一个与"bending"有关的插曲。2009年春天，英国威廉王子（Prince William）代表女王访问澳大利亚，在悉尼的一个社区活动中心，一个六岁小女孩问他一个问题。

When he landed in Sydney and visited a community centre, William handled with aplomb a six-year-old girl who asked if his mummy had died. "Yes, she did," he said bending down to her height. "It was pretty sad."

小女孩问了一个可爱的问题，戴安娜早在小女孩出生前好几年已经死了。这里的"bending down to her height"是一个动作，但"bending"用在这个语境里是一个鲜明的画面，高高的威廉王子向着六岁小女孩弯下腰来回答她的问题，多么慈祥、多么优雅的形象。

让我们回过来再谈布莱克的译文。

好的作家和译家都追求文字之美，特别是翻译中国古代文言文，写好英语句子，再现文字之美，对谁都是挑战。有人说，写句子是艺术，这个见解很好。不经其事，不知其难，写句子确实是艺术。英国作家毛姆（W. Somerset Maugham）在他的文章"Lucidity"里说，"Words have weight, sound and appearance; it is only by considering these that you can write a sentence that is good to look at and good to listen to"。他要求写句子既要好听又要好看，这是他经过一生的写作对英语句子的感悟。

布莱克翻译的这个句子不仅听着好听、看着好看，而且成功塑造了一个旧时贤淑女子的形象，也创造了一个优美的意境。

沈复与芸婚后不久，遵从父命，离别妻子赴杭州赵省斋先生门下读书。

［原文］居三月，如十年之隔。

［译文］The next three months, as I dragged my way through them, felt like ten years of unendurable separation.（p.11）

"如十年之隔"之类，汉语里表达离别之痛时常这样说，译文在"separation"之前加了形容词"unendurable"，而且，这个译句还补了"as I dragged my way through them"，虽然原文字面上没有这句，但译者在作者的平叙之中感觉到他身处异地、思乡思妻、度日如年的心情，译文也就将这一心情充分地表达出来了。

［原文］每当风生竹院，月上蕉窗……

［译文］Every time the wind rustled the bamboos in my courtyard or the moon silvered the leaves of the banana trees beside my window...（p.11）

"风生竹院，月上蕉窗"，不是诗句，但其声响节奏、其形式对仗，以及其意象意境，皆具诗之美感。这里对风竹、月蕉的环境描写，"情景交融"，衬托了作者当时的心绪。

首先是"竹院"和"蕉窗"如何译，需要考虑，从何处落笔，怎么用英语把这种情景写出来，又富有诗意。在这些方面译文也努力取得原文的效果，尤其在再现原文意象意境上是很成功的。其中"the wind rustled"和"the moon silvered"里的两个动词也用得好。前者让我们听见风中竹丛的窸窣作响；后者让我们看见蕉叶上的斑驳月光。

[原文]对景怀人，梦魂颠倒。

[译文] I remembered other moons and other nights until my soul became entranced with an unreal world of dreams and fancies.（p.11）

译者理解"怀人"的含义，作者想起了往日与妻子在皎洁的月光之下度过的美好夜晚，这样的理解和处理是合理的，也符合实际，译文成功阐释了"怀人"的含义。

对于"梦魂颠倒"，依照字面翻译比较困难。译者发挥她的想象力，译出了沈复此时的思绪万千，进入梦幻世界的情景。译文将沈复思念妻子的心情写得真实感人。

第二，关于"to be as meticulous as I could in expressing the exact meaning of the Chinese words"，一丝不苟地将汉语字、词的确切含义表达出来。很多情况下，文言词语在英语里找不到词义相当的对应词（equivalent），即使在词典里找到意思相近的词，也很难表达它的隐含意思。译者为自己树立这样的目标，是对自己提出的一个很高的要求，翻译过程中她确实也在努力这样做。

乾隆乙未冬，即1775年冬天，芸堂姐出嫁，沈复随母前去送亲，见到芸时有这样一段描写：

[原文]……时但见满室鲜衣，芸独通体素淡，仅新其鞋而已。

[译文]The house was gay, on this ceremonious occasion, with the rainbow-hued new robes of the family and the wedding guests. Yuen alone, looked her quiet, simple self, having added nothing to her everyday dress but a pair of bright new shoes.（p. 5）

译者运用想象，将"满室鲜衣"译作"The house was gay, on this ceremonious occasion, with the rainbow-hued new robes of the family and the wedding guests"，送亲时，家人和客人身穿色彩鲜艳的新衣，译文用了两个语义一致的形容词，"gay"和"rainbow-hued"，亮丽、多彩；"芸独通体素淡"，译文"Yuen alone, looked her quiet, simple self"，这不只是指芸的穿着打扮，更指她历来以"素淡"为美的品质，意义似更深了一层。

［原文］见其绣制精巧，询为己作，始知其慧心不仅在笔墨也。

［译文］When I had admired the artistry of their embroidery and learned that she had made the shoes herself, I began to understand that Yuen was extremely capable and practical; that reading, writing, and composing poetry were only a few of her many accomplishments.（p. 5）

译文将"慧心"译作"extremely capable and practical"，心灵手巧。

"笔墨"，"指文字或诗文书画等"，这里译者将其译作"reading, writing, and composing poetry"，用具体而确切的词语表达原文中一个笼统的概念，而且符合原文所指。译者如此细致地拆解文字完全是为了让译文读者明白，好的用心。

再如：

［原文］余性爽直，落拓不羁；芸若腐儒，迂拘多礼。

［译文］I am naturally straightforward and easy-going, unhampered by convention; but Yuen, like a pedantic old Confucian scholar, firmly believed in propriety and ceremony, and insisted on observing many old-fashioned formalities in our daily life.（pp. 14-15）

［原文］余性爽直，落拓不羁……

［译文］I am naturally straightforward and easy-going, unhampered by convention...

这个译文把原文所包含的意思几乎都包括了。"爽直"，译作"straightforward"，表示人品性格时，意为"honest and frank"；"落拓"，为"豪迈，不拘束"，也即"落拓不羁"，译文用了"easy-going"和"unhampered by convention"。"easy-going"有"relaxed and tolerant in approach and manner"之意，也有潇洒的成分。虽然句子形式不同，但原文意思表达得准确无误。

第三，关于"to approximate the feeling of the author's own way of expressing himself"，即，尽量对作者特有的表达自己情感的方式有所感觉，这种感觉对准确再现原文所描写的情绪至关重要。

芸临死前对沈复有一番诀别之语，继而又说：

［原文］"愿君另续德容兼备者，以奉双亲，抚我遗子，妾亦瞑目矣。"

［译文］"I hope you will marry again—someone both kind and beautiful, who will serve your parents and take my place with my forsaken children. Then at last I can close my eyes."（p. 96）

沈复与芸曾一起游园，偶遇浙江歌妓温冷香之女憨园，芸喜其美貌与修养，便竭力为沈复物色为妾，后"憨为有力者夺去，不果，芸竟以之死"，芸因未能了却此愿，伤心欲绝。当此临死之际，仍不忘嘱咐沈复续弦，说了以上的话。

"德容兼备"译作"both kind and beautiful"，这里的"德"，在芸的心目中就是"心地善良"，婚后能善待沈复，这是她最为关切的事情。译文未深究"德"的含义，对一个普通妇女来说，"德"主要是指"心地"好。这样简单而直白的译文足够了，把原文意思说清楚了。

［原文］言至此，痛肠欲裂，不觉惨然大恸。

［译文］At these words, my body felt as if it were being ripped apart, and I lost control of myself completely, overcome with grief.（p. 96）

抚今追昔，芸之死让沈复肝肠欲断，译文"my body felt as if it were being ripped apart"，充分表达了他的悲痛心情。

　　嘉庆癸亥三月三十日（1803 年 5 月 20 日），芸执沈复之手而逝，作者说：

　　［原文］当是时，孤灯一盏，举目无亲，两手空拳，寸心欲碎，绵绵此恨，曷其有极。

　　［译文］From that moment, I have been utterly alone; a solitary lamp, a stranger in a strange place; my lifted eyes seeing no beloved face, my outstretched arms clasping only the empty air. This agony—this heartbreak—will it never end?（p. 97）

　　译文中的"I have been utterly alone"，是译者的补充；芸死后，沈复感到十分孤独、十分痛苦，译者对作者当时的心情做了这个概括性的描述，后面的细节描写便不觉突兀。

　　将文学作品译成文学作品，这是文学翻译的境界，也是对译者的挑战。能否"将文学作品译成另一种语言的文学作品"，取决于译者的翻译理念和文字技巧，所谓"翻译理念"，指译者对翻译的认识，以及他面对一个具体作品所采取的翻译策略。而译好一个作品需具备两个前提，一是译者对原文的理解深度，包括对原文的思想感情和语言特征的感觉，这决定译文的深度和语言质量；二是译者的文学修养和审美修养，译者要有语言的审美意识，要知道话如何说、如何写才具有美感。就文学作品翻译而言，只译出原文意思，尽管句法正确，也是远远不够的；文学作品是语言艺术，译文要有美感，要有艺术感染力。这是文学作品翻译成功与否的关键标志。

　　文学作品原文的故事情节是作者组织起来的，原文的思想感情是作者表达的，译者对原文的情节和思想只有尊重。但在语言的转换上（当然也包括译者对原文作品中文化元素的阐释，但文化因素也是以语言为载体表达出来的），就布莱克所译《浮生六记》而言，在不违背原意的前提下，译者发挥想象，在用英语对原文进行阐释的过程中，也体现了明显的创作倾向，因而使译文具有较强的可读性。

译文中这样的例子多，书里有这样一个情节：

七月望，俗谓之鬼节，芸备小酌，拟邀月畅饮。夜忽阴云如晦，芸愀然曰："妾能与君白头偕老，月轮当出。"

［原文］余亦索然。但见隔岸萤光，明灭万点，梳织于柳堤蓼渚间。

［译文］I, too, felt depressed and apprehensive, looking across the water to the darkness of the opposite shore, where will-o'-the-wisps, shining in the blackness like thousands of tiny, bright lanterns, wove in and out among the tangled willows.（p. 21）

这段原文运用诗一般的语言创造了诗一般的意境。仔细阅读译文，我们感觉也同样具有诗一般的韵味。简单的用词，自然的搭配，紧凑的衔接，漂亮的组织。这样的译文让我们认识到译者运用英语创造了一个神秘莫测的夜景，也让我们认识到，英语和汉语一样，同样具有神奇的表现力。

译者为译好《浮生六记》，遵循自己提出的三条努力方向，在运用今日英语表达汉语文言文方面下了功夫。其译文不追求字面上和句子形式上的忠实，而追求在语义深层和审美层面上尽量与原文保存一致。在布莱克看来，这似乎更为重要，在我们读来，也感觉这很重要。

当然，其他的文学作品未必都可以采取她的这种译法译，其他译家也未必都赞成这样译。但她在翻译中所遵循的几条原则，她所探索的翻译途径，对文学作品的英译有启发，有参考价值。

至于译者在译文中所做的增与减，对原文所做的重新编排，译文中也难免有误译和不妥，这些都可以作为话题，但不在这里讨论了。

完成于农历庚子年三月三十日

［陈芸于嘉庆癸亥年（1803）三月三十日

去世，距今日 217 年整］

阅读凯蒂·尼科尔（Katie Nicholl）：
The Making of a Royal Romance

简介

这本书写英国威廉王子（Prince William）和凯瑟琳·米德尔顿（Catherine Middleton）的爱情故事。

作者凯蒂·尼科尔（Katie Nicholl），记者和广播员，《名利场》杂志（*Vanity Fair*）和《星期日邮报》（*Mail on Sunday*）撰稿人，在英国的 BBC 和 Sky News、加拿大的 CBC，以及澳大利亚的 Channel 9 都有兼职。

在过去的二十年里，她专门采访英国王室成员，连续发表了《创造王室浪漫史》（*The Making of a Royal Romance*）、《威廉和哈里》（*William and Harry*）和《新王室》（*The New Royals*）等王室传记作品，被认为是报道王室事务的权威作家。

The Making of a Royal Romance（paperback edition published by Arrow Books 2011），此书为传记文学作品，用实用英语写今日故事，是一本学习英语的好读物。

她的英语雅俗共赏，既通俗又文雅，既简洁又刚劲，既是口头用语，又是书面用语，读来饶有趣味，对提高我们的英语写作水平和汉英翻译能力很有帮助。

我们做汉英翻译，要把英语写好，且能让英美读者认可，甚至喜欢，这是很大的挑战，也是译者应有的追求。

读英语有两个环节：一是会读，读得懂；二是为了写好译好，这是目的。读懂原文，一般情况下不是很困难，但读过的东西会用，这个比较困难。所以，读书过程中消化吸收尤为重要。

读英语有两种方法，一是多读，二是精读，至于哪个方法好，因人而异，要看哪种方法适合自己。

现在选取书中一些句子，并做简要说明，供学习研究。

例句 1. William promised Kate she was the one, but he wanted to complete his military training before they got married. Kate put her trust in William and waited.（p. 2）

说明　作者在 *The Making of a Royal Romance* 的前言里介绍了关于威廉和凯特（即 Catherine Middleton，爱称 Kate）恋爱的一个细节：

威廉和凯特的恋爱经过反反复复、分分合合，后来终于定下来了。威廉答应凯特"she was the one"，他的决定表露了他对凯特的感情和忠心，这是凯特多年来所期待的，可以想象此时凯特的心情。

这句话很容易懂，句中的"the one"是一个简单的代词。

若将"she was the one"译成汉语，并具有原文的情感内涵，如何译，值得思考。

例句 2. Harry assured her that she was the one, and for the first time Charles gave his seal of approval, allowing Harry and Chelsy to share a room at Highgrove.（p. 210）

说明　哈里曾经与在津巴布韦长大的切尔西（Chelsy）恋爱，他也曾向切尔西保证说，"she was the one"；这句话里的"seal of approval"是一个固定的表达方式，"批准"的意思，查尔斯王子批准了哈里和切尔西的恋爱关系，《牛津高阶英汉双解词典》有例句：

The project has been given the government's seal of approval.

项目已由政府正式批准。

例句 3. But in the end there is a great sense of loyalty and dedication among the family and it rubs off on me.（p. 1）

💡 说明　威廉王子在庆祝自己二十一岁生日讲话时用过"rubs off on"这个短语，作者在书的前言中引用了这句话。

威廉谈到君主制时说，它与人民的生活息息相关，而且在王室内部有"a great sense of loyalty and dedication"，这种"sense"也传给了他。这是书中第一次使用这个短语，此外还有，如：

例句 4. William discovered he had rather a lot in common with Camilla. She was down-to-earth, and her sense of humour appeared to have rubbed off on his father, who seemed happier than he had been in years.（p. 92）

💡 说明　这里的"to have rubbed off on his father"也是说卡米拉的幽默感传给了威廉的父亲。

《牛津高阶英汉双解词典》里有一个类似的例句：

Her sense of fun has rubbed off on her children.

可见，"to rub off on sb"这个短语使用频率不低，做汉英翻译时不妨学着用。

例句 5. While they recognise the unique privileges their royal titles bring, they both still crave normality.（p. 4）

💡 说明　这个句子里的"normality"是形容词"normal"的名词形式。"... they both still crave normality"，"他们兄弟俩（威廉和哈里）都渴望过正常生活"，或"普通人生活"。我们做汉英翻译表达这个意思时，可能会使用比较多的文字，英语名词的这种用法给我们启示。英美作家常常使用动词或形容词的名词形式，文字简练，听起来很有力量。还有类似的例子，如：

1. William just wanted to forget the awfulness of what had happened. Many of us wrote letters and William was genuinely touched.（p. 81）

💡 **说明** 此处的 "awfulness" 指威廉的母亲戴安娜遇车祸致死之事。"awfulness" 是形容词 "awful" 的名词形式。

2. ... Harry was left to his own devices. William had left Eton and was on his gap year, leaving Harry with the run of Highgrove.（p. 85）

💡 **说明** 查尔斯因公经常在外，有时和卡米拉躲在另外的住处，威廉王子正享受一年假期，留下哈里王子一个人照看 Highgrove（梅洛罗夫庄园，查尔斯的私人住宅）。

作者没有说 "leaving Harry to run Highgrove"，而是用了 "run" 的名词形式，这大概是出于行文方式和叙事语气的考虑，其中的微妙可慢慢体味。

3. William, in shorts, T-shirt and flip-flops, loved the anonymity of the trip and checked in as "Brian Woods" at Le Domaine de Decide, a small and basis resort where he stayed for a month.（p. 101）

💡 **说明** "anonymity" 来自形容词 "anonymous"，意为 "匿名" 等。威廉王子外出旅行时，穿着普通的衣服，他不想让人认出他是谁。

4. He had no need to worry about being recognised; there were no photographers on the island. William was left in peace to enjoy the simplicity of living in a spartan hut with a corrugated-iron roof and two single beds for twenty-six pounds a night.（p. 101）

💡 **说明** 同样，这里的 "simplicity" 是形容词 "simple" 的名词形式，在小岛上，他安静地享受着简单的生活。

例句 6. Some royal observers have been quick to compare Kate to the young Diana Spencer, but the truth is they could not be more different. While Kate is just as glamorous and intriguing as the late princess, she is headstrong and confident. Lest we forget, this is the young woman who when told she was lucky to be dating William retorted, "He's lucky to be going out with me." (p. 5)

💡 **说明**　这是一个编织严密的段落，一共三句话，写中产阶级家庭出身的凯特倔强的性格，并不因为威廉是王位继承人而低三下四地去高攀他。有人说她跟威廉王子谈恋爱是幸运，她反驳说，"是他有幸和我谈恋爱"，这个凯特很有个性，也让我们了解了"headstrong and confident"的含义。

1. ... they could not be more different...

💡 **说明**　一些王室的观察者把凯特比作年轻时的戴安娜，但作者认为她们的性格很不同，这是一个强调的说法。这个意思用汉语表达时，可能是她们的性格"很不一样"，或者是她们的性格有"天壤之别"。两种语言所强调的意思都是"very different"。这个表达方式我们不妨学着使用。

2. ... this is the young woman who when told she was lucky to be dating William retorted...

💡 **说明**　以"who"开始的定语从句之后插入了以"when"起始的状语从句（"when"后面省略了"she was"），请注意，"who"的谓语动词是"retorted"，虽然二者距离比较远，但句子所表达的意思是清楚的，这种复杂句式的写法值得学习。

例句 7. When she gave birth to William she was still navigating the maze of royal life and coming to terms with the fact that home was no longer a flat in west London but a grand palace. It was a steep learning curve and she had yet to master the confidence and sophistication she would acquire in later life. (p. 10)

💡 **说明**　戴安娜与查尔斯结婚后，对于宫廷生活的繁文缛节、清规戒律很不习惯，很不适应，有时为了吃饭和应酬，一天要更换四五次衣服，所以就有了"navigating the maze of royal life"的描述。

这两个句子所含内容较多，但作者所写的英语读起来并不觉浓重，其用词和句子组织对我们有启示：

1. ... navigating the maze of royal life and coming to terms with the fact...

💡 **说明**　这两个过去进行时动词中间用一个"and"连接，使句子有一种平衡感和节奏感。

书中还有一处也用了"navigate"和"maze"，这里是指学校的建筑：

It took William several months before he could confidently navigate the school and its maze of corridors, but he managed to cope academically.（p. 56）

2. It was a steep learning curve...

💡 **说明**　"learning curve"是一个固定的英语搭配，英语词典的解释是"the rate at which you learn a new subject or a new skill"，即"学习曲线"。戴安娜从普通妇女变为王室成员，从普通民房搬进豪华宫殿，生活发生了这样的变化，为了适应宫廷生活，她需要学的东西很多，所以说她的"learning curve"是"steep"。

例句 8. While Diana had wanted to blend into the background, the British public positioned her centre stage, a role the baby prince would later also struggle with. The minutiae of her daily life was now public consumption.（pp.10-11）

💡 **说明**　戴安娜不愿意太显眼，"to blend into the background"，想躲进背景，但公众却把她放在舞台中央，"positioned her centre stage"，"the background"和"centre stage"形成对照。

1. 关于 blend in/into，《新牛津英语词典》有解释，"be an unobtrusive or harmonious part of a greater whole by being similar in appearance or behaviour"，意为悄悄地融入进来，并给出例句：

She would have to employ a bodyguard in the house, someone who would blend in.

2. "... public consumption"，她的生活细节都成了公众所关注的事情。《牛津高阶英汉双解词典》例句：

Her speech to party members was not intended for public consumption (to be heard by the public).

例句 9. She could not get to grips with the etiquette of changing her clothes sometimes as many as four or five times a day.（p. 13）

💡 说明　短语 "to come/get to grips with"，意为 "to begin to understand and deal with sth difficult"，开始理解并着手处理难题。

书中还有一个类似的例句：

The uniform was actually rather comfortable once you got used to it, and the trickiest thing was getting to grips with the timetable, which changed from week to week.（p. 52）

例句 10. "I want to bring them up with security... It's so important." Like Charles, Diana had been raised by a governess, but for her security meant being hands on.（p. 15）

💡 说明　这里的 "hands on"，意思是自己动手，也说 "事必躬亲"，或 "亲力亲为"，对于戴安娜来说，所谓 "安全"，就是自己亲自带孩子才有安全感。

书中另外一处谈到威廉时，也用了这个说法：

According to one senior royal aide who was present, he chaired every meeting with confidence and authority. "William was very hands on..."（p. 225）

威廉王子逢事总是亲力亲为。

例句 11. While those around her put her doubts and anxieties down to pre-wedding nerves, it was apparent from the start that Diana and Charles had entered into the marriage with polarised expectations.（p. 13）

💡 **说明**　这句话可译为"她周围的人把她的怀疑和焦虑归因于婚前的紧张情绪"，或"她的怀疑和焦虑是由于婚前的紧张情绪造成的"等。"to put sth down to sth"既是口语，也是很别致的书面语。

英语词典解释"to put sth down to sth"："to consider that sth is caused by sth"，即"把……归因于……"，并有例句：

What do you put her success down to?

此短语和"attribute sth to sth"意思相近。

例句 12. The couple had not stopped criss-crossing the world, and eighteen months of tours and states visits on top of motherhood had left the vulnerable Diana tired and drained.（p. 18）

💡 **说明**　戴安娜一方面要抚养孩子，另一方面还要和查尔斯一起出国访问，有时在外的时间很长，这让她身心疲惫。在这个上下文里，"... states visits on top of motherhood"有国事重于母子情之意。

再看下面一个例子：

Diana was used to her husband's habit of putting duty before family, but the press turned on the prince. WHAT KIND OF A DAD ARE YOU? asked the *Sun* on its front page.（p. 41）

💡 **说明**　这里的"... putting duty before family"和"on top of motherhood"所表达的几乎是同样的意思。这种短语能表达用较多文字才能说清的内容。

文字的"简洁"和"力量"互为因果，简洁的文字一定有力量，有力量的文字以"简洁""含蓄"为特征。汉语有"意则期多，字则期少"之说，英语也一样。运用文字应有"以简为美"意识。

例句 13. The Queen, more astute in such matters, was aware that the transition from carefree young woman to the goldfish bowl of royalty was taking its toll on the sensitive young princess.（p. 14）

💡 **说明**　短语 "taking its toll on"，意为 "to have a bad effect on"，在这本书里，作者多次使用这个短语，如：

By now the strains in the marriage had taken their toll on William.（p. 45）

💡 **说明**　这里指查尔斯和戴安娜紧张的婚姻关系给威廉造成负面影响。

例句 14. Publicly the Waleses had put on a united front, but behind the wrought-iron gates of Kensington Palace the tears in the fabric of their marriage were beginning to show.（p.18）

💡 **说明**　"... put on a united front"，他们的夫妻关系表面上形成了统一战线（看上去很和谐），但实际上 "the tears in the fabric of their marriage were beginning to show"，这里的 "fabric"，意为 "the basic structure of their marriage"，而 "tears" 意为 "裂痕"，即他们的婚姻出现了裂痕。很好的修辞方式，值得借鉴。

例句 15. Diana, who was aware of their friendship when she first met Charles, became increasingly paranoid about Camilla during her marriage. When Charles disappeared, she would anxiously question their staff on his whereabouts.（p.18）

💡 **说明**　关于 "paranoid"，英语词典这样解释："afraid or suspicious of other people and believing that they are trying to harm you, in a way that is not reasonable"，多疑，恐惧。

因查尔斯婚后仍然幽会他的情人卡米拉，引起戴安娜的怀疑，用 "paranoid" 描写戴安娜在这种情况下的心态很恰当，作者选词很考究。

例句 16. As he furiously pedalled his brightly-yellow plastic truck along the upstairs corridor of Craigowan Lodge he let out a squeal of delight before crashing the toy into the wall for the umpteenth time.（p. 21）

💡 说明　人们有时因为激动或兴奋而发出尖叫声，在英语中，这种状况如何表达？我们做汉英翻译时有时会遇见这种情况。在英语作品里偶尔会有这样的表达方式，像上面这个句子里的"he let out a squeal of delight"就是一例。还有，如：

When they played hide-and-seek or big bad wolf this was the most popular hiding place, and the boys would shriek with excitement as their father dived into the colourful sea of balls to pluck them out in time for tea.（p. 25）

这里的"shriek with excitement"也是一例。再如：

Diana exclaimed as she scooped Harry into her arms and planted a kiss on his head.（p. 21）

这里的"exclaimed"是一个动词，表达了同样的意思。

《牛津高阶英汉双解词典》里有一个很好的例句：

She opened her eyes and exclaimed in delight at the scene.

例句 17. While the Queen had noticed that William had become quite a handful, she adored her grandsons and encouraged them to let off steam at Balmoral.（p. 23）

1. a handful...

💡 说明　我们阅读时偶尔见到"a handful of sth"，但"a handful"作为独立名词并不多见，其意为"a person or an animal that is difficult to control"，难控制，不好管，这里是说威廉王子变得不听话。这个小词用在这里读来很有趣味。

2. ... let off steam

💡 说明　女王鼓励她的孙辈们到离宫巴莫拉尔宫（Balmoral）去尽

情宣泄。字面意思似乎是"泄汽"，这里喻为"释放（精力）""宣泄（情绪）"等，很形象的表达。类似的例子还有，如：

Harry also let off steam playing the Eton wall game, a sport exclusive to Eton that is both lawless and dangerous...（p. 95）

这句用了同样的表达方式"let off steam"。再如：

If the military could not find a place for him, Harry would find another outlet for his passions and talent.（p. 217）

这里的"find another outlet for..."表达与"let off steam"同样的意思。

在英语里，这种形象的修辞很多，文字生动、耐读。学习汉英翻译者，在日常阅读中应留意并积累这种修辞，并学会使用这些表达方式。

例句 18. The Princess pottered around in the house with the children while Charles would spend hours in the garden, tending his impressive beds of hydrangeas, sweet peas and roses...（p. 24）

💡 说明　"to potter around"，也可以说"to putter around"，英语词典的解释："to do things or move without hurrying, especially when you are doing sth that you enjoy and that is not important"。

在这个上下文里，这个词组来得很自然，似乎是作者信手拈来，但翻译成自然的汉语却需要斟酌。

例句 19. The Queen was increasingly aware that her grandson, now four, misbehaved and reminded Nanny Barnes that it was her job to instil discipline.（p. 28）

💡 说明　女王发现威廉开始调皮不听话，她提醒保姆说，她的责任是教育威廉守规矩，对他加强管教。这里的动词"instil"和名词"discipline"搭配，有时也可以和"confidence"搭配，"instil confidence in/into sb"，即"使某人有信心"，一个很好的动宾短语。

例句 20. It was bitterly cold and the four-and-half-year-old prince was a bundle of nerves as he stepped out of the chauffeur-driven car tightly clasping his mother's hand.（p. 31）

💡 说明　这里的 "a bundle of nerves" 指四岁半的小王子很紧张。英语词典里有 "a bundle of laughs, fun, joy, etc." 的用法，指风趣的人，或有意思的事等。

在凯蒂·尼科尔的新著《哈里王子与梅根》（*Harry and Meghan*）里就有一个句子，用了 "a bundle of fun"：

According to a member of the nursery staff, Harry was "a bundle of fun who was very bright and much smarter than his brother at that age."（p. 9）

例句 21. Diana called him "my little Spencer" and despite rumours that later surfaced about Harry's paternity he was a Spencer through and through.（p. 30）

💡 说明　这里的 "through and through" 意思很清楚，"地道的""彻底的""完全的"等。哈里是地地道道的斯宾塞，Spencer 是戴安娜的姓，她这样说可能是有情感方面的隐情。

例句 22. Harry being Harry wanted a chocolate bar *and* a packet of chewy sweets, but his mother reminded him that he would only have enough money for one.（p. 32）

💡 说明　句子以 "Harry being Harry" 做主语很新鲜。如果将其理解为 "Harry who was Harry after all" 似乎也说得通，但如何将其翻译成汉语，需要斟酌。

请看另外一个句子：

But, being Harry, it wasn't all work, and in April 2004 he made his first of many trips to Cape Town, where he met up with the girl he had been hoping to bump into.（p. 123）

💡 **说明**　哈里对去非洲莱索托做慈善事业，表现出很高的热情，做得很成功，也受到媒体的好评。除了工作，他也要玩，所以他也去了开普敦找他的女朋友。此句中的"being Harry"，意为哈里毕竟是哈里，这个用法与前者类似，但它在这里是用作状语。

例句 23. I do remember William being distracted by what was going on at home. At the time there was a lot in the newspapers about Charles and Diana's marriage being in trouble（p. 40）

💡 **说明**　句中第一个"being"是做"remember"的宾补，第二个"being (in trouble)"相当于一个定语从句"which was in trouble"，以分词短语做宾补和做定语的写法可以借鉴。

例句 24.

1. For William, who had matured from a boisterous child into a sensitive boy, school proved to be a relief from the turmoil at home.（p. 36）

2. Arabella had blossomed into a gorgeous-looking girl, and as she sashayed past him, her perfume lingering in the air, he wondered why he hadn't noticed her properly until now.（p. 141）

3. While she had never counted herself as pretty, those around her often made a point of commenting on her natural beauty, especially her mother. "Kate morphed into something of a beauty that holiday, and we all saw it."（p. 168）

💡 **说明**　以上三个句子表达类似的意思，但作者所使用的动词不同。描写威廉时用"matured... into"，描写阿拉贝拉时用"blossomed into"，描写凯特时用"morphed into"。这三个表达方式都是描写年轻人的成长变化，但用的是不同动词短语。

"matured... into"比较常见，无须多做解释。

关于"blossom"，英语词典用"develop""mature""flourish"来解释其意义；这个词经常用来描写"花开"，因此用它描述女孩的成长时有一种修辞效果，在英语中，这是一个自然而又具有美感的句子。我们单译"Arabella had blossomed into a gorgeous-looking girl"时，如何也能再现英语的修辞效果，值得思索。

"blossomed into"与汉语的"出落"意思相近。词典说："青年人（多指女性）的体态、容貌向美好的方面变化"。

至于如何翻译句中的"a gorgeous-looking girl"，既要把它的意思准确译出来，又能和"出落"形成自然而恰当的搭配，似乎需要斟酌。

"morphed into"，变化。

例句 25. She always had a lovely willowy figure, but now she had filled out and the colour was back in her cheeks. She never wore particularly fashionable or revealing clothes—just jeans and jumpers but she had an innate sense of style. （p. 166）

🔎 说明　这个描写女孩子身材的句子值得揣摩，"a lovely willowy figure"，杨柳细腰，或"苗条"；"she had filled out"，她现在变得丰满些了；"the colour was back in her cheeks"，脸色也红润起来；"revealing clothes"，暴露的衣服；"... she had an innate sense of style"，凯特具有一种内在风采、内在的风韵，即她无须特意打扮或特意表现。这些表达方式在写作或翻译中可以模仿。

例句 26. Lessons did not start until 9 a.m., and William liked to fit in a quick game of football before the first class. Lessons continued until 5:20 p.m., when the boys were free to play more sport before supper, and after chapel it was lights out at 8 p.m. （p. 37）

🔎 说明　"to fit in"，即"to find time to do sth"，早晨第一节课之前

抓空踢会儿球。一个小动词"fit"，与介词"in"搭配表达这个意思。用"to find time to play..."也行，但"to fit in a quick game"，这种平易、活泼的 Anglo-Saxonism 很新颖。

例句 27. His protection officers... lived in private accommodation on the perimeter of the school grounds next to the tennis court and the art school. Both had been told to keep their distance from William and allow him space and time with his peers.（p. 37）

💡 **说明**　威廉的保镖被告知与威廉保持距离，"to keep their distance from..."，汉语里也有类似说法，"和某某保持距离"，但往往是提醒，"不要和某某接近"，或"防备某某"的含义。用英语表达汉语的这层意思，可用"to keep your distance from sb"这个说法。

"... allow him space and time with his peers"，让他有和同伴在一起的空间和时间，初读这个句子不觉有什么出奇之处，但"allow"和介词短语"with his peers"却构成一个最简洁的搭配；这个意思可以用其他形式表达，但不如这个好。

例句 28. Both Diana and Charles were delighted with how well William settled in at Ludgrove. He was in the top stream for most of his subjects and one of the best swimmers at the school.（p. 39）

💡 **说明**　我们说某某学生成绩好，总是排在前几名，或名列前茅，英语说"in the top stream"。还有，如：

1. Academically, Catherine fared well and although she wasn't always in the top stream she was a good all-rounder.（p. 162）

虽然凯特不在前几名，但她是全面发展的好学生。

2. But Harry's tomfoolery came with a price, and by the end of his second year he had slipped into the bottom group for nearly every subject.（p. 84）

指哈里在课堂上非常淘气，经常捣乱，于是，功课不行了，几乎每门功课都是垫底，这就是他所付出的代价（price）。

英语词典里有一个例句很好：

She was put into the fast stream. 她被分在快班。

例句 29. There was never a big deal when she showed up at the school and she seemed to like that. For us boys she was just William and Harry's pretty mummy, not a princess.（p. 39）

♥ 说明　威廉王子的一个同学回忆说，戴安娜去学校看威廉踢球时，学生们从来不太在意，他们从不把她看作王妃，只是把她看作威廉和哈里的漂亮母亲，而戴安娜似乎也喜欢这样。

关于"deal"，陆谷孙《英汉大词典》这样解释："局面，情况，事情"，并给了一个例子说明它的用法："make a big deal out of..."（极端重视；对……小题大做）。这个解释能帮助我们恰当理解此文中的"a big deal"，学生们没有把王妃的到来看作什么了不起的大事。

书中还有几处也出现了"a deal"：

1. If people made a deal about who he was he would colour up and move the conversation away from him.（p. 94）

这是指威廉王子，当人们大谈威廉的身份时，"made a deal about who he was"，他会脸红，赶紧把话题引开。

2. It was a big deal and all of the girls, even the not so sporty ones, would rush to the playing fields to get a glimpse of William.（p. 162）

威廉王子上小学时，经常来凯特的学校踢球。每次威廉来学校踢球，都会引起轰动，凯特一定要到场观看。全校的女孩子们，即使不爱好体育，也都跑来一睹王子的风采，所以这里用了"It was a big deal..."。

3. For William it was no big deal, but for Kate the cancellation was a sign of something more sinister to come.（p. 199）

有一年，威廉已经答应参加凯特 12 月 31 日的庆祝活动 Hogmanay，但最后一分钟威廉变卦，他决定和自己的家人在一起，这对威廉不算回事，这里说"For William it was no big deal"，但对凯特则是莫大的打击。

例句 30. Harry had come out of his shell. He was more talkative and confident in class...（p. 42）

💡 **说明**　查尔斯说，他的小儿子哈里"was the one 'with the more gentle nature'"，但他在学校的最后一年，性格有了变化。"Harry had come out of his shell"，这是一个比喻用法，英语词典这样解释："to become less shy and more confident when talking to other people"，文中后面的一句话也解释了这个意思。

例句 31. The cameras clicked away, but it was only the photographs of Diana with the boys which made the papers the next day. "It was a great pity that they didn't also show the pictures of Charles embracing the boys..."（p. 45）

💡 **说明**　戴安娜在王室游艇上拥抱孩子的时候，记者不停地拍照，第二天这些照片登上了报纸，但遗憾的是，报纸没有登查尔斯和孩子拥抱的照片。戴安娜在很多场合尽显风采，而查尔斯经常被冷落，这让他感到尴尬。

英语动词的多义性带来了其用法的灵活性，也为学习者制造了困难。动词"make"就是一例，它有很多意思，这里的"make the papers"基本意思是"reach"，或"appear on"，即"登上报纸"。我们或者不会想到这样写，但它确实很简单、很灵活，因而很有魅力。词典里也有例句：

The story made the front pages of national newspapers.

如果我们信仰"Beauty lies in simplicity"，我们可以从中体会英语之美。

例句 32. *Diana—Her True Story* had shaken the House of Windsor to its foundations and ensured the princess's exclusion from the circle of the royal family for good.（p. 47）

💡 **说明** 1992 年 6 月，安德鲁·莫顿（Andrew Morton）出版了一本关于戴安娜的书，*Diana—Her True Story*，披露戴安娜的很多隐私，这本书的出版对于英国王室是一个灾难性的事件。

"foundations" 本来指建筑 "地基"，也指 "基金会" 等，当用其引申意思时，常与 "shake" 或 "rock" 连用，例如：

［原文］1. 乱烘烘人来人往，里面哭声摇山振岳。（《红楼梦》）

［译文］Despite the hour, a multitude of people were hurrying through it in both directions, while from inside the house issued a sound of lamentation that seemed to shake the very buildings to their foundations.（霍克斯译）

［原文］2. 士隐意欲也跟了进去，方举步时，忽听一声霹雳，有若山崩地陷。（《红楼梦》）

［译文］Shi-yin was on the point of following them through the archway when suddenly a great clap of thunder seemed to shake the earth to its very foundations, making him cry out in alarm.（霍克斯译）

例句 33. Young, energetic and attractive, Tiggy, who had grown up in Wales and was a close friend of Charles, loved shooting, hunting and fishing, more than enough to secure the affection and trust of the young princes.（p. 49）

💡 **说明** 查尔斯为他的两个儿子请了一个保姆，叫 Tiggy Legge-Bourke，这段文字是对她的描写。

这里的 "... more than enough" 指什么，特别是 "... more than enough to secure the affection and trust of the young princes" 如何翻译，值得考虑。

Tiggy（蒂姬）不但 "Young, energetic and attractive"，而且 "loved shooting, hunting and fishing"，这些都表现在一个保姆身上实为难得，才貌双全，所以她赢得了小王子们的喜爱和信任。

试译如下：

查尔斯的好友 Tiggy 在威尔士长大，她年轻、漂亮、精力充沛，喜欢射击、打猎和钓鱼。这些都足以让她赢得小王子们的喜爱和信任。

关于"attractive"，词典说法笼统，为了行文顺畅，这里译作"漂亮"；结合上下文，似乎译作"有魅力"更好些，但行文方式需要调整。而"more than enough"，根据汉语的通俗说法，译作"足以"即可。

翻译的乐趣在于译文可以反复推敲，推敲的过程是寻找"好"的过程，直到自己比较满意为止，说是"为止"，实为几近"无止境"，因为译文很难做到十全十美。

翻译还有一个特点，那就是：原文只有一个，译文可以是多个；不同译者根据同一个原文所译出的文字常常不相同。某个措辞或句子有可能相同，但就一个语段（或段落）而言，其行文方式和叙事语气总是不一样的。一个人有一个人的译法，即使同一个译者在不同时期翻译同一篇文章，也会译出不同版本。所以，读译文应是取其优长，弃其不足。

例句 34. Above his desk, the thirteen-year-old prince straightened the picture of Cindy Crawford which took pride of place on the wall.（p. 51）

说明　威廉王子来到伊顿公学，住进宿舍后开始布置他的房间，他把美国超级模特辛迪·克劳馥（Cindy Crawford）的照片挂在墙上最显眼的地方。

"pride of place"，指最显著或最重要的位置，这里用的动词是"took"，而且"pride of place"之前不用冠词。

下面例句中的"pride of place"用的动词是"had"：

... and as Kate raised her champagne flute to toast the birthday prince at the aptly themed Out of Africa celebration at Windsor Castle, it was Jecca who had pride of place next to William at the head table.（p. 155）

在宴会桌上坐在王子身边是一种殊荣。

例句 35. At Manor House little fanfare was made about the royal arrival at William's request. He was deeply embarrassed by the attention and wanted nothing more than to slip seamlessly into the background.（p. 54）

说明 威廉进了伊顿公学以后，校方为了威廉的人身安全在校园各个角落以及他的住宿地 Manor House 安装了各种安保设施。

翻译这两个句子需要弄清楚三个关键词："fanfare""seamlessly"，以及"background"，特别是"seamlessly"如何译是个问题。

"fanfare"，意思是大张旗鼓地宣传庆祝，但按照威廉的要求，在他住进宿舍时不搞庆祝活动，这就是文中所说的"little fanfare was made"；"seamlessly"，是形容词"seamless"的副词形式，其本来意思是"无缝地"，有时也引申作"周密地"，是一个很好的英语副词，在英语著作里偶尔能见到。威廉作为英国王室王子来到伊顿公学上学，这不仅是校方的一件大事，也会引起媒体的关注，制造轰动全国的新闻。但威廉不喜欢这样，他希望能够悄悄地、不声不响地住进来。

"background"，按照英语词典的解释，"less important position"；"to slip seamlessly into the background"，是说威廉希望像平常人一样，别把他的入住弄成一个轰动事件，自然而然地、不声不响地住进来就行了，意思大概如此。

翻译时，先是把单个的词译好，然后还要考虑句子的组织和整体的叙事语气，都要和原文保持一致，这个更重要。

可比较一下例句8中的"While Diana had wanted to blend into the background, the British public positioned her centre stage..."。

例句 36. "There were three of us in this marriage, so it was a bit crowded," she said, famously referring to Camilla Parker Bowles.（p. 57）

说明 戴安娜与查尔斯结婚后，发现查尔斯与他的旧日情人卡米拉仍在幽会，因此，戴安娜说了上面的话。

戴安娜谈论自己的婚姻悲剧时没有使用任何粗鲁暴躁的语言，只是说 "There were three of us in this marriage, so it was a bit crowded"，苦涩之中不乏幽默，从语言可以窥见她的修养。

［补充说明］查尔斯写过一本自传，他在书里承认和戴安娜结婚以后又开始跟卡米拉幽会，英国媒体公开了他们的电话通话录音。这对王室声誉影响很坏，英国公众开始怀疑君主政体，要求实行共和的声浪席卷全国。下面这段文字说的就是这件事：

The reputation of British monarchy was at its lowest ebb for decades, and it was not just William who could take no more of this farcical and public warring. Polls in national newspapers questioned the need for a monarchy that didn't pay taxes and a tide of republicanism washed over the country. (p. 59)

请留意这段文字中的 "... washed over..."，下面的文字也用了这个搭配。

蒂姆·克莱顿（Tim Clayton）写的 *Diana—Story of a Princess* 中关于戴安娜婚礼的盛况曾写道，戴安娜在父亲陪同下去圣保罗大教堂举行婚礼，广场上人们高呼 "Good luck, Diana" "You look fabulous" "Congratulations!" 等。书中描写戴安娜此时的心情时，也用了 "wash over"：

Diana shared the famous Glass Coach with her father. They waved continuously as they passed through the crowds. In Trafalgar Square there were so many people, and the cheering grew so loud... The general feeling of optimism and pleasure was washing over her. (p. 82)

葛浩文翻译莫言《师傅越来越幽默》时也用了这个表达方式：

［原文］他的心里泛起一丝悲凉之情，好似微风吹过湖面，水上皱起波纹。但这丝悲凉很快就过去了，即将开始的崭新生活就像那个买小猪的女人一样让他浮想联翩，没有工夫伤感。

［译文］Waves of melancholy washed over him, like the ripples on a breezy lake. But only for a moment. A new stage in his life was about to begin, and the new life, like the woman who bought the little pigs, filled his mind with too many lustful thoughts for him to get sentimental.

［说明］英美作家和翻译家都用"wash over"，看来这个搭配已经从"比喻"演变成常用语。学习这个说法，写作、翻译时不妨试着使用。

例句 37. On 13 January 2002 the *News of the World* had gathered enough evidence to run the story and splashed HARRY'S DRUG SHAME across the front page.（p. 88）

💡 说明　这是指哈里吸毒丑闻，文中的"splashed"与"washed over"有异曲同工之妙。

例句 38. William was also fascinated by the notion that people could see into the future, and when he was younger would often make secret calls to his mother's psychic, begging her for a reading.（p. 66）

💡 说明　戴安娜有几个信奉"招魂说"（spiritualists）和几个占星家（astrologers）的朋友，还有一个有"通灵术"的人（psychic），经常接受他们的指导。这些人能够"预知未来"，威廉感觉很神奇，有时背着母亲给那个有"通灵术"的人打电话，"begging her for a reading"，请求她给自己说说自己的未来。

汉语文化里有"算命"的说法，《现代汉语词典》说，"凭人的生辰八字，用阴阳五行推算人的命运，断定人的吉凶祸福（迷信）"，《新时代汉英大词典》将其译作"fortune-telling"。

汉语文化里也有"算卦"的说法，意思是"根据卦象推算吉凶"，《新时代汉英大词典》译文，"to practise divination"；林语堂的《当代汉英词典》译文是"to practise divination by *baguah*"，而"算卦先生"则译作"a practioner of *baguah*"；"算命"，林语堂译作"to tell fortune"，"算命先生"，译作"fortune teller"。

"算命"或"算卦"，在汉语，既可用作名词，也可用作动。做名词时翻译比较好处理，但用作动词时，如何翻译是个问题，比如，"我去算个命（或算个卦）"，如何将这句汉语译成英语呢？

此例中的"reading"值得借鉴，可能源自动词"read"（in the sense of reading one's mind/thoughts），或也有"interpret"之意。如何翻译汉语的"算命""占卦"，如果是使用动词，而且还要符合英语表达习惯，这也许很需要思索。但"... for a reading"这个说法似乎很可取，如"去找算命先生算个命"，"go to the fortune teller for a reading"，或"找占星家占个卦"，"go to the astrologer for a reading"。这个短语解决了用什么动词翻译"算命""占卦"之困惑。

凯特在圣安德鲁斯大学上学时表现出表演天赋（a natural flair for acting），曾在一个家庭录像节目里扮演请算命先生算命的角色，其情节是这样的：

... she speaks to a fortune teller. "Soon you will meet a handsome man, a rich gentleman," the soothsayer tells her. "It's all I ever hoped for. Will he fall in love with me?" asks the teenage Kate. "Indeed he will," the fortune teller assures her. "And marry me?" she enquires clasping her hands to her chest. "And marry you," confirms the soothsayer. At the end of the play her beau, William, gets down on a bended knee and proposes. Kate responds, "It's all I've ever longed for. Yes, oh yes, dear William."（p. 159）

这段文字里谈算命先生时用了两个词，"fortune teller"和"soothsayer"，而且是交替使用，看来翻译汉语文化中的"算命先生"时，选择其中任何一个都可以。

例句 39. Harry had heard all about Sandhurst from Mark Dyer. The college was formed in 1947 by the amalgamation of two previous army training colleges...（p. 179）

💡 说明 我们在前面谈到具有动词或形容词意义的名词的运用，这里的"amalgamation"又是一例。它是动词"amalgamate"的名词形式，其意思相当于汉语的"联合""合并"。英语词典里有例句：

A number of colleges have amalgamated to form the new university.

我们国内前些年有不少大学合并的例子，从学科建设考虑，几个学院合并到某个大学里，使它的学科更加全面、更有竞争力。今后翻译有关学校合并或别的单位合并内容时，可以放心使用动词"amalgamate"或名词"amalgamation"，因为以英语为母语国家的作者是这样写的，英语词典里也有类似的例句。

例句 40. The Palace tried its hardest to bury the story but inevitably Charles's parenting was called into question. Diana's death was still fresh in people's minds, and if anyone was to blame it was Charles...（p. 89）

💡 说明　哈里吸毒被媒体曝光，那时戴安娜刚刚死去不久，人们自然开始质疑查尔斯的为父之道。"Charles's parenting was called into question"，这个表达方式很好，值得借鉴。

关于哈里因吸毒而被谴责，有几种不同的表达方式，值得学习：

1. "... it was Harry who took the flak and had to suffer the indignity of being front-page news..."（pp. 89-90）

💡 说明　关于"flak"，英语词典解释为"severe criticism"，严厉批评。

2. "The Palace had to be seen to protect Charles and William, so it was Harry who took the stick..."（p. 90）

💡 说明　挨棍子，即遭受严厉批评、谴责等。

3. William felt guilty that his brother had taken all the blame.（p. 90）

💡 说明　"to take the blame"，意为挨批、接受谴责。

例句 41. He was very easy-going and very humble; he didn't go around using his title to get him anywhere, if anything he downplayed it.（p. 94）

🔖 **说明**　这段文字，用一系列简单词语和表达方式，描写威廉王子，写得好。如 "easy-going"（随和）、"humble"（谦虚）、"he downplayed it"（他低调对待）。威廉如此随和、谦虚、低调，一个王位继承人具有这样的品质很难得。

关于 "if anything"，陆谷孙《英汉大词典》里有一个解释："要说有什么区别的话"，并有例句："His family, if anything, was poorer than mine." 这个解释也适用。

《牛津高阶英汉双解词典》说，"if anything shows a tentative opinion"。

本文里的 "if anything" 的意思大约相当于 "相反"。

这个 "if anything" 用得很广，但要用得恰当，要审视上下文。

葛浩文翻译萧红的《王阿嫂的死》也用了 "if anything"：

［原文］五岁的小环，开始做个小流浪者了。从她贫苦的姑家，又转到更贫苦的姨家。

［译文］So Little Huan had become a homeless waif at the age of five. She had lived for a while with some impoverished paternal relatives, then had been bundled off to some maternal relatives who were, if anything, even worse off.

这个译法译出了原文的行文语气，地道的英语。

> **例句** 42. ... and Charles had hated the limitations of a life dictated solely by duty. "You can't understand what it is like to have your whole life mapped out for you," he had said. "It's so awful to be programmed."（p. 98）

🔖 **说明**　查尔斯作为王位继承人，他的前途是由英国王室的继承传统安排好的，他的生活是被王室的清规戒律束缚住的，他要按照宫廷规矩行事，没有选择自由，所以他说 "You can't understand what it is like..."。

这个段落里有三个表达方式，意思类似：

1. "dictated"，英语词典解释："to tell sb what to do, especially in an

annoying way"，意为指使、强行规定。

2. "mapped out"，规划。

3. "programmed"，事先安排规划好。

但值得注意的是，这三个动词的含义都是"由别人安排、规划"。

例句 43. It was training that would serve William in good stead and make him realise just how much he loved army life. The only reminder of home was when Charles emailed William his A-level results.（p. 100）

💡 说明　威廉在军队里参加训练，当他看见周围的士兵射击机关枪时，他没有惊慌失措，表现得很从容。"... that would serve William in good stead"，这是说，军队生活对他有益。

这是一个固定短语，准确表达"某事对某人有益"这个概念，有时也说"stand sb in good stead"，英语词典里有这样的例句：

Your languages will stand you in good stead when it comes to finding a job. 当你找工作时，你的多语能力对你有利。

例句 44. The first week tested everyone's resolve, and at one point William, like the others, just wanted to come home. The weather had closed in and it rained for days. They tried their hardest to entertain themselves, but their spirits flagged and William spent most of his time in his tent. "The wind whipped up into a storm. The tents were flapping so violently that we thought they were going to blow away," he said afterward... "It was so demoralising even though we managed to keep ourselves going by singing and stuff like that."（p. 106）

💡 说明　威廉王子与朋友们一起去南美旅游，或者说是野营，所去之处是一个荒野而孤立的地方，他们到达目的地后天气骤变。这段描写天气和人的情绪的文字都很好，可学着用在我们的英语写作和汉英翻译中。

［原文］1. ... tested everyone's resolve...

［说明］考验每个人的决心。

［原文］2. The weather had closed in...

［说明］在谈到天气时，"to close in"的意思是"to get worse"，雨下起来没完没了，天气情况越来越糟糕。

［原文］3. ... but their spirits flagged...

［说明］此处的"flagged"是说人们变得"less enthusiastic"，情绪低落。

［原文］4. The wind whipped up into a storm...

［说明］我们可能说"The wind became a storm"，或"The wind escalated/rose into a storm"等，这里的"whipped up"更口语化；英语词典说"whip up"和"rouse"是同义词，并举例："He was a speaker who could really whip up a crowd."（他是一个极具煽动力的演说家。）

［原文］5. The tents were flapping...

［说明］"flapping"这个词酷似象声词，甚至让我们能听见大风吹打帐篷时发出的噼啪声。

［原文］6. demoralising

［说明］天气让人情绪低落，与"their spirits flagged"所表达的意思类似。

例句 45. We got on well but I think we would have got on well even if nothing had been going on romantically. It was very much a university thing, just a regular university romance.（p. 140）

说明 这段话是威廉曾经的女朋友卡利（Carley）所说。"... going on romantically""a university thing""a regular university romance"，这几个英语表达方式出自一个年轻学生之口，语气比较随意，表达方式简单而又有内涵，但翻译到中文如何处理是好，在中国的大学里，当学生们谈论这些话题时是怎么表述的，有没有与此类似的说法，可以想一想。

例句 46. The Queen and the Duke of Edinburgh were kept abreast of the situation. "He needs to knuckle down and not wimp out" was Philip's typically blunt response.（p. 143）

说明　威廉不喜欢学校的艺术课程，女王丈夫爱丁堡公爵说了以上的话。这里的"to knuckle down"，英语词典说："to begin to work hard at sth"；而"wimp out"，英语词典说："to not do sth that you intended to do because you are too frightened or not confident enough to do it"，因为畏缩或没有信心而不敢做。这两个表达方式出自女王丈夫之口一定是地道英语；他没有用具有同样意思的"to work hard"，也许因为这个说法用得很多，已经没有新鲜感。类似的例子还有：

1. With his military training due to end in October, Harry had to knuckle down to some serious work.（p. 212）

2. Unsurprisingly the teenage prince was more interested in having fun than knuckling down, and it was no great surprise when he failed two of his AS levels at the start of his final year.（p. 113）

威廉正在享受大学入学前的一年假期，哈里急切地等待着学校放假，他只想玩而不想努力学习，但他进入大学前的资格考试 AS levels 有两门没有通过。

看来"to knuckle down"这个表达方式使用频率颇高，当我们做汉英翻译想表达"努力工作"或"努力学习"时，不妨替换一下习惯使用的"to work hard"，尝试使用"to knuckle down"。

注释：

1. A levels：Advanced level，英国中学毕业年级的单科考试。

2. AS levels：Advanced Subsidiary level，英国学生在 17 岁时参加的考试，通过此考试及 A2 证书考试的学生才有资格入大学。

例句 47. "Kate looked amazing," recalled one of the models. "Her hair was slightly frizzy and with her wasp-like waist and washboard stomach she stole the show. She always had a complex about her legs, which she complained were too short..."（p. 146）

［原文］1. wasp-like waist and washboard stomach...

［说明］蜂腰和搓板肚，两个很形象的形容词。

［原文］2. She always had a complex about her legs, which she complained were too short...

［说明］这句话可以理解为"她总是忧虑自己的腿，抱怨她的腿太短"。

关于名词"complex"，英语词典里有两个重要解释：

1. "if sb has a complex about sth, they are worried about it in a way that is not normal"，非正常忧虑；

2. "a mental state that is not normal"，情结，比如："a guilt complex"（内疚情结）、"an inferiority complex"（自卑情结）、"a persecution complex"（受迫害情结）等。

这个意义上的"complex"是一个常用词，也是一个表现力很强的词，应该学会使用它。

例句 48. According to one of her friends at St Andrews, she remained level-headed and kept her feet on the ground during the early months of their courtship. "She never got above her station, and even though she had secured the most sought-after boy at St Andrews she never gloated."（p. 170）

💡 说明 英语里一些很普通的名词，孤立看，并没有特别的意义，但当它们和动词或介词搭配使用时，就能表达特定的意思。这种搭配很灵活，在英语著作里用得很多。这种现象体现英语之妙用，也体现英语之难学，这是其中一个原因。

［原文］1. she... kept her feet on the ground...

［说明］"ground" 是一个很寻常的名词，但当它和 "keep sb's feet on" 搭配时，就衍生出 "讲究实际""从实际出发" 等新意。凯特是一个平民，而威廉是英国王子，她很实际，并未因为王子追她而变得飘飘然。

［原文］2. She never got above her station...

［说明］"station" 常用来表示 "车站"，火车站、地铁站、汽车站等，这里是表示人的身份、社会地位等，而 "above her station" 则具有 "超出她的身份" 之意；英语词典给了一个类似的例句：

She was definitely getting ideas above her station.

意为 "她的想法超出了她的身份"。

学英语掌握词汇固然重要，但掌握词汇的搭配更重要，好搭配有助于创造好句子。英语里各种不同形式的搭配很多，如主语与动词搭配、动词与副词搭配、名词与形容词搭配等。学英语要培养学习 "搭配" 的意识。

例句 49. "She was debating whether or not she should text or call him. She got quite drunk on white wine and really let her guard down," recalled one of the group. "She said how sad she was and how much she was missing William, but she never mentioned it after that."（p. 173）

📍 **说明** 一年暑假，威廉和他的朋友去希腊度假，未带凯特，凯特心里不快。她和朋友们去了法国，她的一个同伴回忆凯特在法国时的心情时说了上面的话。

这个段落里有几个常用的表达方式，如 "debate""text""let her guard down" 等。在这里，"debate" 相当于汉语常说的 "考虑"，我们习惯于说 "think""consider" 等，较少想到使用 "debate"，这对我们可能是一个新用法；"text" 是动词，意为用手机发短信；"let her guard down"，指凯特因喝了酒而说话不太谨慎，把自己内心的想法都说了出来，表达这个意思有时也说 "unguarded"，如 *Diana—Story of a Princess* 中有这样一句话：

There were times when she was so frustrated that she would become unguarded in her criticism, for example, towards the Queen.（p.155）

这些简单而地道的表达方式在我们的写作和翻译中偶尔会用得上。

例句 50. You may have met your husband or wife. Our title as the top matchmaking university in Britain signifies so much that is good about St Andrews, so we rely on you to go forth and multiply.（p. 178）

💡 **说明**　这是圣安德鲁斯大学校长（vice-chancellor）布赖恩·兰博士（Dr Brian Lang）在毕业典礼上给毕业生致辞的最后一段文字。

这个"multiply"很有意思，在数学里它是"乘法"，也含成倍增加的意思，在生物学里意为"繁殖"。在这个致辞里，校长以这样的用词鼓励学生们结婚生子，不乏幽默。

例句 51. He had brought with him several jars of polish, which he would use daily to buff his army boots, and his own ironing board. For a boy who had never had to press a shirt or shine his shoes, it was a rude awakening.（p. 181）

💡 **说明**　这个"a rude awakening"在我们的阅读中比较少见，英语词典是这样解释的："an occasion when you realize sth or become aware of sth"，醒悟，觉悟；这个短语在本文里的意思是，在军队里参加训练时，威廉认识到自己擦鞋是怎么回事，体会到自己擦鞋的滋味。

《牛津高阶英汉双解词典》有例句：

If they had expected a warm welcome, they were in for a rude awakening. （They would soon realize that it would not be warm.）要是他们以为会受到热烈欢迎，他们很快就会醒悟并非如此。

例句 52. The last thing anyone wanted was the newspapers running pictures of Charles and Diana alongside Charles and his new bride. It would cause unnecessary hurt to everyone, especially William and Harry.（p. 175）

💡 **说明**　戴安娜死后，查尔斯和他的情人卡米拉筹备结婚。王室的婚事，各路媒体争相报道，抢登照片，人们最不想看到的是报纸上把查尔斯和戴安娜的照片与查尔斯和他的新娘的照片并排登出来，因为那会对人们，特别是对威廉和哈里造成不必要的伤害。

"the last thing/person" 是英语的一个习惯用法，其中的 "the last..." 不是 "最后的……"。形式上它是肯定的，意思却是否定的。《牛津高阶英汉双解词典》里有一个例句，能帮助我们了解它的用法：

He's the last person I'd trust with a secret. 我要是有什么秘密，告诉谁也不能告诉他。

陆谷孙《英汉大词典》也有一个例句：

An actress is the last thing she will ever be. 她最不愿意干的就是当演员。

这是一个很有表现力的表达方式，写作和翻译时可以试着使用。

例句 53. The Queen, who had been "under the weather" according to William, had asked her private secretary to request that the ninety-minute ceremony was moved from the morning to the afternoon to ensure that she had plenty of time to get to St Andrews.（p. 177）

💡 **说明**　动词 "move" 不但可用于表示挪动在空间上的位置，也可用于表示改变时间，与 "put off" "postpone" 为同义词。英语词典有例句：

Let's move the meeting to Wednesday.

陆谷孙《英汉大词典》例句：

We have to move the date of the party.

动词 "move" 的这种用法在词典里得到印证。

例句 54. It was not long before rumours were circulating among their friends that something was going on. William had apparently had a secret crush on Jecca since the first time he met her. She was beautiful, with long blond hair, deep-blue eyes and legs like a gazelle. (p. 154)

💡 **说明** "William had apparently had a secret crush on Jecca"，是说威廉曾经"暗恋"过杰卡（Jecca）。"暗恋"，一般是指男女之间一方暗恋另一方，当然也不排除相互"暗恋"的情况。

林语堂的《当代汉英词典》未收入"暗恋"一词，吴景荣、程镇球主编的第一版《新时代汉英大词典》也未收入此词，潘绍中主编的第二版《新时代汉英大词典》增补了这个词，它是这样解释和翻译的："to love secretly"，并有示例："an old couple who fell in love secretly and then got married"。

这里可能是指两个人的恋爱没有公开，也可能是指两个人在彼此暗恋。

我们做汉英翻译时，习惯借助副词；但英语常用固定短语表达。

书中还有一个例句使用了"crush"：

Her first schoolgirl crush was on Andrew de Perlaky, who now sings with musical group Teatro, using the stage name Andrew Alexander. (p. 160)

这里的"first schoolgirl crush"，指凯特上学时最初的暗恋对象是安德鲁·德伯拉基（Andrew de Perlaky），表达此类意义时，"crush"后面总是用介词"on"。

例句 55. Always impeccably dressed, she was advised never to talk to the press, but to politely smile at photographers, who she handled with aplomb. (p. 195)

💡 **说明** 因为记者很难缠，凯特被告知不要理睬他们，但在摄影记者面前要有礼貌地微笑。这里的"with aplomb"是英语固定短语，常与动词"handle"搭配使用，意思是沉着应对。又如：

When he landed in Sydney and visited a community centre, William handled with aplomb a six-year-old girl who asked if his mummy had

died. "Yes, she did," he said bending down to her height. "It was pretty sad."
（p. 309）

2009 年春天，威廉王子访问澳大利亚，在悉尼一个社区活动中心遇见一个六岁小女孩，小女孩问威廉："你的妈妈是否死了？"小女孩的问题很天真，这对威廉是个敏感话题，但他的回答很得体，所以用了"handled with aplomb"。

例句 56. With her impressive knowledge of sport and her ability to drink most grown men under the table, Natalie immediately hit it off with Harry.（p. 208）

说明 "to hit it off with..."，英语固定短语，意为"to have a good friendly relationship with sb"，即，电视节目主持人纳塔利（Natalie）立即和哈里成了朋友。

作者的新书 *Harry and Meghan* 里也有一个例句：

His arrival attracted the paparazzi, however, and while the two of them hit it off, the zoom lenses clicked and clacked, sending back photos of the Princess entwined with Dodi...（pp. 23-24）

戴安娜与查尔斯离婚后，与埃及富商的儿子多迪（Dodi）发生恋情，这段文字是描写他们在豪华游艇上被媒体拍照的情景。这里也用了"hit it off"这个短语。

例句 57. William is a young man thinking of his future, thinking of his career, thinking of his responsibilities, thinking of holding on to what freedoms he can. Thinking, his comments suggested, of marriage.（p. 311）

说明 这里重复使用了五个以"thinking"开始的排比结构，这个例句说明，必要时，英语是可以这样写的，写好了可以避免重复感。

例句 58. "His Royal Highness Prince William of Wales and Miss Catherine

Middleton are engaged to be married," it said. "The Prince of Wales is delighted to announce the engagement of Prince William to Miss Catherine Middleton. The wedding will take place in the spring or summer of 2011 in London."（p. 333）

💡 **说明** 因为查尔斯和卡米拉提前走漏了订婚的消息，媒体得以大肆炒作，威廉与凯特的婚事不想再出现这种情况。上面的文字是按照威廉的示意，克拉伦斯宫通过王室脸书和推特发表的一个声明，正式宣布威廉与凯特已经订婚，并通报他们结婚的大约日期和地点。

这个声明使用的是正式文体，与一般叙述文字风格不同。

注释：

1. Clarence House，克拉伦斯宫，在伦敦，是王室住所。

2. the Prince of Wales，即威廉王子的父亲查尔斯。

例句 59. While Harry's career hung in limbo following his return from Afghanistan, William's had been meticulously planned.（p. 259）

💡 **说明** 关于 "limbo"，《牛津高阶英汉双解词典》解释："a situation in which you are not certain what to do next... especially because you are waiting for sb else to make a decision"，处于不确定状态。而 "hung in limbo"，意思是 "悬而未决"，把一个抽象的概念说得如此形象，很妙。

例句 60. It was the closest William and Kate had come to domestic bliss since their university days... As Kate darted around the kitchen searching for utensils, William would give her a kiss when he thought no one was looking.（p. 263）

💡 **说明** 每逢周末，威廉和凯特邀请同学到宿舍里共进晚餐，自己做英国风味的饭菜。描写凯特在厨房里寻找用具 "searching for utensils" 时，作者用了 "darted around"，一个简单的动词词组把行动迅速、动作敏捷的凯特在厨房的忙碌情景写活了，可考虑一下这句话如何翻译。

E. B. 怀特在他的散文 "Once More to the Lake" 里描写蜻蜓在鱼竿上

的动作时，也用了"darted"这个动词：

... the fly... darted two feet away, poised, darted two feet back, and came to rest again a little farther up the rod.

The Making of a Royal Romance 为我们提供了很多好的英语表达方式，通过阅读这本书，我们也能体会到英语之简、英语之美，因而也感受到学好英语需要下很大的功夫。

阅读斯特林·西格雷夫（Sterling Seagrave）：
Dragon Lady（片段）

简介

斯特林·西格雷夫，美国作家，他从1980年开始写作此书，至1992年出版，历时12年。书的正文长达463页，注释有100页之多，涉及有姓名、有身份的中外人物180人。

作家掌握史料翔实，对围绕慈禧皇太后的这段清末历史研究到家，文笔娴熟、流畅。

研究英美作家如何用英语写中国，对学习汉英翻译尤其有帮助。

斯特林·西格雷夫此前还写有《黄雨》（*Yellow Rain*）、《马科斯王朝》（*The Marcos Dynasty*）、《宋氏王朝》（*The Soong Dynasty*）等。

我们从书中选取关于晚清名臣李鸿章和曾国藩的三段文字，作家对他们做了细致的刻画，创造了多维的人物形象。作者的句子写得好，他的叙事方式值得研究、学习。

［原文］1. Now seventy-six years old, Li Hung-chang was the richest and most powerful political boss in the empire; he controlled railways, telegraphs, mines, shipping lines, and had a private army and legions of secret agents. Many leading mandarins and Manchu princes had accepted money from the viceroy to bail them out of financial difficulties and were in thrall to him ever after. (p. 4)

💡 **说明**　这段文字写七十六岁老臣李鸿章是一个有钱有势的朝廷要员。

1. 此处的 "mandarins" 指政府要员；

2. "legions of..."，即 "a large number of people of one particular type"，指某种类型的人，这里指大批特务；

3. "... to bail them out of financial difficulties..."，很多官员和满族亲王为了摆脱经济困境向李鸿章借钱，这个 "bail out of..." 是有用的表达方式；

4. "... were in thrall to him"，由此受制于他，或受他的影响，等。

「原文」2. As it was still hot, Li wore a hat of woven bamboo covered with cream gauze, resembling a lampshade, decorated with a peacock feather fastened by a tube of Burmese jade. His robes were covered by a long silk coat, slit up the sides to allow horseback riding, embroidered front and back with a mandarin square emblematic of rank—in Li's case a white crane, for the first rank.（p. 4）

💡 **说明**　这段文字写李鸿章的穿着打扮。

1. 李鸿章戴一顶竹帽（"a hat of woven bamboo"），蒙一层淡黄色薄纱（"covered with cream gauze"），样子好像一个灯罩（"resembling a lampshade"）；

2. 帽子上装饰着用翡翠翎管固定下来的（"fastened by a tube of Burmese jade"）花翎（"a peacock feather"）；

3. 长袍外面穿着丝织外罩（"His robes were covered by a long silk coat"），为了便于骑马两边开衩（"slit up the sides to allow horseback riding"）；

4. 前后有标识官员级别的方形图案（"embroidered front and back with a mandarin square emblematic of rank"），李鸿章的是标识一品官员的一只白色仙鹤（"in Li's case a white crane, for the first rank"）。

［原文］3. Tseng looked less like a warlord than he did a venerable sage. At five feet nine inches he was strongly built, with a broad chest and square shoulders but with a large head exaggerated by the Manchu fashion of shaving the brow and raiding the hair in a queue down the back. He wore a full beard that hung over his chest, adding to the impression of great sagacity. His sad hazel eyes were keen and penetrating, and his mouth was tightly compressed into thin lips. The overall impression was of strong will, high purpose, great dignity, and total self-possession. He was not a man to be trifled with.（p. 106）

例句 1. Tseng looked less like a warlord than he did a venerable sage.

💡 说明 "... than he did"，这个说法是为了避免重复前半句的 "looked less like"，也精简了文字。这个写法并不新鲜，但在写作或翻译中有意识这样写，就是好英语。

例句 2. ... but with a large head exaggerated by the Manchu fashion of shaving the brow and raiding the hair in a queue down the back.

💡 说明 这个句子在 "a large head" 之后的修饰语写得好，其中短语 "exaggerated by" 是构建这个句子的关键成分，有了这个短语就把为什么曾国藩的头看起来很大说清楚了，这是一个好句子，前后平衡，节奏感好。

例句 3. He wore a full beard that hung over his chest, adding to the impression of great sagacity.

💡 说明 此句中的分词短语 "... adding to the impression..." 虽然形式上是句子的次要成分，但它所传达的意思却非常重要：曾国藩是一个具有智慧的人，他胸前的胡须更增强了人们的这个印象。

例句 4. The overall impression was of strong will, high purpose, great dignity, and total self-possession.

💡 **说明**　此句"was of"之后一系列"形容词＋名词"词组所表达的意思有很强的表现力。

1. "strong will"，坚强的意志；

2. "high purpose"，崇高的志向；

3. "great dignity"，令人印象深刻的尊严；

4. "total self-possession"，沉着镇定。

这个"be of"后面加名词或名词词组的形式运用较广，有时比具有同样意义的形容词更具表现力。

例句 5. He was not a man to be trifled with.

此人不可小觑。

"to trifle with"意为"怠慢""小看"，这个动词词组多用于否定句，《牛津高阶英汉双解词典》有一个类似的例句：

He is not a person to be trifled with.

他这个人怠慢不得。

戴维·霍克斯（David Hawkes）翻译《红楼梦》：
The Story of the Stone

简介

　　戴维·霍克斯（David Hawkes, 1923—2009），英国汉学家、翻译家、红学家，一生从事中国文学的研究与翻译。曾翻译过包括《楚辞》及唐诗等在内的很多中国古代诗歌作品，特别是倾其一生翻译的中国古典小说《红楼梦》，成就了一项浩大的翻译工程，为中国文学西介、中英文化交流、汉英翻译研究做出了重要贡献，使其成为举世公认的翻译家。

　　戴维·霍克斯曾于 1948—1951 年在北京大学读研究生，1960—1971 年，在牛津大学教授汉学。为翻译《红楼梦》，霍克斯提前从牛津大学退休，花费 10 年时间，翻译完《红楼梦》前八十回，分三册，分别于 1973 年、1977 年、1980 年作为"企鹅经典"丛书的一部分在英国出版；后四十回由约翰·闵福德（John Minford）翻译，分两册，分别于 1982 年、1986 年出版。

　　英译本书名为 *The Story of the Stone*。

　　美国翻译理论家尤金·奈达说，翻译理论一定要建立在翻译实践的基础之上，换句话说，有关翻译的原则需要反映受尊敬的翻译家实际上是如何翻译的（We are convinced that theories about translation must be based primarily on practice. In other words, principles about how to translate need to reflect the ways in which highly respected translators have actually translated.）。

对戴维·霍克斯丰富的翻译实践进行理论研究和总结，会对探讨汉英翻译有重要意义。

这里所选例句皆出自上海外语教育出版社于2012年出版的由戴维·霍克斯和约翰·闵福德合译的汉英对照本《红楼梦》。

所选例句按内容分六个部分：经典句子；人物描写；对话；概念的具体化、形象化；汉英对应；听黛玉说诗，读霍克斯英译。

一．经典句子

译例 1

▶ **原文** 看官：你道此书从何而起？——说来虽近荒唐，细玩颇有趣味。（卷Ⅰ，第一回，第2页）

▶ **译文** GENTLE READER, What, you may ask, was the origin of this book? Though the answer to this question may at first seem to border on the absurd, reflection will show that there is a good deal more in it than meets the eye.（Vol. Ⅰ, chap. 1, p. 3）

1. ［原文］看官……
   ［译文］GENTLE READER...
   ［说明］"看官"是对读者的尊称，古代尊重读书人；译文"GENTLE READER"也是对读者的尊称，符合原文称呼。陆谷孙《英汉大词典》里对"gentle"有一个解释："有礼貌的；有教养的；文雅的"，这个解释对理解"看官"和"GENTLE READER"之间的关系有帮助。

2. ［原文］你道此书从何而起？

［译文］What, you may ask, was the origin of this book?

［说明］"you may ask" 作为插入语放在句中，行文产生一个停顿，正是问句的需要。此外，这样安排可使句中重读音节间隔均匀，节奏感明显，读起来好听。

3.［原文］说来虽近荒唐，细玩颇有趣味。

［译文］Though the answer to this question may at first seem to border on the absurd, reflection will show that there is a good deal more in it than meets the eye.

［说明］"近荒唐" 用 "to border on the absurd" 表示，"细玩" 用 "reflection" 表示，而 "颇有趣味" 的译文不是字面形式的对应，"其中味" 不是通过直观就能看得出来，需要通过思考、琢磨、玩味才能悟得出来。这个译文准确译出了原文意思，而且表达方式富有文学色彩。这是一个好译文。

译例 2

二人归坐，先是款酌慢饮，渐次谈至兴浓，不觉飞觥献斝起来。（卷 I，第一回，第18页）

▶ **译文** ... and the two men took their places and began to drink. At first they were rather slow and ceremonious; but gradually, as the conversation grew more animated, their potations too became more reckless and uninhibited.（Vol. I, chap. 1, p. 19）

1.［原文］二人归坐，先是款酌慢饮……

［译文］... and the two men took their places and began to drink. At first they were rather slow and ceremonious...

［说明］中秋夜，甄士隐邀贾雨村到家中小酌，开始，因顾及礼节，二人"款酌慢饮"，慢慢斟酒慢慢饮，译文用"slow and ceremonious"表示，把他们因拘泥礼节而举止谨慎的状态描画出来。

2.［原文］……渐次谈至兴浓，不觉飞觥献斝起来。

［译文］... but gradually, as the conversation grew more animated, their potations too became more reckless and uninhibited.

［说明］后来谈兴渐浓，不顾身份、场合，便"飞觥献斝"，畅快痛饮，译文用了"reckless and uninhibited"，描绘了他们无拘无束、无所顾忌的生动情景。汉语是"款酌慢饮""飞觥献斝"，译文是"slow and ceremonious""reckless and uninhibited"，意义和形式对应恰到好处。

译例 3

▶ **原文** "十九日乃黄道之期，兄可即买舟西上，待雄飞高举，明冬再晤，岂非大快之事。"（卷 I，第一回，第 20 页）

▶ **译文** "The almanac gives the nineteenth as a good day for travelling," he went on, addressing Yu-cun again. "You can set about hiring a boat for the journey straight away. How delightful it will be to meet again next winter when you have distinguished yourself by soaring to the top over all the other candidates!" (Vol. I, chap. 1, p. 21)

💡 **说明** "待雄飞高举，明冬再晤，岂非大快之事"，这是一个汉语感叹句，感叹语气在句尾；译者也将其译作一个英语感叹句，感叹语气在句首："How delightful it will be to..."

更难得的是"待雄飞高举"的处理，既体现了金榜题名，"distinguished yourself"，也译出了"雄飞"之寓意，"by soaring to the top"。

总之，这是一个出色的译文，不但意思译得准确，读起来也很有感叹句应有的气势。

译例 4

▶ **原文** 彼时虽有军民来救，那火已成了势了，如何救得下？（卷Ⅰ，第一回，第22页）

▶ **译文** ... and though the firemen came to put it out, by the time they arrived the fire was well under way and long passed controlling.（Vol. I, chap. 1, p. 23）

💡 **说明** "那火已成了势了"，即大火已经烧起来了，英语词典对 "under way" 有解释："having started"。译文 "the fire was well under way"，表达意思准确，和汉语说法几乎一致。

"如何救得下"，在汉语是反问句，意即"无法救了"，只好眼看着火烧下去，汉语的这种反问句在英译时常译作叙述句，所以，此处译为 "... and long passed controlling"。

译例 5

▶ **原文** 老老你放心，大远的诚心诚意来了，岂有个不教你见个真佛儿去的呢？（卷Ⅰ，第六回，第148页）

▶ **译文** Don't you worry, Grannie! After you've made such a long pilgrimage, we won't let you go home without seeing a real Buddha!（Vol. I, chap. 6, p. 149）

💡 **说明** 《红楼梦》第六回，《贾宝玉初试云雨情　刘老老一进荣国府》，刘老老先是见了周瑞家的，周瑞家的问道："今日是路过，还是特来的？"刘老老说："原是特来瞧瞧嫂子；二则也请请姑太太的安。"刘老老会说话，其实，她的本意是来见贾母的。

"大远的诚心诚意来了"，译作 "After you've made such a long pilgrimage"，这个 "pilgrimage" 好，比 "journey" 好，大老远的来朝圣，

和后面的"真佛儿"（"a real Buddha"）呼应，"we won't let you go home without seeing a real Buddha"，创造性的翻译。

译例 6

▶ **原文**　凤姐听了，眼圈儿红了一会子，方说道："'天有不测风云，人有旦夕祸福。'这点年纪，倘或因这病上有个长短，人生在世，还有什么趣儿呢！"（卷 I，第十一回，第 248 页）

▶ **译文**　Xi-feng's eyes became moist and for a moment she was too overcome to speak. "I know 'the weather and human life are both unpredictable'," she said at last, "but she's only a child still. If anything should happen to her as a result of this illness, I think all the fun would go out of life!"（Vol. I, chap. 11, p. 249）

1. ［原文］"天有不测风云，人有旦夕祸福。"

　［译文］"the weather and human life are both unpredictable"

　［说明］这个中国民间谚语据说始于宋代，已经流传近千年。大意是天气变化不可预测，人的祸福也不可预测。霍克斯抓住这个谚语的要义，译文简洁，属于意译。

　是否可以采取直译方法在译文里反映原文形式的对仗呢？不妨试一试。

2. ［原文］还有什么趣儿呢！

　［译文］I think all the fun would go out of life!

　［说明］用英语的"fun"译汉语的"趣儿"，很巧；用英语的固定短语"go out of life"表示生活没意思了，也是很准确的译法。

译例 7

▶ **原文** 大家看时，只见帮底皆厚八寸，纹若槟榔，味若檀麝，以手扣之，声如玉石。（卷Ⅰ，第十三回，第 286-288 页）

▶ **译文** The planks for the base and sides were at least eight inches thick. The wood had a grain like areca palm and a fragrance suggestive of musk and sandalwood. When rapped with the knuckles it gave off a hard, ringing sound like jade or stone.（Vol. Ⅰ, chap.13, p. 287）

1. ［原文］纹若槟榔，味若檀麝……

［译文］The wood had a grain like areca palm and a fragrance suggestive of musk and sandalwood.

［说明］第十三回，秦可卿死，家人寻找上好木料做棺材，薛蟠说他的木店里有好木料，据说是铁网山上的，做棺材万年不腐。此时大家正在观看刚刚从薛蟠那里抬来的木料。

"纹若槟榔，味若檀麝"，其中"纹若"是直观的，用"（looking）like"，看着像槟榔；"味若"是感观的，闻着像"檀麝"，译作"suggestive of musk and sandalwood"。逻辑和传译都很周密。

2. ［原文］以手扣之，声如玉石。

［译文］When rapped with the knuckles it gave off a hard, ringing sound like jade or stone.

［说明］译者用"hard"和"ringing"译了声音的性质，而"like jade or stone"则把原文的意思说透了，引起读者的听觉反应，再好不过的译文。

译例 8

▶ **原文**　贾政笑道："倒是此处有些道理。虽系人力穿凿，而入目动心，未免勾引起我归农之意。我们且进去歇息歇息。"（卷Ⅰ，第十七回，第 380 页）

▶ **译文**　"Ah, now, here is a place with a purpose!" said Jia Zheng with a pleased smile. "It may have been made by human artifice, but the sight of it is none the less moving. In me it awakens the desire to get back to the land, to a life of rural simplicity. Let us go in and rest a while!" (Vol. Ⅰ, chap.17, p. 381)

📍 **说明**　第十七回《大观园试才题对额》，贾政带领众客及宝玉来到大观园。

1.［原文］倒是此处有些道理。

［译文］Ah, now, here is a place with a purpose!

［说明］所谓"有些道理"，是说这个地方可以做文章，译作"a place with a purpose"，意为此处有文章可做，译者的理解和表达都符合原文。

2.［原文］人力穿凿……

［译文］made by human artifice...

［说明］指有人工巧做痕迹。

3.［原文］入目动心……

［译文］... but the sight of it is none the less moving

［说明］此处"入目"的译法很巧妙，看见此景让人心动，以一个完整的英语句子表达了汉语的"入目"和"动心"两个词组所表示的两个动作。

4.〔原文〕……归农之意。

〔译文〕.... the desire to get back to the land, to a life of rural simplicity.

〔说明〕译文译出了"归农"的意义，并补充了归农之后过简单的田园生活的意愿。

特别值得指出的是"倒是……"的翻译，此开头语并无实在意义，只是一种表示喜出望外的语气，译文"Ah, now"也并无实在意义，但准确再现了原文语气。

这段文字的译文可供学习、借鉴的东西不少。

译例 9

▶ **原文**　话说宝玉在黛玉房中说"耗子精"，宝钗撞来，讽刺宝玉元宵不知"绿蜡"之典，三人正在房中互相讽刺取笑。（卷 I，第二十回，第 470 页）

▶ **译文**　We have shown how Bao-yu was in Dai-yu's room telling her the story of the magic mice; how Bao-chai burst in on them and twitted Bao-yu with his failure to remember the "green wax" allusion on the night of the Lantern Festival; and how the three of them sat teasing each other with good-humoured banter.（Vol. I, chap. 20, p. 471）

💡 **说明**　中国古代章回小说和北方评书里常以"话说"开关，有承前启后的功能。这个"话说"用英语如何表达，值得研究。译者没有寻求它的英语对应词，在英语里也许未必有；他用了"how... how... and how..."，这个结构很符合原文的"意义"，也很符合原文的语气。英语的这个译法很有启示。

译例 10

▶ **原文** 宝钗在亭外听见说话，便煞住脚，往里细听……（卷 Ⅱ，第二十七回，第 6 页）

▶ **译文** Hearing voices inside the pavilion, Bao-chai halted and inclined her ear to listen.（Vol. Ⅱ, chap. 27, p. 7）

💡 **说明** 第二十七回，小红和坠儿在园中亭子里正偷偷说着手绢事，宝钗因追蝴蝶碰巧来到亭旁，听见里面有人说话，"便煞住脚，往里细听"。译文将"往里细听"译作"inclined her ear to listen"，这个译文把宝钗的姿势、神态写活了，我们甚至可以看见宝钗屏气敛声、往亭子里细听的样子，生动如画。一个"incline"写活了一个句子。霍克斯从他庞大的词库里将这个词信手拈来，一个词创造了一个形象，可谓"神来之笔"。

译例 11

▶ **原文** 这先生方伸手按在右手脉上，调息了至数，凝神细诊了半刻工夫，换过左手，亦复如是。（卷 Ⅰ，第十回，第 240 页）

▶ **译文** The doctor stretched out his hand and laid it on her right wrist, then, having first regulated his own breathing in order to be able to count the rate, he felt the pulse with great concentration for the space of several minutes, after which he transferred to the left wrist and spent an equal amount of time on that.（Vol. Ⅰ, chap.10, p. 241）

💡 **说明** 第十回，张太医为秦可卿号脉，这里所说"至数"可能是指中医所说的"脉数"或"息数"。关于"息数"，网上有这样的解释：中医说，一息就是一个呼吸之间。一呼一吸之间有一个停顿。一呼脉跳两下，一吸脉跳两下，中间停顿时脉跳一下，所以正常人一息是脉跳五下。超过五下就是"数脉"，少于五下就是"迟脉"。所以这个一息的时间就是一个呼吸的时间。但是这个时间要以正常人的呼吸时间为准，一般是以健康的医生的呼吸为准，不能用病人的呼吸来算。

译者在翻译"调息了至数"之前，一定做了研究，或请教了行家。他的译文，"having first regulated his own breathing in order to be able to count the rate"，很专业，可见他在这部小说的翻译上下了功夫。

二、人物描写

译例 1

▶ **原文**　第二个削肩细腰，长挑身材，鸭蛋脸儿，俊眼修眉，顾盼神飞，文彩精华，见之忘欲。（卷Ⅰ，第三回，第 56 页）

▶ **译文**　The second girl was rather tall, with sloping shoulders and a slender waist. She had an oval face under whose well-formed brows large, expressive eyes shot out glances that sparkled with animation. To look at her was to forget all that was mean and vulgar.（Vol. Ⅰ, chap. 3, p. 57）

1.［原文］削肩细腰，长挑身材……

　　［译文］rather tall, with sloping shoulders and a slender waist

　　［说明］第一印象是"长挑身材"，比较高，"rather tall"，细观其特征是"削肩细腰"，"with sloping shoulders and a slender waist"，先后次序合乎英语的叙事逻辑。

2.［原文］鸭蛋脸儿，俊眼修眉，顾盼神飞，文彩精华……

　　［译文］She had an oval face under whose well-formed brows large, expressive eyes shot out glances that sparkled with animation.

　　［说明］译文 "well-formed brows"，译出了"修眉"的意思；"顾盼

神飞，文彩精华"，这两个词组把探春的神采写活了，令读者印象深刻，但不好译。霍克斯译的这个句子，几乎每个实词都重要。一般有神的眼睛都大，所以译作"large, expressive eyes"，有神的眼睛都放光，而且充满活力，所以译作"shot out glances that sparkled with animation"。不仅写了眼神，也写了眼神所折射出来的智慧。

译例2

▶ **原文** 一会儿，果然带来个后生来，比宝玉略瘦些，眉清目秀，粉面朱唇，身材俊俏，举止风流，似更在宝玉之上，只是怯怯羞羞有些女儿之态，腼腆含糊的向凤姐请安问好，凤姐喜的先推宝玉笑道："比下去了！"（卷 I，第七回，第178页）

▶ **译文** ... (and Jia Rong disappeared for a while) and presently came back leading a youth who, though somewhat thinner than Bao-yu, was more than his equal in freshness and liveliness of feature, in delicacy of complexion, handsomeness of figure, and grace of deportment, but his painful bashfulness created somewhat a girlish impression. He approached Xi-feng and made his bow with a shy confusion which delighted her. "You've met your match!" she said to Bao-yu with a laugh, nudging him playfully.（Vol. I, chap. 7, p. 179）

1. [原文] 眉清目秀，粉面朱唇，身材俊俏，举止风流，似更在宝玉之上……

[译文] ... more than his equal in freshness and liveliness of feature, in delicacy of complexion, handsomeness of figure, and grace of deportment...

[说明] 针对原文四字语的排列，译文用了相应的名词词组，译文意义与原文相符，形式相当，而且照顾了原文行文节奏；"似更在宝玉之上"，原文是结论性的概括，放在句尾，而译文则是放在句首，表示秦

钟在以下这些方面在宝玉之上，从这个句子译文的安排可见霍克斯用心之苦。

2. [原文] "比下去了！"

[译文] "You've met your match!"

[说明] 凤姐说宝玉比不上秦钟。只几个字就把她的快人快语性格写出来了。译文很不错，但原文说法有上下之分，译文未分伯仲。或者可以说 "You're outshone!"，或 "Outshone!" 等。

译例 3

▶ **原文**　……"不公道，欺软怕硬！有好差使派了别人，这样黑更半夜送人就派我，没良心的忘八羔子！瞎充管家！你也不想想焦大太爷跷起一只腿，比你的头还高些。二十年头里的焦大眼里有谁？别说你们这一把子的杂种们！"（卷 I，第七回，第 184 页）

▶ **译文**　... while Big Jiao... accusing him of being unfair, and of always dropping on the weakest, and so on and so forth. "If there's a cushy job going you give it to someone else, but when it's a question of seeing someone home in pitch bloody darkness, you pick on me. Mean, rotten bugger! Call yourself a steward? Some steward. Don't you know who Old Jiao is? I can lift my foot up higher than your head! Twenty years ago I didn't give a damn for anybody, never mind a pack of little misbegotten abortions like you!"（Vol. I, chap. 7, p. 185）

1. [原文] 二十年头里的焦大眼里有谁？别说你们这一把子的杂种们！

[译文] Twenty years ago I didn't give a damn for anybody...

[说明] 第七回，秦钟来到贾府拜见宝玉，晚上管家赖升派焦大送秦钟回家，焦大发了脾气。从语气上一听就是一个居功自傲的粗人在说话。

关于"not give a damn"，《新牛津英语词典》说，"not care at all"，意即"谁我也不在乎"，与原文的意义和语气一致。

2. ［原文］……别说你们这一把子的杂种们!

　　［译文］... never mind a pack of little misbegotten abortions like you!

　　［说明］用"never mind"译"别说"，意义和语气都与原文一致。

3. ［原文］一把子的杂种们

　　［译文］a pack of little misbegotten abortions like you

　　［说明］陆谷孙《英汉大词典》里有个例子，"a misbegotten child"，译为"私生子"，霍克斯的"misbegotten abortions"的骂法比"私生子"更甚。

　　如何用英语翻译粗话是个问题，我们没有在英语文化中特定阶层里生活的经验，不知道用英语如何骂人。遇到这种情况，只好向说英语者询问或通过阅读积累，因为用英语骂人也要骂得像，否则尴尬。

译例 4

▶ **原文**　如此亲朋你来我去，也不能计数。只这四十九日，宁国府街上一条白漫漫人来人往，花簇簇官去官来。（卷 I，第十三回，第 292 页）

▶ **译文**　From then on there was a continuous stream of arrivals, and throughout the whole forty-nine-day period the street in front of the Ning-guo mansion was thronged with family mourners in white and mandarins in their colourful robes of office, milling in and out and to and fro all day long.（Vol. I, chap. 13, p. 293）

💡 **说明**　这是第十三回《秦可卿死封龙禁尉　王熙凤协理宁国府》中的一段文字，写秦可卿死后，人们来吊唁的情景。

1.［原文］白漫漫人来人往……

　　［译文］family mourners in white...

　　［说明］译文"family mourners"指明吊唁者是贾家的亲朋好友，一律身穿白衣。

2.［原文］……花簇簇官去官来。

　　［译文］... mandarins in their colourful robes of office.

　　［说明］"花簇簇"用"colourful robes of office"表示，指带着各种图案的官服，译得准确。

3.［原文］"人来人往""官去官来"

　　［译文］milling in and out and to and fro

　　［说明］用英语常用的表达方式把"人来人往"和"官去官来"这些叠词表达清楚了，取得了很好的修辞效果；这里的"milling"和"moving"是同样的意思。

译例 5

▶ **原文**　宝玉有一搭没一搭的说些鬼话，黛玉只不理。（卷Ⅰ，第十九回，第 462 页）

▶ **译文**　He tried to arouse her interest with desultory chat—talking for the sake of talking. Dai-yu took no notice.（Vol. Ⅰ, chap.19, p. 463）

📍 **说明**　第十九回，宝玉来到黛玉房间恋着不走，黛玉让他去，宝玉说："要去不能。咱们斯斯文文的躺着说话。"

"有一搭没一搭"，北方方言，意为没话找话，或随便聊聊，"desultory chat"，漫无目的，东拉西扯，为了清楚起见，译文补充了"talking for the sake of talking"，把"有一搭没一搭"的意思说透彻了。

"He tried to arouse her interest"，译者根据上下文需要，为做成一个完整句子的补充。

三、对话

译例 1

▶ **原文**　"扬州有一座黛山，山上有个林子洞……"

黛玉笑道："这就扯谎，自来也没有听见这山。"（卷 I，第十九回，第 464 页）

▶ **译文**　"Near the city of Yangzhou there is a mountain called Mt Yudai, in the side of which is a cavern called the Cave of Lin."

"That's false, for a start," said Dai-yu, "I've never heard of a mountain of that name."（Vol. I, chap.19, p. 465）

💡 **说明**　鲁迅说："《水浒》和《红楼梦》的有些地方，是能使读者由说话看出人来的。"（《花边文学·看书琐记（一）》）

《红楼梦》的语言处处传神，通过对话刻画人的性格更出色。如能把原文中人物的神态翻译出来是很难得的，霍克斯有很多传神译笔。宝玉顺口胡诌故事，黛玉一听就知道他在扯谎，她的一声"这就扯谎"，对宝玉的胡诌表示惊诧。译文"That's false, for a start"也一样，把黛玉的即时反应和语气都译出来了，行文节奏也和原文相符，连她的神态也展现出来。

这是一个通过对话展现人物性格的好例句。

译例 2

▶ **原文**　既来了，没有空回去的理，好歹尝一点儿，也是来我家一趟。（卷 I，第十九回，第 444 页）

▶ **译文** "Since you've decided to come," she said to Bao-yu with a smile, "we can't let you go without having tasted *something* of ours. You'll have to try *something*, just to be able to say that you have been our guest!"（Vol. I, chap.19, p. 445）

📍 **说明** 第十九回《情切切良宵花解语 意绵绵静日玉生香》里有很多袭人的语言。袭人是来自社会底层的贫家女孩，没有文化，说的话都是民间语言。她对母亲倾诉衷情时说的话，她规劝宝玉时的推心箴言，言不修琢，语不拿腔，句句在理，句句情真。她的语言是怎么形成的呢？有时代的印记，有家庭的熏陶，还有她对语言的敏感，才说得一口自然美妙的民间口语。笔者小时候常听母亲和邻里的妇女们在一起聊天，冬天坐在炕头上，夏天坐在家门口，那时常听见她们说类似的话，使用类似的词。现在农村老年妇女们说话时也许还能听见这种语言的余音。《红楼梦》这种来自民间的语言翻译起来很难，如果没有这种语言环境的熏陶，体会不出这种语言的韵味，翻译起来确实很难。有作家说，外国人要读《红楼梦》，让他先来中国学好汉语。霍克斯对《红楼梦》的语言和文化下了功夫，有很多地方译得确实很好。这里举的例句不太好译，比如，"也是来我家一趟"，意思比较充分地译出来了。

> **译例3**

▶ **原文** 宝玉（被黛玉拒之门外）问道："凡事都有个原故，说出来人也不委屈。好好的就恼，到底为什么起呢？"（卷 I，第二十二回，第520页）

▶ **译文** "There's always a reason for everything," he said. "If you tell people what it is, they don't feel so bad about it. You can't suddenly get angry with me for no reason whatever. What is all this about?"（Vol. I, chap. 22, p. 521）

译例 4

▶ **原文** 宝玉看见袭人两眼微红，粉光融滑，因悄问袭人道："好好的哭什么？"（卷 I，第十九回，第 444 页）

▶ **译文** Bao-yu noticed that Aroma's eyes were slightly red and that there were recent tear-stains on her powdered cheeks. "Why have you been crying?"（Vol. I, chap.19, p. 445）

📍 **说明** 宝玉有个口头语，常爱说"好好的"，近似"无缘无故的（地）"。但他多是和亲近的人说话时才说这个口头语，这里一个是黛玉，一个是袭人，都是他生活中非常亲近的人。所以，这个口头语隐含着说者与听者的亲密关系。在英语里有无对应的说法，我们说不出。一是因为我们读书不够，不能举出适当的例句；二是因为我们多数人没有在英美民间生活过，不知道在英语国家民间的英语里是否有类似的口头语，作为一种高度发达的语言，应该有，只是我们不知道而已。就霍克斯的译文看，是可以用英语把这个口头语的意思表达出来的。在译例 3 的译文里，他在努力这样做："You can't suddenly get angry with me for no reason whatever." 句中的"suddenly"和"for no reason whatever"很接近"好好的"原意，效果也是好的。但在译例 4 的译文中只是一个问句"Why have you been crying?"我们从中读不出说话者之间的感情，而且语气略显生硬。汉语里的这类口头语，也许不一定都需要翻译，但需要译的时候译好了可以把原文的语气译出来。同样的话用不同的语气说出来，能表达不同的意思，所以，译出语气很重要。

译例 5

▶ **原文** 那先生说："大奶奶这个症候，可是众位耽搁了！"（卷 I，第十回，第 242 页）

▶ **译文**　"I am afraid my colleagues have allowed your mistress's condition to deteriorate," said the doctor.（Vol. I, chap. 10, p. 243）

💡 **说明**　此处"众位"之称指先前来给可卿看过病的几位大夫，语气客气、礼貌、婉转。虽没有讥讽，但"耽搁"一词却暗含锋芒，道出他们的责任和对他们的埋怨。译文用"my colleagues"，很客气、很礼貌、很婉转地表达了同样的语气和分寸；"allowed your mistress's condition to deteriorate"也以平和的语气表达了"耽搁"的含义。译者对原文意义和语气把握准确，译得好。

译例6

▶ **原文**　小红笑道："奶奶有什么话，只管吩咐我说去；要说的不齐全，误了奶奶的事，任凭奶奶责罚就是了。"（卷Ⅰ，第二十七回，第8-10页）

▶ **译文**　"Tell me the message, madam. If I don't get it right and make a mess of it, it will be up to you to punish me."（Vol. Ⅱ, chap. 2, pp. 9-11）

💡 **说明**　第二十七回，凤姐要找一个丫头传口信，对小红说："不知你能干不能干？说的齐全不齐全？"于是小红说了上面的话。

从小红干脆利落的话语，可以听出她是一个聪明、自信、大胆的女孩。译文短促而明白无误的句子再现了小红的这种性格。

四、概念的具体化、形象化

《红楼梦》中有些概念词，译者翻译时将其具体化、形象化，效果很好。

译例1

▶ **原文**　今见女婿这等狼狈而来，心中便有些不乐。（卷Ⅰ，第一回，

第 22 页）

▶ **译文**　He was somewhat displeased to see his son-in-law arriving like a refugee on his doorstep...（Vol. I, chap. 1, p. 23）

💡 **说明**　"狼狈"这个概念可以译出来，但译者将其形象化，译作 "like a refugee"，描画出甄士隐的狼狈相，而且意义与原文贴切，不得已寄人篱下很像"难民"。

译例2

▶ **原文**　众人劝说："人已辞世，哭也无益，且商议如何料理要紧。"（卷 I，第十三回，第 286 页）

▶ **译文**　"Now that she's gone, crying isn't going to bring her back again. The important thing now is to make your plans for the funeral."（Vol. I, chap. 13, p. 287）

💡 **说明**　秦可卿死了，大家悲痛，自然是哭，于是有人劝说，"人已辞世，哭也无益"。汉语的一些概念，特别是一些朦胧概念，以英语为母语的译者翻译时常将其具体化，为的是让译文读者明白，这可能也属所谓的"归化"之类。此处的"哭也无益"，意即人死了，哭也没用，而 "crying isn't going to bring her back again" 意为反正也救不活了，将原文的委婉说法直白、具体地表达出来。

"料理"是一个很好的词汇，很概括，译文 "to make your plans for the funeral" 将其具体化，效果是好的。

译例3

▶ **原文**　只嫡妻贾氏生得一女，乳名黛玉，年方五岁，夫妻爱之如掌上明珠，见他生得聪明俊秀，也欲使他识几个字，不过假充养子，聊解膝下荒凉之叹。（卷 I，第二回，第 32 页）

▶ **译文** His chief wife, who had been a Miss Jia, had given him a daughter called Dai-yu. Both parents doted on her, and because she showed exceptional intelligence, conceived the idea of giving her a rudimentary education as a substitute for bringing up a son, hoping in this way somewhat to alleviate the sense of desolation left by the death of their only heir. (Vol. I, chap. 2, p. 33)

1. 〔原文〕不过假充养子……

〔译文〕as a substitute for bringing up a son...

〔说明〕说白了，就是让黛玉读点书，受点教育，把女儿当儿子养，译文中的"substitute"用词恰当。

2. 〔原文〕聊解膝下荒凉之叹

〔译文〕somewhat to alleviate the sense of desolation left by the death of their only heir

〔说明〕此处"荒凉"指因家中无子嗣而感凄凉。旧时家中无子传宗接代意味"无后"，被视为家族悲剧，自然让人感觉凄凉。因此，前文中曾提到"今如海年已五十，只有一个三岁之子，又于去岁亡了"，所以，译文中有了"left by the death of their only heir"之说。

此处的"聊"意为"略微"，译文的"somewhat"很好地解释了它的含义。

译例 4

▶ **原文** 雨村不耐烦，乃退出来，意欲到那村肆中沽饮三杯，以助野趣，于是移步行来。(卷I，第二回，第34页)

▶ **译文** Yu-cun walked out again in disgust. He now thought that in order to give the full rural flavour to his outing he would treat himself to a few cups of wine in a little country inn and accordingly directed his steps towards the near-by village.（Vol. I, chap. 2, p. 35）

译例 5

▶ **原文** （雨村）交代过了公事，将历年所积的宦囊，并家属人等，送至原籍安顿妥当了，却自己担风袖月，游览天下胜迹。（卷 I，第二回，第 30 页）

▶ **译文** ... and when the business of handing over was completed, he took his wife and family and the loot he had accumulated during his years of office and having settled them all safely in his native Hu-zhou, set off, free as the air, on an extended tour of some of the more celebrated places of scenic interest in our mighty empire.（Vol. I, chap. 2, p. 31）

📍 **说明** 以上两个例句中"以助野趣"和"担风袖月"是两个富有诗意的汉语词语。汉语里，这类语义朦胧、蕴涵丰富的词语较多，尤其在古文里，或是在描述书画艺术、描写戏剧表演艺术时使用得比较多。翻译时首先需要确定其词意，用英语表达时颇费斟酌，看看霍克斯如何确定其词意、怎么翻译，对我们会有启发。

"以助野趣"，译作"in order to give the full rural flavour to his outing"，在村野小馆里喝两杯酒，酒后微醺，可为乡间的信步而行增添些许乡野情趣，这也许是经验者很自然的感觉。译文把这个意思准确地表达出来了。"担风袖月"，意即轻松自在地漫游天下，译作"free as the air"，这样解释很是恰当。

五、汉英对应

汉、英两种语言里有一些意思对应的词语，翻译时用好了很有意思，可视为巧译。

译例 1

▶ **原文**　宝玉笑道：“凡我说一句，你就拉上这些。不给你个利害也不知道，从今儿可不饶你了。”（卷 I，第十九回，第 462 页）

▶ **译文**　"Whatever I say, you are always dragging in things like that," said Bao-yu. "Very well. You will have to be taught a lesson. From now on, no mercy!"（Vol. I, chap. 19, p. 463）

📍 **说明**　译文中的 "dragging in things like that" 对应原文的 "拉上这些"。

译例 2

▶ **原文**　家中虽不甚富贵，然本地也推他为望族了。（卷 I，第一回，第 8 页）

▶ **译文**　The household was not a particularly wealthy one, but they were nevertheless looked up to by all and sundry as the leading family in the neighbourhood.（Vol. I, chap. 1, p. 9）

📍 **说明**　译文的 "were... looked up to by all and sundry as the leading family" 对应原文的 "望族"。"望族" 为有名望之家族，人皆仰望，虽二者不属同一词性，但其意思和内涵都表达出来了。

译例 3

▶ **原文**　迎春：“林妹妹怎么不见？好个懒丫头！这会子难道还睡觉不成？”

宝钗道：“你们等着，等我去闹了他来。”（卷 I，第二十七回，第 4 页）

▶ **译文**　... Bao-chai volunteered to go and fetch her: "The rest of you wait here; I'll go and rout her out for you," she said.（Vol. I, chap. 27, p. 5）

💡 **说明**　译文的"rout her out for you"对应原文的"闹了他来"。陆谷孙《英汉大词典》有解释，将睡者从床上唤起或拖出。

六、听黛玉说诗，读霍克斯英译

关于《红楼梦》翻译，已经讨论了霍译的部分佳句。现在讨论第四十八回黛玉关于诗歌和写诗的见解。香菱搬进大观园以后，来找黛玉，表示要跟她学写诗。黛玉对香菱谈了怎么学诗、什么是好诗等，发表了一些观点，很有见解，此时的黛玉简直是个深谙古诗三昧的学问家。

选择这个内容意在接触一些关于诗歌的术语，培养用英语讨论中国古诗的能力。

译例 1

▶ **原文**　黛玉说："什么难事，也值得去学？不过是起、承、转、合，当中承、转是两副对子，平声的对仄声，虚的对实的，实的对虚的。若是果有了奇句，连平仄虚实不对都使得的。"（卷 II，第四十八回，第570 页）

▶ **译文**　"There's nothing in it really,"said Dai-yu, "There's really hardly anything to learn. In Regulated Verse there are always four couplets: the 'opening couplet', the 'developing couplet', the 'turning couplet' and the 'concluding couplet'. In the two middle couplets, the 'developing' and 'turning' ones, you have to have tone-contrast and parallelism. That's to say, in each of those couplets the even tones of one line have to contrast with oblique tones in the other, and *vice versa*, and the substantives and non-substantives have to balance each other—though if you've got a really good, original line, it doesn't matter all that much even if the tone-contrast and parallelism are wrong."（Vol. Ⅱ, chap. 48, p. 571）

1.［原文］起、承、转、合……

［译文］"起"，译作"the 'opening couplet'"；"承"，"the 'developing couplet'"；"转"，"the 'turning couplet'"；"合"，"the 'concluding couplet'"。

［说明］在介绍"起、承、转、合"之前，译者增加了一句话，"In Regulated Verse there are always four couplets"，这句话原文里没有，也不需要，因为说者、听者，以及小说读者都熟悉，但译文读者需要有个完整的概念，所以，译者增加了这句话，很必要。

2.［原文］平声的对仄声……

［译文］the even tones of one line have to contrast with oblique tones in the other...

［说明］"仄"是一个很特殊的汉字，指古汉语中的"上""去""入"三声，在英语里难以找一个能表达这三层意思的词，译者用了"oblique"来表示。

3.［原文］虚的对实的，实的对虚的……

［译文］... the substantives and non-substantives have to balance each other...

［说明］译文与原文意思吻合。

译例2

▶ **原文**　香菱笑道："难怪我常弄本旧诗，偷空看一两首，又有对的极工的，又有不对的。又听见说，'一三五不论，二四六分明……'"（卷Ⅰ，第四十八回，第570页）

▶ **译文**　"Ah, that explains it!" said Caltrop, pleased. "I've got an old poetry-book that I look at once in a while when I can find the time, and I long ago noticed that in some of the poems the tone-contrast is very strict, while in others it's not. Someone told me the rhyme:

> For one, three and five
>
> You need not strive;
>
> But two, four and six
>
> You must firmly fix.
>
> ..."

（Vol. Ⅱ, chap. 48, p. 571）

1. ［原文］难怪……

［译文］Ah, that explains it!

［说明］经黛玉解释，香菱明白了，"难怪"二字的语气用一个句子来表现，"Ah, that explains it!"，意思是，这就清楚了，其语气与原文的"难怪"相一致。译者的处理方式很到家。

2. ［原文］一三五不论，二四六分明……

［译文］For one, three and five

You need not strive;

But two, four and six

You must firmly fix.

［说明］"指旧体律诗的平仄格式。往往每句一三五字的平仄声要求相对宽松，而二四六字较严，必须合韵。"（张俊、沈治钧，评批:《新批校注红楼梦》，卷Ⅱ，第四十八回，第870页）

"一三五不论，二四六分明"，属行业口诀之类，译者追随原文形式，将其分行翻译，很活泼。

译例 3

▶ **原文**　黛玉道："正是这个道理。词句究竟还是末事，第一是立意要紧。若意趣真了，连词句不用修饰，自是好的，这叫作'不以词害意'。"（卷Ⅱ，第四十八回，第 570–572 页）

▶ **译文**　"You've hit it exactly!" said Dai-yu. "As a matter of fact even the *language* isn't of primary importance. The *really* important things are the ideas that lie behind it. If the ideas behind it are genuine, there's no need to embellish the language for the poem to be a good one. That's what they mean when they talk about 'not letting the words harm the meaning'." (Vol. Ⅱ, chap. 48, pp.571-573)

1. ［原文］第一是立意要紧。

　［译文］The *really* important things are the ideas that lie behind it.

　［说明］这里将"立意"译作"ideas"，《现代汉语词典》说，"立意"是"命意"，例句："这幅画立意新颖"；译者用"idea"传达"立意"的意思是好的。

2. ［原文］若意趣真了，连词句不用修饰，自是好的……

　［译文］If the ideas behind it are genuine, there's no need to embellish the language for the poem to be a good one.

　［说明］这里将"意趣"也译作"ideas"，在汉语，"立意"和"意趣"似乎不完全相同，"意趣"是"意味和兴趣"，但译者为什么将其也译作"ideas"呢？一方面，黛玉刚说了"立意"，紧接着就说了"意趣"，此时她的所指也许并无明显差异；另一方面，译者可能有他的考虑，因为原文说"立意要紧"，所以一以贯之地强调这个"要紧"的"ideas"。这样，除衔接效果好，也突出了这句话的关键意思，译文读者读起来感觉连贯性更好些。

译例 4

▶ **原文** 黛玉道："断不可看这样的诗。你们因不知诗，所以见了这浅近的就爱；一入了这个格局，再学不出来的。"（卷Ⅱ，第四十八回，第572页）

▶ **译文** "Good gracious! You mustn't go reading *that* sort of stuff!" said Dai-yu. "It's only because of your lack of experience that you can think shallow stuff like that any good. Once you get stuck into *that* rut, you'll never get out of it." (Vol. Ⅱ, chap. 48, pp. 571-573)

💡 **说明** 香菱道："我只爱陆放翁的'重帘不卷留香久，古砚微凹聚墨多'。说的真切有趣。"然后黛玉说了上面的话。

1.〔原文〕断不可看这样的诗。

〔译文〕Good gracious! You mustn't go reading *that* sort of stuff!

〔说明〕"Good gracious!"为译者所加，很自然的句子开头用语，表示惊讶，也带有警示的语气。若一上来就说"You mustn't go reading *that* sort of stuff!"语气上会显得突兀。

2.〔原文〕一入了这个格局，再学不出来的。

〔译文〕Once you get stuck into *that* rut, you'll never get out of it.

〔说明〕黛玉是说，如果开始学的路子不对，那会将错就错，将来是学不好的。译文中的"rut"意为"车辙"，英语词典也有另外一个解释："a habit or pattern of behaviour that has become dull and unproductive but is hard to change（figurative）"，即"老套路"。鉴于此，将"格局"译作"rut"，很好地传达了原文意思。

译例5

▶ **原文** "你只听我说，你若真心要学，我这里有《王摩诘全集》，你且把他的五言律一百首揣摩透熟了，然后再读一百二十首老杜的七言律，次之再李青莲的七言绝句读一二百首，肚子里先有了这三个人做了底子……你又是这样一个聪明伶俐的人，不用一年工夫，不愁不是诗翁了。"（卷Ⅱ，第四十八回，第572页）

▶ **译文** "You do as I tell you. I've got the *Collected Works of Wang Wei* here. You take a hundred of Wang Wei's pentasyllabic poems in Regulated Verse and read and re-read them, carefully pondering what you read, until you are thoroughly familiar with them all. After that read a hundred or two of Du Fu's Regulated Verse heptasyllabics and a hundred or two of Li Bo's heptasyllabic quatrains; then, with a firm foundation of those three poets inside you... with your quickness and intelligence you should have no difficulty in turning yourself into a fully-fledged bard within less than a twelvemonth."（Vol. Ⅱ, chap. 48, p.573）

1.［原文］五言律

　　［译文］pentasyllabic poems in Regulated Verse

　　［说明］"pentasyllabic"，意为英诗中的五音节诗行，用来翻译汉语的"五言"有类似效果。

2.［原文］揣摩透熟

　　［译文］read and re-read them, carefully pondering what you read, until you are thoroughly familiar with them all

　　［说明］译者强调"read and re-read""carefully pondering"，以取得"thoroughly familiar"的效果，为了把"揣摩透熟"说透，译者唯恐说得

不够周到。

3.［原文］<u>肚子里先有了这三个人做了底子……</u>

［译文］with a firm foundation of those three poets inside you...

［说明］"肚子里"译作"inside you"，"做了底子"译作"with a firm foundation"，用英语的对应方式表达出汉语意思，而且行文自然。

《红楼梦》是语言和文化的海洋，我们的讨论只涉及一小部分词句。这部书所蕴涵的文化和使用的语言不好译，对任何译者都是挑战；因为一个民族的文学与其历史、文化紧密相关，最适合表达其民族思想和民族情感的是伴随它的历史、文化而发展起来的带有民族性格特征的语言。用另一种语言翻译《红楼梦》，译好了可以讲好故事，但再现其语言风格以及融合在语言中的文化、典故等诸多元素很困难。同时，任何民族的语言都有只能意会难以言传的成分，《红楼梦》尤其如此。从这个意义上讲，翻译《红楼梦》，这里仅就《红楼梦》的翻译，不好要求译者做到对等或等效，意义上的对等或等效或可努力争取，语言形式和意趣的对等或等效比较难，有些情况下不太可能。

总体上看，霍克斯为我们奉献了难得的好译文，可供我们学习的东西很多，对汉、英翻译研究，对汉、英翻译事业，对中英文化交流都做出了可贵的贡献。

阅读蒂姆·克莱顿（Tim Clayton）和菲尔·克蕾格（Phil Craig）：

Diana—Story of a Princess

简 介

戴安娜王妃于 1997 年香消于法国巴黎，蒂姆·克莱顿和菲尔·克蕾格两位作家经过长时间的调查、采访，搜集了比较全面的关于戴安娜的生平材料，合作写了《戴安娜：王妃的故事》（*Diana—Story of a Princess*），全面介绍戴安娜王妃的生活细节。该书于 2001 年由英国霍德－斯托顿出版公司（Hodder & Stoughton, Ltd.）出版，畅销于英语世界。

这本书用今日流行的英语写成，有大量地道的英语表达方式，现选取其中部分句子来学习和研究，对提高我们的英语写作和翻译将大有裨益。

例句 1. And I walked towards her, a real English rose with her eyes downcast, and blushing furiously. And she was very polite and shook my hand and then we were able to lose ourselves in the fuss of loading up the car. (p. 8)

说明 戴安娜的父母离异后，她和弟弟轮流跟着父母过活，跟父亲过一阵，再跟母亲过一阵。父母为他们雇了一个保姆，保姆来的时候戴安娜正在住宿学校上学，她们没有见过面，但保姆看过她的照片。放假时保姆去学校接戴安娜回家，上面这段文字描写保姆在学校见到戴安娜时的情景。两个句子里用了五个连接词 "and"。

对于"and"的用法和功能，阅读时略加留意，会有所感觉。

1. "and"基本功能是连接，在句子之中，把句子连接成一个整体，或在句子之间，把句子连接成一个完整的语段；

2. 多数情况下，"and"是弱读音节，在句中，特别是用在句子开头，读起来给人一种和缓、婉转、自然的感觉，否则会感觉突兀；

3. 正因为它是弱读音节，它能和句中的重读音节协同产生一种节奏或律动，使英语味道更浓，更具美感。

例如：一个负责为戴安娜拍照的报社记者对她说，他要为她拍一张"full-face, big, smiling picture"，然后整幅登在报纸头条，戴安娜同意了。下面是他们的对话，其中三个"and"是用在句子开头：

And she said, "I'll look out of the window tomorrow morning at six-thirty, and if you're the only one here, I will come down and get into my car. I'll put the window down, and let you have some close-ups, with a big smile. And that'll allow you to get home for Christmas." I said, "Right, I'll be here." And she did it.（p. 55）

设想一下，如果这几个句子不用"and"开头，读起来会有不同的感觉。

例句 2. In her second term she was treated to some of her own medicine, being picked on by some older girls, and then she settled down into boisterous popularity as the leader of a small gang in her class of about fifteen.（p. 13）

💡 **说明**　戴安娜在西希斯学校（West Heath School）上学时，承认自己是个"bully"，欺人者。

到了第二学期，"she was treated to some of her own medicine"，这是一个成语，曾是欺人者，现在被人欺。《牛津高阶英汉双解词典》有例句："Let the bully have a taste of his own medicine."

例句 3. Diana was different. She was tall and lithe and enthusiastic and she had been trained to dance.

Diana actually danced backward and drew the wheelchair towards her, by holding the arms of the wheelchair. Now that is incredibly agile and clever and there are not many people who could maintain their balance. And she kept an extremely good rhythm.（p. 18）

💡 **说明**　学生志愿者来到医院和坐在轮椅上的病人跳舞，她们被告知跳舞时要俯下身子和轮椅保持一个高度，并且要拉着病人的手跳。这个动作不太容易，所以多数学生都是从后面推着轮椅和病人跳舞。戴安娜从小就喜欢公益事业，她表现出发自内心的热情和真诚。她的做法与众不同，她虽然个子高，但身体柔软灵活，又学过舞蹈。她不是从后面推轮椅，而是面对病人双手抓住轮椅扶手倒着走，且能保持平衡，跳出节奏来，这很不容易。

这段英语文字有技巧，虽然简单，但细节描写生动。

例句 4. In the late 1970s one writer was allowed to sample Charles's lifestyle. A *Sunday Times* journalist named Anthony Holden was researching a biography to mark the Prince's thirtieth birthday. He flew in Charles's helicopter, dined at Buckingham Palace, met many of Charles's friends.（p. 20）

💡 **说明**　文中的动词"sample"，陆谷孙《英汉大词典》解释为"体验"，这个解释确切，并给了一个例子："to sample the pleasures of country life"，体验乡村生活乐趣。

"to sample Charles's lifestyle"，体验查尔斯的生活方式。

"体验"一词在汉语里使用率很高，这个"sample"很有用，要学会使用它。

例句 5. As all this happened, Earl Spencer beamed his weak approval while his heir and daughters looked on, steaming with sullen fury. The final affront to family pride came when the famous portrait of Robert, first Lord Spencer, which had dominated the grand staircase for centuries, was replaced by a full-length picture of Raine in her beauteous youth. (p. 24)

💡 **说明** 戴安娜父母离婚后，父亲斯宾塞伯爵（Earl Spencer）和一个叫雷恩（Raine）的女人再婚。这个女人很霸道，她要重新装修房子，自作主张贱价处理掉很多家具，引起孩子们的不满。

1. Earl Spencer beamed his weak approval...

💡 **说明** 关于动词"beam"，陆谷孙《英汉大词典》有一个很好的解释：以微笑表示。而"weak approval"，勉强表示同意。

2. ... while his heir and daughters looked on, steaming with sullen fury.

💡 **说明** 动词"steam"一般解释为"蒸发"，但在这个上下文里，"steaming with sullen fury"是生气的意思，孩子们眼看着继母如此霸道，敢怒不敢言，一个很形象的表达方式。

3. The final affront to family pride...

💡 **说明** 最令人不能容忍的是，雷恩装修房子时竟然把几个世纪以来一直挂在楼梯间的第一代斯宾塞勋爵罗伯特的肖像取下来，换上她自己年轻时的全身像，这对斯宾塞家族的荣耀是极大的侮辱，这里的"affront"指的是这个意思。

例句 6. She was very good at getting down to the children's level both physically and mentally. She was quite happy to sit on the floor, have children climbing all over her, sit on the low chairs beside them, and actually talk to them. That's very important, to be able to talk to them, at their level. And they responded incredibly well to her. (p. 27)

💡 **说明** 戴安娜学历不高，连中学也没念完。她姐姐为她在幼儿园找了一份工作，每周去三个下午。因为她表现出色，很会以平等身份和孩子们一起玩、一起说笑，孩子们喜欢她，家长们也表扬她，幼儿园便邀请她上午也来上班。她有一种天赋，能让孩子们展示最好的自己，"her flair for bringing out the best in the children"，以及她与生俱来的耐心、幽默感和直觉，"her natural patience, good humour and intuition"，这些都给同事们留下深刻印象。上面这段文字写她和孩子们在一起的情景，作者用简单的文字描写具体的行为，这里的文字功夫，值得揣摩。若将这段文字译成汉语，可能也有一定的难度，特别是第一个句子：

1. She was very good at getting down to the children's level both physically and mentally.

💡 **说明**　这是一个很妙的句子，妙在简单、易懂，但不好译，有兴趣者可试试看。

2. ... to be able to talk to them, at their level.

这句话同样简单、易懂，但译好了不容易。

例句 7. It was a huge step to hand over Patrick to a stranger in a strange city where we had no neighbours, we really didn't know anybody. But Diana just struck me as so sensible and grounded and committed to Patrick. I really had no concerns about her being flighty or irresponsible.（p. 28）

💡 **说明**　戴安娜曾给在英国工作的美国人玛丽·罗伯逊（Mary Robertson）的儿子帕特里克（Patrick）做保姆。玛丽·罗伯逊住在一个人地两生的城市，又没有邻居。在这种环境里把自己的孩子交给一个陌生人确实有点不放心，所以她说"It was a huge step"。但经过一段时间的考察，戴安娜给她留下特别好的印象。上面的文字是她对戴安娜的评价，她说戴安娜"sensible"，明白事理，通情达理；"grounded"，明智而现实，踏踏实实；"committed to Patrick"，对她的儿子帕特里克尽心尽力，尽职尽责；"... had no concerns about her being flighty or irresponsible"，不担心她轻浮或不负责任。

她评价戴安娜的这几个词很好，在汉语里也常见，可借鉴使用。

例句 8. But this particular weekend came where there didn't appear to be a current girlfriend and we went to this particular match and Arthur spotted this girl sitting in the crowd with a "D" round her neck and had a vague recollection he'd seen her somewhere before.（p. 32）

 说明　查尔斯王子每逢周末要去打马球，每次都要带一个女友，常常是不同的女友。这次亚瑟在人群中看见一个女孩，他影影绰绰记得似乎在哪儿见过她，这里的 "had a vague recollection" 是一个好的表达方式，汉语里也有这个说法。

例句 9. Charles's assistant private secretary, Oliver Everett, received an early impression that this romance might go the distance. Robert Spencer remembers his cousin Johnny telling him at the same time that "he was thrilled that Prince Charles seemed to be so keen on Diana."（p. 36）

 说明　查尔斯和戴安娜开始接触时，他的助理秘书埃弗里特（Everett）就看好他们的关系，认为这段关系能够走得远，"go the distance" 是一个很新鲜的搭配。

例句 10. Life was relaxed and stylish: riding horses through woods or along riverbanks, early evening drinks in the garden, an excellent dinner to follow.（p. 37）

 说明　这句话描写查尔斯的朋友们与他在一起时轻松而高雅的生活方式，这里值得注意的是英语不完全句的写法。在林中或河边骑马漫游；傍晚在花园里小酌；接下来是美味晚餐。

回忆我们学习英语的过程，多是如何依据英语句法写完全句，少有写不完全句的经验。由于不完全句简洁的特征，或没有人称，或没有完整的动词形式，只用不同形式的词组，其表现力反而特别强，这个例句值得品读。

例句 11. All the world and all the glory of it, whatever is most attractive, whatever is most seductive, has always been offered to the Prince of Wales of the day, and always will be. It is not rational to expect the best virtue where temptation is applied in the most trying form at the frailest time of human life. （p. 38）

💡 **说明** 立宪历史学家沃尔特·贝奇霍特（Walter Bagehot）在二十年前曾这样预言查尔斯王子。

这个小段由两个句子组成，所表达的概念比较复杂，句子结构也比较复杂。

整个世界，全世界所有的荣光，凡是最具吸引力的，凡是最有诱惑力的，都给了当今的威尔士亲王（指查尔斯王子）而且终究是要给他的。在人类生活处于最脆弱的年代，在各种诱惑以最考验人的形式无处不在的情况下，期待（他）具有最优秀的人品是不合情理的。

这两句话说得很绕，但有很强的逻辑和很强的说服力。文中的"where"不是表示地点的代词，词典将其列为连接词，"（in）the place or situation in which"，在某某地方，在某某情况下。下面这个"where"表示同样的意思：

The love affair was evidently precious to Diana but in Devon she had also found something else that she craved—a relaxed and informal family life of a kind that was just not available where your husband was the future King. （p. 165）

戴安娜和她丈夫查尔斯关系不好，也不愿受王室清规戒律的约束，她希望和她的情人休伊特（Hewitt）在德文郡（Devon）找一个温馨舒适的小房子，过一种轻松、安逸的生活，但她的丈夫是未来的国王，在这种情况下，她的梦想不可能实现。

阅读时注意观察上下文，把握好"where"的用法，学会在写作和翻译时使用它。

例句 12. After the train story, the papers rallied round Diana again, the *Sun* to the fore. They implored Charles not to let a catch like this slip through his fingers.（p. 51）

说明　在和戴安娜结婚之前，查尔斯同时与几个女人有暧昧关系，公众和媒体特别好奇到底谁是他的未婚妻。后来有传闻说，戴安娜曾与查尔斯在王室列车上共度了两个夜晚，戴安娜否认有此事，但这个消息还是上了报纸。文中的 "After the train story" 即指这个传闻。

1. 这里的 "... the papers rallied round Diana again"，是说媒体对戴安娜又表示关注或支持，而 "the *Sun* to the fore"，是说在这件事情上《太阳报》表现很抢眼、很突出，或扮演了重要角色。

关于 "to the fore"，词典有解释："to be/become important and noticed"，或 "to play an important part"。

2. 文中的 "catch" 是一个很有意思的词，英语词典说："a person that other people see as a good person to marry"，在别人看来是很好的婚姻人选。

我们常说的 "地道英语"，这里的 "to the fore" 或 "come to the fore" 以及 "catch" 就是地道英语，若不知道这个说法，表达这个意思就会很麻烦，或不知所措。

例句 13. And it seemed even more suitable because the Prince seemed like somebody who would want a younger girl to be his wife. She was young enough to be trained, and young enough to be helped, and young enough to be moulded.（p. 57）

说明　这是谈查尔斯的择偶标准，他希望找一个比他年轻的女孩子做他的妻子，戴安娜比他小十几岁，正合他的心意。这里用了三个排比形式的 "young enough"，同样的句式，用两个 "and" 连接。

例句 14. He got bounced into this, make no bones about it. The combination of press and public pressure, he conned himself into thinking he was in love with her. Alarm bells should have been ringing all over the place. We are as guilty as everybody else.（p. 58）

💡 **说明** 作者通篇使用简单平易的英语（Anglo-Saxionism）来叙述，这和美国作家 E. B. 怀特的文风有相同之处。学习英语，需培养这种能力。

1. He got bounced into this...

这个句子用的是一个英语固定短语"to bounce sb into sth"，英语词典是这样解释的："to make sb do sth without giving them enough time to think about it"，这里指查尔斯与戴安娜的婚姻，没有给他足够的时间慎重考虑就定了。实际上，他的婚姻在很大程度上是他父亲菲利普亲王的意志。

2. ... make no bones about it.

意为"to not hesitate to do sth"，没有犹豫，二话没说就决定了。

3. ... he conned himself into thinking he was in love with her.

动词"to con"的基本意思是"to trick"，这句话是否可以译作"他自以为他是爱她的"，有待斟酌。

例句 15. I went straight to the flat, Coleherne Court, and got a really nice picture of her leaving for the last time. She gave a smile, I promise you it just lit up the whole street. She was such a happy girl.（p. 60）

💡 **说明** 这里的"it just lit up the whole street"是夸张手法，形容戴安娜的笑容使满街生辉，虽是夸张，但读来却给人一种美感。

例句 16. I would stand up when she came, and she'd just come bouncing into the room, and the whole place would light up and change and she'd come over and hug and her whole energy would be very evident.（p. 154）

💡 **说明** 这是描写戴安娜到她的情人休伊特家里时的情景。"she'd just come bouncing into the room"，英语词典这样解释"bounce"："to move somewhere in a lively and cheerful way"，描写她来时活泼喜兴的样子；"the whole place would light up"，她一进门就使得全家欢乐起来，虽属夸张，也是写实，因为戴安娜一来，家里的气氛就变了。

例句 17. The Palace is a very gossipy place and Diana was soon made aware that staff provided information to the newspapers. It was difficult to know who to trust, and it did not come naturally to Diana to remain distant and buttoned up.（p. 65）

💡 说明　宫廷是个是非之地，戴安娜身边的工作人员常向媒体透漏内部信息，她弄不清谁是可信之人。在这种情况下，戴安娜自然不会心不在焉，或沉默不语。

这里的 "it did not come naturally to Diana..."，如译作 "戴安娜自然不会……" 或 "当然不会……"，符合原文语气。

例句 18. Journalist Christopher Hitchens remembers the fevered atmosphere in the build-up to the royal wedding.（p. 66）

💡 说明　这里的 "fevered atmosphere"，即 "exciting atmosphere" 或 "atmosphere filled with excitement"；"in the build-up to the royal wedding"，在准备婚礼的过程中，很好的表达方式。

例句 19. For photographers Diana was a gold mine and for the most part they... were just very excited about it... Everyone in the world wanted pictures of her.（pp. 66-67）

💡 说明　对于摄影记者，戴安娜的照片是金矿，发到报纸上可以赚钱，有的可以赚很多钱。这个比喻很恰当。

读英语作品，偶尔有类似的比喻，如美国作家 E. B. 怀特，曾经有一本他的英语老师威廉·斯特伦克编写的 *The Elements of Style*，多年不见，在他重新发现这本书以后说了下面的话：

"Am now delighted to study it again and rediscover its rich deposits of gold."

他将这本书比作丰富的金矿，比喻这本书有丰富的内容，很值得阅读。英语和汉语一样，都喜欢使用这种比喻，表现力强。

例句 20. The wedding was the province of Lord Chamberlain and Lord Maclean, the head of the royal household. For him and his staff, this would be the biggest event of their career, a moment of defining glory. All agreed that it was to be a splendid occasion, but their ideas of what was splendid did not always coincide.（p. 70）

💡 **说明**

1. "province"，词典解释这个词时这样说："a person's particular area of knowledge, interest, or responsibility"，这里是说查尔斯与戴安娜的婚礼是张伯伦勋爵（Lord Chamberlain）和迈克林勋爵（Lord Maclean）操办的事情。"province" 这个用法新鲜，学会使用它。

2. "... a moment of defining glory"，理解这个句子需弄清 "define" 的含义，词典有一个解释说得很明白："describe or show sth accurately"，按照这个解释，我们不妨将其译作这是给他们 "带来荣光的时刻"，或更直白地说，这是他们 "大显身手的时刻"。

3. 动词 "coincide"，在多数情况下，用来表示多个事情同时发生，这里它表示另外一个含义，即 "(of ideas, opinions, etc.) to be the same or very similar"，相同的想法或意见，在这个上下文里它的意思是，对于什么是 "splendid"，他们的想法并不相同。

例句 21. ... but Diana evidently went over her conversations with Camilla again and again in her mind. Her analysis suggested that Camilla saw hunting and country life as her opportunity to maintain her affair with Charles. She appears to have interpreted Camilla's "Will you hunt?" as a code for "Do you accept he will be mine some weekends?"（p. 76）

💡 **说明**　查尔斯的情人卡米拉在与戴安娜交谈时有时这样问她："你去打猎吗？"戴安娜琢磨她说这话是什么意思，认为她这样问实际上是一种暗示："有些周末查尔斯是属于我的，这个你接受吗？"卡米拉之问就是我们常说的有"言外之意"，即英语所谓"understatement"。

例句 22. Everywhere Mary looked were lace-trimmed gowns, dazzling jewels and tall, handsome men in ribbons and medals. Charles looked regal in his red dress uniform, Diana was ravishing in deep pink ruffled taffeta with the most enormous diamond necklace sparkling at her neck.（p. 78）

💡 **说明**　这个段落描写在查尔斯与戴安娜婚前举办的一次舞会上与会者华丽的着装。这个玛丽（Mary）就是戴安娜曾经为其当过保姆的美国人，她也应邀参加舞会，这段文字是描写她在舞会上见到的情景。

1. 这里的"regal"是个很有讲究的形容词，词典这样解释："typical of a king or queen, and therefore impressive"，查尔斯身穿红色礼服，王子派头十足。

2. 这里的"ravishing"，是描写戴安娜的一个形容词，意为"extremely beautiful"，美若天仙。

例句 23. Mary almost bumped into Prime Minister Margaret Thatcher, standing alone at the edge of the dance-floor, surveying the scene and looking as if she felt a little out of place among the cream of Europe's aristocracy.（pp. 78-79）

💡 **说明**　玛丽撞见英国首相撒切尔夫人，她孤零零一个人站在舞池边上，在欧洲贵族精英面前显得不合时宜，或格格不入。此处的"out of place"是常用词组，"cream"作"精英"讲，常以"the cream of..."短语形式出现。

例句 24. Those accompanying him thought that he did not know whether to break the rules to please his wife or try to coax Diana into coming to terms with the necessary facts of royal life.（p. 87）

💡 说明　早在查尔斯向戴安娜求婚时，他就提醒过她，要学会习惯王室生活方式，但天天面对王室的运作方式，戴安娜还是感觉乏味无聊，查尔斯也同样觉得 "irksome"，即 "irritating"。陪同查尔斯的人们认为此时他不知如何是好，是为了取悦他的妻子而打破王室的清规戒律呢，还是劝戴安娜接受王室生活的现实呢？

"to coax ... into"，一般译作 "哄劝"，这里就是 "劝" 的意思，查尔斯或者为了取悦妻子而打破王室的清规戒律，或者劝戴安娜接受王室生活的现实。

短语 "come to terms with..." 表示顺从、接受等，这是一个常用短语，这里用得恰当。

例句 25. Anthropology introduced Charles to the writings of Laurens van der Post, who became a mentor during the 1970s. He now hoped to share these enthusiasms with his young wife. But Charles's attempts to read Laurens van der Post aloud to Diana, and his attempts at intellectual discussion, triggered her inferiority complex and she left him to it.（p. 88）

💡 说明　查尔斯好学，爱读书，他学过人类学，读过南非作家、人类学家劳伦斯·普司特（Laurens van der Post）的作品，他想和妻子朗读他热衷的这位作家的书，并与她进行讨论。但戴安娜没有上过大学，没有这方面的知识，对此也不感兴趣，查尔斯的建议让她产生自卑感：你还是自己读吧。

这个 "complex" 意为 "情结"，"inferiority complex" 正是汉语所谓的 "自卑感"。而 "to trigger" 相当于汉语的 "引起"，或 "触发" 之意，用于 "inferiority complex" 是很好的搭配。

例句 26. In any marriage there are rows. Of course, they were royal and they were not supposed to row, and certainly not in public and certainly not where the servants can hear. But you see, Diana was very volatile, she just let it rip when she felt she should.（p. 103）

💡 **说明** 戴安娜个性很强，情绪易变，反复无常，作者用 "volatile" 描述她的这种性格；"let rip" 是固定短语，"to speak or do sth with great force, and without control"，这里是指戴安娜激动地说、不管不顾地说，有时甚至是粗鲁地说。这两个词和词组所表达的意思很准确，是很新鲜的表达方式，写作或翻译时不妨借鉴。

例句 27. "... whoever I choose is going to have a jolly hard job, always in my shadow, having to walk a few steps behind me, all that sort of thing."（p. 123）

💡 **说明** 以上是查尔斯关于择偶曾发表过的陈旧观点。

此处的 "jolly" 是副词，表示 "very" 的意思，他说，不论谁做他的妻子都是很艰难的事情，总是生活在他的影子里，跟在他的身后，诸如此类。

例句 28. But now the spotlight was being continuously beamed away from the heir to the throne and on to his dazzling wife. Once again the crowds cheered if they were on her side of the road and groaned if they were on his, once again he laughed it off, saying he needed two wives to cover both sides of the street.（p. 123）

💡 **说明** 但在很多场合下戴安娜总是抢他的风头。当他们两个并肩走在街上，两侧欢呼的人群表现截然不同，戴安娜一侧的人们欢呼雀跃，"cheered"，查尔斯一侧的人群则怨声载道，"groaned"，这让查尔斯感觉很尴尬。

1. the spotlight... beamed away...

人们的注意力从查尔斯移到戴安娜身上……

2. ... he laughed it off...

他只是笑笑而已。

例句 29. "Hi, I am sitting in bed with Wills and we are watching telly." If it was later she was always on her own, but she would just have a little chit-chat. I suppose it was the mother/daughtery thing.（p. 126）

💡 说明　珍尼特·菲尔德曼（Janet Filderman）是戴安娜的朋友，晚上家里只剩下戴安娜和威廉时，特别晚的时候只是她一个人时，她便经常给菲尔德曼打电话，多是闲聊，无非是些家长里短、婆婆妈妈之类。

此处的"mother/daughtery"目前没有在词典里查到，许是作者的杜撰，其意有可能相当于汉语"家长里短""婆婆妈妈"之类，因为前面用了"chit-chat"这个词。不管词典里有没有，既然英国人这样用了，我们也可以尝试这么用，否则用英语表达"家长里短"或"婆婆妈妈"不太容易。

例句 30. Warming to his wife's more easy-going style, Holden would become one of Diana's great champions in the years that followed, one of many who came to identify her with the spirit of the times, and Charles with the past.（p. 130）

💡 说明　安东尼·霍尔登（Anthony Holden），美国传记作家。

1. Warming to his wife's more easy-going style...

关于短语"to warm to sth"，英语词典解释："to become more interested in or enthusiastic about sth"，"对……更感兴趣"，或"更热衷于……"，因为对他（查尔斯）夫人更随意的风格很感兴趣，他变成戴安娜的一个拥护者。

2. ... who came to identify her with the spirit of the times...

可以理解为"他认为戴安娜体现时代精神"，而查尔斯已经过时了。

"to identify sb with sth"，这里意为"把某人视为……"。这个表达方

式在英语里用得很多，阅读时注意观察。

例句 31. It happened before our very eyes, the transformation from this shy teenager, who hid beneath big hats, and hung her head, into the self-assured woman and mother, confident in her beauty.

📍 **说明** 杰恩·芬彻（Jayne Fincher）曾经见过戴安娜，当再次见到她时，说了上面的话。

这里的"transformation from... into..."就是我们常说的"change from sth to sth else"，但英语词典说"transformation"是"a complete change"，完全变了，彻底变了，这两个词的词意有差别。

例句 32. It never struck me that she was conceited about this, I think she just enjoyed being who she was, and I'm sure too, *grateful* for being as beautiful as she was. I really saw no evidence of vanity in her...（p. 131）

📍 **说明** 戴安娜是人们公认的漂亮女人，但她绝不因此而自负，这更增添了她的内在之美，非常难得。一些女孩因略有一点姿色便千方百计显摆、卖弄，十分浅薄。

1. conceited

意为"having too much pride in yourself"（自负）。

2. vanity

词典说是"too much pride in your own appearance"，因长相而自负、虚荣，和"conceited"意思相近。

3. ... she just enjoyed being who she was...

这句话似乎也包括"she just enjoyed doing what she did"的意思。

作为一个女子，戴安娜身上有人类的共性，也有属于她自己的个性，尤其作为王室成员，她的这种个性更加突出。比如，她鼓励她的儿子们接近普通人，和他们聊天，和他们玩耍，这与王室传统不同；她对普通人有感情，同情弱势群体。她走进艾滋病房时，敢于和病人握手，而且不戴手套，这在世界范围引起轰动效应。英国王室哪个成员肯这样做？她死后，有人这样说："... she was taken by many to represent human nature at its caring best"，很多人认为她体现了最佳状态的人类相互关怀的本性，说她有"an instinct for popular spirituality"，她有根植于本能的崇高的普众精神。

基于她的这些个性，"enjoyed being who she was"的基本意思是"做自己""她只喜欢做自己"，即坚持自己的信念，按照自己的信念做事。

例句 33. There's no doubt that Diana *did* become strongly anti-Windsor, but throughout her life she was an aristocrat to her fingertips.（p. 148）

💡 说明　戴安娜虽然强烈反对英国君主制，但综观她的一生，她自己是地地道道的贵族。

1. "to her fingertips"，意为"in every way"，完全地，地道地。

2. Windsor：温莎城堡，英国君主行政官邸，此处代表英国君主政体。

例句 34. We'd discuss minor politics or people, or events that were going on in the news, or where she had been. Occasionally she'd point someone out and talk about them or what they were wearing, in an idle sort of chit-chat way.（p. 151）

💡 说明　这是戴安娜的骑马教练休伊特（Hewitt）的述说，练习间歇时他们聊天，聊政治，聊新闻，聊眼前之所见等，随意闲聊。"in an idle sort of chit-chat way"，这个表达方式听着就很随意，可以借鉴。

例句 35. It was important for both of us. I became deeply in love with her, and that's a great thing to happen. It's a great thing to be in love with someone. And if they're in love with you, I mean, you know, it makes you want to sing and walk with a bounce in your step.（p. 153）

💡 **说明** 戴安娜和休伊特在骑马训练过程中产生了感情，这是休伊特谈他和戴安娜恋爱的感受。"it makes you want to sing and walk with a bounce in your step"，爱情对他产生了一种神奇的力量，他有唱歌的冲动，走起路来步子也欢快起来，这个描述很真实，也很形象。

例句 36. There were times when she was so frustrated that she would become unguarded in her criticism, for example towards the Queen. Any of us can get in a bit of a paddy about something and say something that we later regret.（p. 155）

💡 **说明**

1. "become unguarded in her criticism"，戴安娜批评女王有时口无遮拦，"unguarded" 这个用法值得借鉴。

The Making of a Royal Romance 里有一个类似的句子："She got quite drunk on white wine and really let her guard down"，这是说威廉王子的女朋友凯特因喝了酒说话口无遮拦，说话放松警惕。

2. "get in a bit of a paddy"，生气，或情绪不好，这个表达方式新鲜，值得借鉴。

例句 37. "The Queen doesn't appreciate what I'm doing. I try to do my job. She's not helping me." But then she would temper that with always sort of trying to show that she was respectful of Her Majesty, which was rather nice and touching, actually.（p. 155）

💡 **说明** 戴安娜说女王不欣赏她的所作所为，女王没有帮助她，然后她又补充说，她还是尊敬女王的，以缓和她的语气。

词典这样解释 "to temper sth（with sth）"："to make sth less severe by adding sth that has the opposite effect"，相当于汉语的 "使缓和"，这是一

个很有用而且很常用的固定短语。

例句 38. But the moment she started meeting patients she relaxed. And, of course, there was that very famous photograph of her shaking hands with a patient who had AIDS. That was wired all over the world. It made a tremendous impact, just a member of the Royal Family *touching* someone.（p. 159）

💡 说明　英国第一间艾滋病房在伦敦开诊时，主管医生迈克·阿德勒（Dr Mike Adler）给王室写信，希望查尔斯王子来主持开幕式，王室回答说查尔斯太忙，问若戴安娜王妃去是否可以，医院巴不得，"we jumped at it"。上面描写戴安娜来到病房时的情况：她刚一进医院时也是很紧张，但一进了病房就放松了。

作为王室成员，戴安娜敢于和艾滋病人握手，而且不戴手套，这个照片传遍全世界，她的这个举动影响太大了。

戴安娜是这样的人，了不起。

例句 39. Nobody in a terminal ward expected to be cured by Diana. Nobody in a battered women's shelter expected her to find them a new apartment. But most claim to have felt better for her presence and some, like Frances Drayton, say they still feel positively joyous to have spent a few moments in the intimate and understanding stillness she carried around with her. Few, if any, have ever said they wanted her to go away and not bother them.（p. 187）

💡 说明　末期病人病房里的病人谁也不会期待戴安娜能治好他们的病。住在破旧房屋里的妇女谁也不会期待戴安娜能给她们找一套新房。但他们都说她的到来（出现）让他们感觉好多了，有的甚至说，在她身上散发出来的那种亲切和相互理解的宁静中与她共处一会儿会让人感到快乐。

弱势群体对戴安娜的这种亲切感和信任感都是发自内心的，说明戴安娜具有一种感染力和亲和力，这是她的内在品质和气质的自然表现，她不是在做给谁看，她是在做自己，"she just enjoyed being who she was"。

这段文字里有几个搭配很新鲜，值得细细琢磨，如"positively joyous""the intimate and understanding stillness"等。

例句 40. If royal healing worked at all it did so because a moment's proximity to greatness lifted the sufferer's morale. In this respect there is a plausible connection to Diana's dazzling arrival in the ward or the shelter.（p. 187）

💡 说明　这里的"greatness"字面上是"伟大"，在这个上下文里不妨理解为"崇高精神""高贵品质"，当病房里的病人或身在避难处的人们看见具有如此"崇高精神"和"高贵品质"的戴安娜时，他们的情绪就好起来。如果说王室成员的到来真有治愈功能的话，可能就是这个道理。

以下两个表达方式值得借鉴：

1. "a moment's proximity to greatness"，瞬时间接触到"崇高精神"。

2. "lifted the sufferer's morale"，提振病人的精神，增强病人的信心。

例句 41. It was a tacit understanding between Diana and Charles that I was a part of her life in the same way that Mrs Parker Bowles was part of Prince Charles's life.（p. 166）

💡 说明　这是戴安娜情人休伊特关于他和戴安娜之间关系的描述，其中的"tacit understanding"很符合汉语"默契"的说法，即戴安娜和查尔斯双方心里都明白，正如卡米拉已经成为查尔斯生活的一部分（或卡米拉已经进入了查尔斯的生活），休伊特也已经成为戴安娜生活的一部分（或休伊特已经进入了戴安娜的生活）。英语的这个习惯用语"in the same way"使用频率比较高，用好了能理清比较复杂的概念。

> **例句** 42. When she died, Diana was taken by many to represent human nature at its caring best. And she did have an instinct for popular spirituality—the way people feel at their children's carol concerts, the way they support each other at a funeral or a hospital bedside. Her friend Rosa Monckton was convinced she could see God in her actions.（p. 187）

📍 **说明**　这里所说的 "human nature at its caring best" 是指处于最佳状态的人类相互关怀的本性，很多人认为戴安娜体现了这个本性，她的本能里就有一种崇高的普众精神，这种精神和父母在孩子们参加的圣诞颂歌音乐会上的精神状态是一样的，也和人们在追悼会上或站在病人床边时那种相互支持的精神是一样的。她的朋友罗莎·蒙克顿（Rosa Monckton）坚信，在戴安娜做这些事情时她能看见上帝，也就是说，她的所作所为符合天意。这也许就是她死后人们如此怀念她的缘故。

下面的两个表达方式真的好呀！

1. "human nature at its caring best"，处于最佳状态的人类相互关怀的本性，从汉英翻译角度看，这个概念处理起来比较困难，特别是只用一个词组就表达出来了，而不用一个完整句子，这种简洁的文字技巧让人赏心悦目，值得学习借鉴。

2. "an instinct for popular spirituality"，根植于她的本能里的崇高的普众精神，又是一个用词组表达复杂概念的例子。

> **例句** 43. In early March a former girlfriend of Hewitt provided the excuse for the *News of the World* to break the story of Diana and James. It stopped just short of saying they were lovers...（p. 206）

📍 **说明**　《世界新闻》（*News of the World*）公布了戴安娜和休伊特的恋情，休伊特的前女友为其找了借口，差一点就说他们是情人了（或者，就差没说他们是情人了）。"差一点就……"在汉语用得很多，而英语的这个固定短语 "stop short of..." 正好表达了这个概念，汉英之间的这种比较对应的表达方式不算少，阅读时可留意。

例句 44. And he said, "Yes, but if you're wrong I'll be in the dock, not you." So he gave me the task of proving to him that the tape was genuine and I spent six weeks doing it... playing it to phonetics experts. We had other experts examine the tape to make sure it wasn't spliced and cobbled together.（p. 241）

💡 说明　媒体拿到查尔斯和卡米拉的电话录音，如获至宝。媒体的理查德·司科特（Richard Stott）找到一个叫哈里·阿诺德（Harry Arnold）的专家辨认，阿诺德说一个声音是查尔斯的，另一个是卡米拉的。司科特认为此事关系重大，不能出错，否则他会被告上法庭。然后阿诺德请了几个语音专家反复研究了六个星期，最后确定这个录音是真实的，不是剪接拼凑的。

1. 这里的"dock"指法庭的被告席，"in the dock"是固定短语，被告上法庭受审的意思，我们在英语作家的作品里看到这个用法，否则我们一般不会想到这个表达方式。

2. "spliced and cobbled together"，剪接拼凑在一起，假图像有这种做法，假录音也有这样的做法，这是个地道的英语表达方式，可借鉴。

例句 45. "Kissinger spoke about Diana's 'luminous personality' and praised her for identifying herself with 'the sick, the disadvantaged and the suffering'".（pp. 288-289）

💡 说明　1995 年 12 月，戴安娜应邀到纽约接受"the United Cerebral Palsy（UCP）Humanitarian of the Year Award"，基辛格为她颁奖，以上是基辛格颁奖词的一部分。

1. "personality"通常解释为"性格或人格"，也有"气质"一说，这里"luminous personality"译作"光彩照人的性格"或"光彩照人的气质"，似乎都可以。

2. "identifying herself with 'the sick, the disadvantaged and the suffering'"，这个 "identifying herself with…" 表示 "支持" "同情"，也表示 "与……有密切联系"，这里指前者，戴安娜支持、同情病人、弱势群体和受苦受难的人们。作为一个地位显赫的王室成员，戴安娜的这种精神十分可贵，十分难得。

这个短语的这种用法值得学习，值得借鉴。

例句 46. The rest of the Royal Family are cold fish, frankly. Diana was a more interesting person because she seemed to have a feeling for people's plights. And she wanted to use her fame and title to do something about it. And she seemed to be trying to fit in to some place that she no longer could.（pp. 288-289）

💡 说明　埃德·马修斯（Ed Mathews）的这段话有几个表达方式很新鲜，值得学习。

1. "cold fish"，根据上下文可以判断这个搭配所表达的意思，"坦率地说，王室是冷漠的"，这一方面是符合实际的描述，另一方面也是衬托戴安娜对普通民众的热情。

2. "have a feeling for people's plights"，这里的 "a feeling" 表示 "同情" "怜悯" 等，"people's plights" 即人们的 "苦难" "艰难的处境" 等，戴安娜对于人们的苦难有怜悯之心。

3. "to fit in to some place"，这里的 "place" 也许有比较宽泛的含义，或者是某种机构、某种位置之类，她为了帮下层的人们做些事情，想方设法进入她不可能进入的这类地方，这里也许有更多的背景，但无论如何，这个表达方式是可以借鉴的。

例句 47. One afternoon he saw her embrace a woman by a graveside and stand motionless with her for what seemed like half an hour. He thought—as Mike Whitlam had thought in Angola—that there was no one else in the world who could have fulfilled this role. Deedes described Diana as a human being with ordinary faults, but an unusually big heart.（p. 336）

📍 **说明**　资深媒体人比尔·迪兹（Bill Deedes）具有五十多年战地采访经历，他陪同戴安娜访问非洲战乱地区的地雷受害者，当她听着受害者家人的叙述让她感到痛苦时，她伸出手去安抚她们时所表现的"silent stillness"，以及她那特有的"soothing tranquillity"，让他感到惊讶。

一天，他看见戴安娜在墓旁拥抱一个妇女，并和她站在一起足有半个小时，他描述戴安娜与常人一样，有她的缺点，但她有一颗超乎寻常的伟大的心。记者迪兹被戴安娜的行为感动了，他对她的评价是客观的。

阅读E. B. 怀特（E. B. White）：
"Once More to the Lake" and Others

简介

E. B. 怀特（E. B. White, 1899—1985），美国散文家。

《纽约客》杂志前总编威廉·肖恩评价 E. B. 怀特时这样说：

"E. B. 怀特是一位伟大的文体家。他的文学风格之纯净，在我们的语言中较之任何人都不遑多让。它是独特的，清晰的，自然的，完全美国式的，极美的。他的人长生不老，他的文字超越时空。"〔引自《夏洛的网》，（美）E. B. 怀特著，任溶溶译，上海：上海译文出版社，2014〕

E. B. 怀特因为他在文学上的贡献，曾获得多个奖项，其中包括美国艺术和文学学会散文与评论金奖（Gold Medal for Essays and Criticism of American Academy of Arts and Letters）和国家文学奖章（The National Medal for Literature）。

1963 年，美国总统约翰·肯尼迪提名授予 E. B. 怀特美国总统自由勋章（Presidential Medal of Freedom），这是和平时期美国授予平民的最高荣誉，奖励那些对提高美国生活品质有重要贡献的人（those who contribute significantly to the quality of American life）。

同年 12 月，林登·约翰逊总统为 E. B. 怀特颁奖时说他是 "An essayist whose concise comment on men and places has revealed to yet another age the vigor of the English sentence"。

以总统名义奖励作家，特别提到"the English sentence"，很不寻常。说怀特的英语展示了"the vigor of the English sentence"，也可以说他的英语展示了"the art of the English sentence"。读他的文字，能体会英语语言之美、英语语言之魅力。

怀特主要作品：

One Man's Meat（1942）

The Wild Flag（1946）

Stuart Little（1945，儿童图书）

Here Is New York（1949）

Charlotte's Web（1952）

The Elements of Style〔1959，与小威廉·斯特伦克（William Strunk, Jr.）合著〕

The Points of My Compass（1962）

一、"Once More to the Lake"

E. B. 怀特有一篇著名散文"Once More to the Lake"，叙事清雅，内涵丰富，文字流畅，节奏感强。这篇散文收录在同年出版的 *Essays of E. B. White* 里，此后出现在他的多个散文集子里，广受读者喜爱。

这篇散文的写作经历了一个漫长的过程。每年秋季开学，英语老师总要给学生出一个作文题目："How I Spent My Summer Vacation"。怀特小时候，每年夏天跟着父母去缅因州的贝尔格莱德湖度假。这是一个很大的湖，长约 16 千米，宽约 8 千米。1914 年，怀特十五岁，便以很高的热情写了一篇作文，描写他在贝尔格莱德湖度假的情景，写了湖区的景色，写了在那里听到的声音和闻到的气息。1936 年，怀特已经是美国知名作家，他又回到贝尔格莱德湖，并给他的兄弟写了一封很长的信，详细描述了他在那里度假的情形。1941 年，怀特带着他的儿子乔尔（Joel）再一次访问贝尔格莱德湖，然后写了著名的"Once More to the Lake"，文中包括不少

1936 年给其兄弟信中的内容。实际上，这篇散文的写作始于 1914 年，终于 1941 年，是在将近三十年的时间里完成的。

文章用词简单，句子结构也简单，所描绘的情景清新淡雅，有中国传统国画之美。*E. B. White Reader* 一书编者说，怀特的语言既新鲜（fresh），又生动（vivid），他的评论既简单（simple），又深刻（profound）。他的语言风格展示了一种独特的境界。

我们从 E. B. 怀特这篇文章中撷取几个段落，欣赏他的英语句子，体会他的英语之美，以提高我们对英语语言的感悟和鉴赏能力。

例句 1. We stared silently at the tips of our rods, at the dragonflies that came and went. I lowered the tip of mine into the water, tentatively, pensively dislodging the fly, which darted two feet away, poised, darted two feet back, and came to rest again a little farther up the rod.

💡 说明　这段文字写蜻蜓落在鱼竿上，钓者把鱼竿沉到水里让蜻蜓飞走，而后它又回来落在鱼竿靠上的地方。作者描写蜻蜓这个动作时用的都是简单词、简单句，如 "came and went" "darted two feet away, poised, darted two feet back" "came to rest again..." 等。用 "darted" 描写蜻蜓飞来飞去动作之迅速，是夏季乡村里常见的景象，一幅活动的画面。

例句 2. There had been no years between the ducking of this dragonfly and the other one—the one that was part of memory. I looked at the boy, who was silently watching his fly, and it was my hands that held his rod, my eyes watching. I felt dizzy and didn't know which rod I was at the end of.

💡 说明　从这段文字可以发现怀特与众不同的叙事角度和与众不同的行文方式。

1. ... the other one—the one that was part of memory.

记忆中的那只蜻蜓，即小时钓鱼曾经见过的那只，这可能是最简洁的表达方式，不但富有诗意，而且有一种自然天成的节奏感。

2. ... it was my hands that held his rod, my eyes watching.

看见儿子手握鱼竿，眼睛盯着鱼漂，作者产生了幻觉，好像是自己的手在握鱼竿，自己的眼睛在盯着鱼漂，作者看着儿子，想起自己儿时跟着父亲一起钓鱼的情景。

3. I... didn't know which rod I was at the end of.

此句的意思是，不知自己手握的是哪根鱼竿，是我的呢还是儿子的？

例句 **3.** I began to sustain the illusion that he was I, and therefore, by simple transportation, that I was my father. This sensation persisted, kept cropping up all the time we were there.

💡 说明　父亲觉得儿子就是小时的自己，而他就是自己的父亲，所以在例句 2 里他说 "I felt dizzy"。

读这段文字，我们不仅看见父子在湖边同钓的画面，也能感觉到此时父亲的幻觉 "illusion"。作者用简单的词句所表达的这种幻觉很微妙。同时注意句中这三个动词 "sustain" "persisted" 和 "kept cropping up" 在意义上的一致性。

例句 **4.** When we got back for a swim before lunch, the lake was exactly where we had left it, the same number of inches from the dock, and there was only the merest suggestion of a breeze.

💡 说明　这里的 "suggestion" 是常用词，《牛津高阶英汉双解词典》这样解释："a slight amount or sign of sth"，并有例句：

She looked at me with just a suggestion of a smile.

"the merest suggestion of..." 和 "just a suggestion of..." 都表示"微微有一点……"，这个用法值得借鉴。

例句 5. I kept remembering everything, lying in bed in the mornings... when the older boys played their mandolins and the girls sang and we ate doughnut dipped in sugar, and how sweet the music was on the water in the shining night, and what it had felt like to think about girls then.

💡 说明　早晨"我"躺在床上，回忆起那些美好的时刻，在明亮的月光下，男孩子们弹奏曼陀林，女孩子们唱着歌，水上飘着甜蜜悦耳的乐声，此时想起女孩子们是一种什么样的感觉啊！

这段抒发浪漫情怀的文字，写得好，很有感染力。

怀特有深厚的语言和美学修养，他所叙述和描写的事物具有美感，他所创造的意境富有诗意。

二、"The Ring of Time"

大约在 1956 年 3 月下旬，E. B. 怀特在佛罗里达观看 John Ringling North's 马戏表演，之后写了散文 "The Ring of Time"。*E. B. White Reader* 一书编者说，作者通过观看骑手的表演向我们展示了"the eternity of youth"。这是一篇好散文，我们从中选几个片段，学习、研究他的句子，揣摩他的写作技巧。

例句 1. The long rein, or tape, by which the woman guided her charge counterclockwise in his dull career formed the radius of their private circle, of which she was the revolving center; and she, too, stepped a tiny circumference of her own, in order to accommodate the horse and allow him his maximum scope.

💡 说明　这是该文的开头部分，写驯马师遛马的情景。她牵着缰绳，让马围着场地逆时针转，为了尽量让马走一个很大的圈，她也在场地中央随着马走一个小圈。

这个句子较长，是一个并列句，意思比较复杂，但句子的构成很清晰。分号之前是一个主从复合句，主干部分："The long rein, or tape...

formed the radius of their private circle"，其中有一个"of which"引导的从句；分号之后的"and she, too, stepped a tiny circumference of her own..."，是并列句的后半部分，也是一个简单句，其中有一个由"by which"引导的从句，并含有一个由"in order to..."引出的短语。

留意一下句中的"to accommodate the horse and allow him his maximum scope"，这里的"to accommodate"意为"to provide enough space"，驯马师这样做是为了给马提供足够的空间让马跑圈；后面的"maximum scope"表达了同样的意思。其中动词"accommodate"用得好，值得揣摩，可以模仿。

在这段文字里，怀特细致而清晰地描绘了一个微妙的场景。他擅长写复杂句子，安排好句子的主干成分之后，特别会用定语从句，或后置的限定、修饰成分，阅读他的作品时可注意这一点。

例句 2. 文中有一个描写骑马女郎穿泳衣在马背上表演的段落，我们以句子为单位分析一下：

1. Twice she managed a one-foot stance—a sort of ballet pose, with arms outstretched.

💡 说明 她曾两次单腿站在马背上，两臂向外伸展，很像芭蕾舞的动作。这里的"stance"是站在马背上的一个姿势；"pose"一般是有意摆出的姿态，在这个上下文里，二者意思相当。

2. At one point the neck strap of her bathing suit broke and she went twice around her ring in the classic attitude of a woman making minor repairs to a garment.

💡 说明 骑马女郎正在表演时，挂在脖子上的泳衣背带断了，这很尴尬。她如何解决这个没有料到的麻烦呢？这里用了"classic attitude"，此处的"classic"有两种解释：一是"typical"，一是"elegant"。根据作者通篇对女孩的赞美，似乎两个解释都说得通，即，她以女孩修补衣服时的那种惯有的（或优雅的）姿态处理了这个意外事故。

3. The fact that she was standing on the back of a moving horse while doing this invested the matter with a clowning significance that perfectly fitted the spirit of the circus—jocund, yet charming.

💡 **说明** 这个意外给她的表演增添了一种滑稽色彩，虽然非常符合马戏场的氛围，然而也显示了马戏的魅力。

关于 "to invest"，《牛津高阶英汉双解词典》的解释为 "to make sb/ sth seem to have a particular quality"（使……具备某种性质），并给了一个例句：

Being a model invests her with a certain glamour. 当模特赋予了她某种魅力。

在这个上下文里，"invest" 是一个恰当的字眼，E. B. 怀特讲究选词。

例句 3. She just rolled the strap into a neat ball and stowed it into her bodice while the horse rocked and rolled beneath her in dutiful innocence.

💡 **说明** 这个 "in dutiful innocence" 将骏马在表演时任劳任怨、忠于职守的姿态呈现在读者面前。神奇的搭配，形象的表达。

例句 4. The richness of the scene was in its plainness, its natural condition— of horse, of ring, of girl...

💡 **说明** 作者通过观察发现表演现场之所以具有丰富的内涵，在于表现在骏马、场地和女孩身上的 "plainness"（可理解为 "简朴、不加修饰"）和 "naturalness"（可以理解为 "自然、不做作"），使作者为之感动。这里只是客观地描述，以展示她们的 "简朴" 和 "自然"，没有评价文字。主观评价是说理，客观描写是艺术，更有说服力。

例句 5. The enchantment grew not out of anything that happened or was performed but out of something that seemed to go round and around and around with the girl, attending her, a steady gleam in the shape of a circle—a ring of ambition, of happiness, of youth.

💡 **说明**　作者被女孩的表演所吸引，所陶醉。同时他也在思考，为什么她的表演如此迷人。不是因为场内正在发生的事情，也不是因为她的骑技，作者似乎看见伴随女孩在场上绕行的光环。何为"a ring of ambition"？因为骑马表演本身是一种"挑战"，从骑者角度说也是一种"征服"，其中自然含有"ambition"；何为"a ring of happiness"？这种喜悦带有职业性质，同时，"征服"也带来喜悦；何为"a ring of youth"？应指女孩所表现出来的青春活力和青春之美。

作者以形而上的眼光，将瞬间的感觉写得可感、可知；怀特的美学思考是深刻的。读经典作家的作品，可以直接吸取他的语言精华，同时探寻他的审美倾向，看他是如何从生活中发现美好，然后用语言将其表达出来。

怀特称自己是"a word man"，他重视字词，讲究用词，仔细推敲他的字词总会有收获。

例句 6. The girl wasn't so young that she did not know the delicious satisfaction of having a perfectly behaved body and the fun of using it to do a trick most people can't do, but she was too young to know that time does not move in a circle at all. I thought："She will never be as beautiful as this again"—a thought that made me acutely unhappy—and in a flash my mind had projected her twenty-five years ahead...

💡 **说明**　作者看着女孩骑着马一圈一圈绕行，循环往复，他想到"the element of time"。对于人生，"time"不是"循环往复"的，而是有始有终。他想到二十五年之后，女孩不再像现在这个样子，于是他发出以上的感慨。一般观众看完表演就完了，但文人多愁善感，这样一次表演却让他对人生进行一番哲学思考，写出这样好的文章。

第一句是比较复杂的长句，其中"The girl wasn't so young that she did not know..."，即女孩不至于年轻到连某某事都不知道；"but she was too young to know that..."，但是因为她还是太年轻，她不懂得（或者没有意识到）"时间不是循环往复的"。作者把这两个小句放在一起，使它们在形式上和内容上形成对比。我们写这种句子的经验可能不多，这种写法值得借鉴。

三、"Will Strunk"

"Will Strunk"是一篇纪念文章，纪念作者在康奈尔大学读书时的英语老师小威廉·斯特伦克（William Strunk, Jr.）。下面是文章的开头文字：

例句 1. Mosquitoes have arrived with the warm nights, and our bedchamber is their theater under the stars. I have been up and down all night, swinging at them with a face towel dampened at one end to give it authority.

🔍 说明

1. theater（或 theatre）

"theater"本来的意思是"剧场"或"戏剧"之类，这里是指"战场"，"我们"的卧室便成了蚊子在星光底下的战场。

2. "up and down"，是说作者因蚊子干扰一夜没睡好觉，一会儿起来一会儿躺下，很简洁的表达方式，简单而达意，可在写作和翻译中学着使用。

3. ... swinging at them with a face towel dampened at one end to give it authority

半夜起来打蚊子是十分讨厌的事，怀特却将这个事情写得饶有风趣。"to give it authority"，意思是把毛巾的一头沾上水打起蚊子来效果更好。

"theater""up and down"和"authority"，这几个英语表达方式的使用，体现了作者的幽默感，结合他的文字功夫，使他的句子生发艺术魅力。

例句 2. This morning I suffer from the lightheadedness that comes from no sleep—a sort of drunkenness, very good for writing because all sense of responsibility for what the words say is gone.

💡 说明

1. "the lightheadedness that comes from no sleep"，因为夜里失眠早晨起来头晕。我们做汉英翻译时，遇到不会的词语要查词典，关于"失眠"，词典给了两个词，一是"sleeplessness"，一是"insomnia"。怀特没有选择这种比较呆板的大词，而是只用了两个小词的搭配，"no sleep"，这个说法活泼，更体现作者的语言特色。

2. ... very good for writing because all sense of responsibility for what the words say is gone.

因为夜里睡不好觉而失眠，因失眠而头晕，在这种状态下写作有一个好处：对文中所说的内容不必担责任，"for what the words say"，怀特不说"for what the author says"，这里又体现他的幽默感。

例句 3. ... I must have once owned a copy, for I took English 8 under Professor Strunk in 1919 and the book was required reading, but my copy presumably failed to survive an early purge. I'd not laid eyes on it in thirty-eight years. Am now delighted to study it again and rediscover its rich deposits of gold.

💡 说明　怀特因搬家需要清理旧书，但有一本书他留了下来——他在康奈尔大学读书时的英语老师小威廉·斯特伦克编写的 *The Elements of Style*。

在这段文字里怀特用了两个比喻：

1. "purge"，有时表示"清洗异己"，有时表示"清除"；怀特在这里借用这个词指他曾经的一次清理书籍，在这个上下文里使用这个词增加了句子的趣味；

2. "its rich deposits of gold"，丰富的金矿，喻 *The Elements of Style* 中有关英语写作方面的丰富内容。

怀特常在文章中使用贴切的隐喻，读者知其意，但又不觉得他是在特意用喻。

英国翻译家赫伯特·翟理斯（Herbert Giles）赞扬中国文学时也用过一个类似的比喻："Untold treasures... lie hidden in the rich lodes of Chinese literature."

这里的 "lodes" 和 "deposits" 词意相近，都指埋在地下的矿藏。

例句 4. "Omit needless words!" cries the author on page 21, and into that imperative Will Strunk really put his heart and soul. In the days when I was sitting in his class, he omitted so many needless words, and omitted them so forcibly and with such eagerness and obvious relish, that he often seemed in the position of having short-changed himself, a man left with nothing more to say but with time to fill...

说明　小威廉·斯特伦克在 *The Elements of Style* 的第二部分列出 22 条 "Principles of Composition"，其中第 17 条专门讨论 "Omit needless words"。

这段文字中的动词 "short-change" 我们可能使用得不多，英语词典这样解释："to treat sb unfairly by not giving them what they have earned or deserve"，意思是 "亏待"。

这段话是什么意思呢？小威廉·斯特伦克在他的书里特别强调说："Omit needless words!" 在他的写作课上也省掉了很多不必要的字词。作为教师，他在课堂上有充裕的时间，本可以详细讲解教材内容或阐明自己的观点，但他的语言很精练，能不用的词不用，能不说的话不说。从这个意义上说，他是 "short-changed himself"，亏待了自己。

鲁迅谈作文时也说过类似的话，"竭力将可有可无的字、句、段删去，毫不可惜。"

有时间可以读一些怀特的散文，学习他体验生活时所表现的敏感，研究他轻巧自然的写作技巧，体会他如何展示英语的句子之美以及他的幽默感等。

通过阅读怀特的散文，感受到他与众不同的写作风格，句子简单，但内涵丰富，耐人寻味。从文章可以看作者的修养和信仰。所谓修养，主要指他的人文修养和审美修养。因为读书多，观察准确，对人、对人际关系、对生活、对社会，看得清楚，从本质上进行分析，写出来的东西给人启示，同时，他把写作当作艺术；所谓信仰，是说他相信，这样写句子有美感（beauty）、有活力（vigor）、有力量（power），这是一种信仰。这对我们有启发，我们写句了、翻译句子，如何做到有美感、有活力、有力量，值得思索。

四、“An Approach to Style”

1959 年，*The Elements of Style* 再版，怀特写了前言，还写了“An Approach to Style”作为独立的一章附在书后。

在文中，他认为，“style is something of a mystery”，并举了一个例句：These are the times that try men's souls.

这是美国革命时期来自英国的宣传鼓动家托马斯·潘恩（Thomas Paine）写的小册子《美国危机》（*The American Crisis*）开头的一句话。怀特说，这句话虽然只有八个简单的小词，但却被人们引用了二百多年，今天人们还在引用。他说，若换一个说法表达同样的意思，无论怎么说都不行。

为说明“style is something of a mystery”，怀特将潘恩的意思用四种不同形式表达：

1. Times like these try men's souls.

2. How trying it is to live in these times!

3. These are trying times for men's souls.

4. Soulwise, these are trying times.

怀特说，以上四种方式尽管语法都正确，但它们的寿命都不会很长，很快就会被人们忘记，这是为什么，值得思考。

同样，我国唐代诗人王维的《渭城曲》中的著名诗句"劝君更尽一杯酒，西出阳关无故人"也是一样。古来写送别的诗很多，唯有王维的这两个诗句流传特别广，虽然用词一样地简单、平白，至今已有一千多年，还将流传下去。这是为什么？也值得思考。

五、"Sootfall and Fallout"

1956 年，怀特写散文"Sootfall and Fallout"。文章开头写邻居搬来一户名叫玛丽·马丁（Mary Martin）的人家。文中有一段描写邻居后院的景象，其中有一句话是这样写的：

例句 1. On every slight stirring of the breeze, the willow behind Mary Martin's wigwam lets drop two or three stylish yellow leaves, and they swim lazily down like golden fish to where Paul, the handyman waits with his broom. （wigwam 比喻玛丽·马丁的房子像印第安人的锥形棚屋）

💡 **说明**　微风吹来，柳叶飘落，如同金鱼懒洋洋飘到保罗跟前，这时保罗正拿着扫帚在那里等着。

怀特把飘落的柳叶比作自上而下游动的金鱼，这是一个很有意境的句子，描绘出一幅动态的画面。

作者能把生活琐事、自然景象，写得生趣盎然，让人爱读。这跟齐白石绘画一样，常见的昆虫，一只蟋蟀、一只蜻蜓，在他的笔下，可以变成妙不可言的艺术品。

表达这个内容，可以把句子写得很花哨，但怀特只用了一个常见的并列句（compound sentence），写得很自然。他在"An Approach to Style"一文中提出几条写作原则，有一条是这样说的：

Write in a way that comes easily and naturally to you, using words and phrases that come readily to hand.

由此看来，句子要写得自然，结构也不是越复杂越好。

E. B. White Reader 一书的编者说：

Simplicity is the key to clarity. The strenuous struggle for deathless prose does not guarantee lively writing. It is better to say what comes naturally than to strain to be impressive.

这话说得很中肯，最好是有话自然地说，自然地写，不必刻意给人留下深刻印象。

例句 2. The impression one gets from campaign oratory is that the sun revolves around the earth, the earth revolves around the United States, and the United States revolves around whichever city the speaker happens to be in at the moment. This is what a friend of mine used to call un-Copernican system.

说明 "Sootfall and Fallout" 写于 1956 年 11 月初，正值美国大选竞争的高潮。文中提到艾森豪威尔，他是美国第 34 任总统，第一个任期 1953 年 1 月 20 日—1957 年 1 月 20 日，第二个任期 1957 年 1 月 20 日—1961 年 1 月 20 日。怀特写此文时，艾森豪威尔正在竞选连任。

竞选者为了拉拢选民而哗众取宠，经常说一些不着边际的话。怀特连用几个排比句嘲讽他们，这种排比方式的讥讽力量很强，也很风趣，体现了怀特式幽默。

un-Copernican：违反哥白尼日心说的

六、"Education"

例句 1. She cooks for the children on the stove that heats the room, and she can cool their passions or warm their soup with equal competence. She conceives their costumes, cleans up their messes, and shares their confidences.

My boy already regards his teacher as his great friend, and I think tells her a great deal more than he tells us.

💡 **说明** 这段文字取自写于 1939 年的 "Education" 一文，赞美乡村女教师。文章开头说，这位女教师不但担任一、二、三年级的全部课程，接着说了上面的话。

1. She cooks for the children on the stove that heats the room...

这句话的意思是，"在为屋子取暖的炉子上给孩子们做饭……"，在汉语是用一个限定词"取暖的"修饰"炉子"；在英语，怀特则用一个从句 "that heats the room" 限定 "the stove"。这个从句与其限定的成分写得如此连贯自然，笔调亦"淡"亦"雅"，怀特的写作风格。

2. ... and shares their confidences.

这里的 "confidences" 意为 "secrets"，"私密话"，此时的这个词常以复数形式出现。

3. My boy... I think tells her a great deal more than he tells us.

与此句中的 "tells" 意思相同的词还有 "speak" "talk" "converse" 等，但怀特用 "tell"，这是说孩子的感情是有倾向性的，他有事对老师讲，有话对老师说，跟老师比跟父母还亲。这里的 "tell" 包含这层意思。

例句 2. When the snow is deep or when the motor is dead or both, he makes it on hoof. In the afternoons he walks or hitches all or part of the way home in fair weather, gets transported in foul.

💡 **说明** 这段文字写得简练，一是使用代词，"both" 代替的不是两个名词，而是两种情况："When the snow is deep" 和 "when the motor is dead"。二是运用省略，"all or part of the way" 是 "all the way or part of the way" 的省略；"in foul" 是 "in foul weather" 的省略。这两个方法很是省略了一些文字。

作者在这两句话里使用了四次 "or" 而不乱，也帮助节省了文字。

怀特的老师小威廉·斯特伦克主张 "Vigorous writing is concise"，有活力的文章莫不简练。这句话可作为写作时的座右铭。

七、"Bedfellows"

例句 1. Although birds fascinated him, his real hope as he watched the big shade trees outside the window was that a red squirrel would show up. When he sighted a squirrel, Fred would straighten up from his pillow, tense his frame, and then, in a moment or two, begin to tremble. The knuckles of his big forelegs, unstable from old age, would seem to go into spasm, and he would sit there with his eyes glued on the squirrel and his front legs alternately collapsing under him and bearing his weight again.

💡 说明　这是 E. B. 怀特描写自己爱犬的一段文字。

1. Fred would straighten up from his pillow, tense his frame...

当弗雷德（Fred，怀特爱犬的名字）看见松鼠，便从枕头上站起来，浑身紧绷，或者浑身变得紧张起来，"tense his frame" 这个说法简单，很形象。

2. ... would seem to go into spasm...

由于弗雷德已经老了，他的前腿站不稳，似乎是出现了痉挛状态。

3. ... and his front legs alternately collapsing under him and bearing his weight again...

它的两条腿一会儿瘫了下去，一会儿又支撑着站起来。

这里的 "alternately" 是 "交替" 的意思，和汉语常说的 "一会儿……一会儿……" 的意思一样。

例句 2. The only time he was discovered in an attitude that suggested affection was when I was in the driver's seat of our car and he would lay his heavy head on my right knee. This, I soon perceived, was not affection, it was nausea. Drooling always followed, and the whole thing was extremely inconvenient, because the weight of his head made me press too hard on the accelerator.

💡 **说明** "he was discovered in an attitude that suggested affection"，这里的"attitude"指弗雷德的姿态，"affection"是亲近的表示，弗雷德把它的头枕在作者的右腿上，这个动作看似和人在亲近，实则是因为它坐车感觉头晕。翻译这两个词时应掌握好分寸。

八、关于 "... say what comes naturally"

1. 关于英语的写作，E. B. 怀特的理论与实践对我们很有启发。我们在前面提过，E. B. 怀特在他的 "An Approach to Style" 一文中曾提出几条写作原则，有一条是这样说的：

Write in a way that comes easily and naturally to you, using words and phrases that come readily to hand.

2. *E. B. White Reader* 一书的编者也说：

Simplicity is the key to clarity. The strenuous struggle for deathless prose does not guarantee lively writing. It is better to say what comes naturally than to strain to be impressive.

其中也提到 "It is better to say what comes naturally..."。

3. "Just say the words."

E. B. 怀特曾经当过《西雅图时报》(the *Seattle Times*) 记者，在写一篇报道时遇到写作方面的问题，于是请教报社编辑，报社编辑想了一会儿说："Just say the words."

后来怀特说：

I always remembered that. It was excellent advice and I am still (sixteen years later) trying to say the words.

4. "I am a word man..."

E. B. 怀特曾经这样说：

Some people, perhaps most people, think words are not really important, but I am a word man and I attach the very highest importance to words.

5. 鲁迅谈"白描"写法：

"白描"却并没有秘诀。如果要说有，也不过是和障眼法反一调：有真意，去粉饰，少做作，勿卖弄而已。——《作文秘诀》

6. 看鲁迅如何"say what comes naturally"。

《孔乙己》中的一段描写：

掌柜仍然同平常一样，笑着对他说，"孔乙己，你又偷了东西了！"但他这回却不十分分辨，单说了一句"不要取笑！""取笑？要是不偷，怎么会打断腿？"孔乙己低声说道，"跌断，跌，跌……"

然后作者说，"他的眼色，很像恳求掌柜，不要再提。"

后面这句话只十几个白描似的文字，便刻画了一个让人同情、令人难忘的孔乙己形象。这句话虽是白话，没有刻意雕琢，但却是经典。

阅读吴延迪编著《英国风情录》（片段）

简介

　　这个段落选自吴延迪编著的《英国风情录》（英汉对照），这是一本全面介绍英国风土人情的书籍，阅读这本书不但可以了解英国社会生活的各个方面，而且这本书的英语写得特别好，字字皆珠玑，句句有诗味，是学习英语的上好材料。

▶ **原文**　The song's cosmopolitan character led to some confusion at a concert at a European resort attended by many English visitors. In Weber's Jubilee Overture, they recognized the National Anthem, and many immediately stood up—to the bewilderment of their Continental hosts. As the tune wove in and out they bobbed up and sat down, puzzled and unsure of what to think and to do.

💡 **说明**　一些英国人到欧洲一个旅游胜地度假，正赶上那里举行音乐会，演奏曲目是德国作曲家韦伯（Weber，1786—1826）的《狂欢节序曲》。英国人发现这个曲子好像是英国国歌，于是他们中的很多人立即起立，这让当地人感到莫名其妙。酷似英国国歌的曲调一会儿出现，一会儿消失，他们一会儿站起来，一会儿又坐下，不知如何是好。

　　这段文字对这个微妙的情景写得很精彩，将英国人当时无所适从的状态写得很具体，我们读这段文字觉得新鲜，其用词、其搭配、其句子都表现出以英语为母语的作家的才华。

例句 1. The song's cosmopolitan character led to some confusion...

💡 **说明**　这个句子里的"The song's cosmopolitan character"，系指韦伯的《狂欢节序曲》和英国国歌的曲调有相似之处，这个说法比较独特；而"led to some confusion..."是说这一相似之处造成了一些混乱，或使得一些人感到迷惑，这里用的是"动词＋名词"词组，而没有用形容词"confused"。

例句 2. ... and many immediately stood up—to the bewilderment of their Continental hosts.

💡 **说明**　这里的"to the bewilderment of their Continental hosts"是一个"介词＋名词"词组，使得欧洲大陆主人感到迷惑，同样，这里也没有使用形容词"bewildered"。

例句 3. As the tune wove in and out they bobbed up and sat down, puzzled and unsure of what to think and to do.

💡 **说明**　这个"wove"是"weave"的过去式，在这个上下文里，它的意思是说，这个曲调一会儿出现，一会儿消失，和我们在翻译时容易想到的动词可能不一样。

例句 4. ... they bobbed up and sat down...

💡 **说明**　此处的"bobbed up"表示速度快，一听见这个曲调他们立即起立。而且，"bobbed up and sat down"和前面的"wove in and out"相呼应，使句子产生一种平衡感和节奏感。

翟理斯（Herbert Allen Giles）
翻译中国古代散文

简 介

> 翟理斯（Herbert Allen Giles，1845—1935），英国汉学家、翻译家，向西方介绍中国文化的先驱。

1867 年，翟理斯来到英国驻华使馆，做一名翻译生。此后，历任中国沿海几个主要城市的英国领事馆翻译、副领事、领事等职。1893 年，在华工作 26 年后，返回英国。回国后，在剑桥大学教授汉学、汉语，长达 30 余年，1935 年病逝。

翟理斯终生著述、翻译，不辞辛劳，向西方介绍中国文学、中国文化，在西方产生较大影响。

他写了很多关于中国的书，翻译了很多中国文学作品，其中有《中国文学史》（*A History of Chinese Literature*，1901），据作者说，他的这本书是古今中外第一部中国文学史，为渴望了解中国文学的西方学者提供了丰富资料。还有《中国文学精华》（*Gems of Chinese Literature*，1883）。该书分散文卷和诗歌卷，散文卷节译了自春秋战国至晚清近 90 个作家的 180 多篇作品。

翟理斯对中国古文和中国古代文学有深入的学习和研究，而且对其评价很高。其译文优雅，译笔流畅，是学习汉英翻译的好材料。

翟里斯在《中国文学精华》（散文卷）里对中国文学、中国语言做过这样的评价：

"Untold treasures," says Professor G. von der Gabelentz, "lie hidden in the rich lodes of Chinese literature." Now without committing myself to exaggeration or misdirection as to the practical value of these treasures, I dare assert that the old pride, arrogance, and exclusiveness of the Chinese are readily intelligible to any one who has faithfully examined the literature of China and hung over the burning words of her great writers... （*Gems of Chinese Literature*，1884 年版序言）

关于翻译，翟理斯说：

It must however always be borne in mind that translators are but traitors at the best, and that translations may be moonlight and water while the originals are sunlight and wine. （*Gems of Chinese Literature*，1884 年版序言）

从这段文字可以看出，翟理斯对中国古代汉语和古典文学之美很有研究、非常赞赏，深知将其译成英语所面临的挑战；也可以看出，他是一个谦虚的学者。

翟理斯从小接受良好教育，打下深厚的英语基础，拉丁文和希腊文也有过严格训练，并广泛阅读古希腊神话，这些使他养成了严谨的治学作风。他极富语言天赋，在华工作二十几年，不但学习了艰深的中国文言文，阅读了大量中国古典文学著作，而且还学会了一些方言。这为他的翻译创造了条件，他的大部分译文不但准确传达原文意义，而且能再现原文风格，行文流畅，少有翻译腔。其译文之好，令人赞叹。但他仍对自己的译文保持低调，对原文和译文的优劣做这样的比喻。他的谦虚品质，十分难得。

再欣赏一段翟理斯评价《聊斋志异》时写的一段英语：

Any reader of these stories as transferred into another language might fairly turn round and ask the why and the wherefore of the profound admiration—to use a mild term—which is universally accorded to them by the literati of China. The answer is to be found in the incomparable style in which even the meanest of them is arrayed. All the elements of form which make for beauty in Chinese composition are there in overwhelming force. Terseness is pushed to its extreme limits; each particle that can be safely dispensed with is scrupulously eliminated, and every here and there some new and original combination invests perhaps a single word with a force it would never have possessed except under the hands of a perfect master of his art. (*A History of Chinese Literature*, p. 342)

作者用清晰而明朗的语言对《聊斋志异》的文字魅力做了精辟分析，逻辑自然，语言流畅，读来有吸引力、有说服力，是一个很有气势的段落，可供阅读、欣赏。

开头提出，为什么中国文人普遍崇拜这部作品？

答案：在它的无可比拟的文字风格里：

1. 包括形成汉语文字之美的所有形式要素；

2. 简洁——凡是可以省略的成分都被剔除；

3. 在《聊斋志异》作者的笔下，随处都有新的和富有创意的词语搭配。

翟理斯下苦功夫研读了中国古典文学，深知其艺术价值，所以，他对中国文学如此热爱、如此赞赏。当代西方学者如果也像翟理斯当年那样阅读、研究一些中国古代文学作品，他们也会肃然起敬。翟理斯讨论中国文学时所写英语如此漂亮，和他对中国文学所持态度不无关系。

翟理斯谈汉唐语言：

For general purposes, however, it is only necessary to state, that since the age of the Hans the meanings of words had gradually come to be more definitely fixed, and the structural arrangement more uniform and more polished. Imagination began to come more freely into play, and the language to flow more easily and more musically, as though responsive to the demands of art. (*A History of Chinese Literature*, p. 144)

这段文字讲汉唐语言，分三个层次：词意、结构、想象；然后他说汉唐语言更加流畅、更有乐感。因为是讲语言的发展变化，其间用了多个比较级的"more"，最后说，"as though responsive to the demands of art"，一个富有美感的短语道出汉唐语言的艺术性。这是翟理斯文章中不难寻觅的好段落，值得揣摩。

一、翟里斯翻译欧阳修《醉翁亭记》

The Old Drunkard's Arbour（from *Gems of Chinese Literature*）

［说明］宋仁宗庆历五年（1045），欧阳修三十九岁，因受诽谤被贬至安徽滁州任太守。《醉翁亭记》是他在那里写的一篇散文，写山水之乐，写与民同乐，以排遣遭贬之郁闷。语言极具特色，历代被尊为古文经典，为文人、读者所称颂。

翟理斯有多方面修养：有英国维多利业时代文学熏陶；有深厚的语言审美修养；对中国古典文学有深入研究。译文有意境，语言有美感，可视为英语翻译文学经典。

译例 1

▶ **原文**　环滁皆山也。其西南诸峰，林壑尤美。望之蔚然而深秀者，琅邪也。

▶ **译文**　The district of Ch'u is entirely surrounded by hills, and the peaks to the south-west are clothed with a dense and beautiful growth of trees, over which the eye wanders in rapture away to the confines of Shantung.

1.［原文］其西南诸峰，林壑尤美。

［译文］... and the peaks to the south-west are clothed with a dense and beautiful growth of trees...

［说明］原文两个部分之间没有动词；译文用"clothed"将二者联系起来，构成一个完整的英语句子。其中"clothed"有修辞效果。《牛津高阶英汉双解词典》有一个类似例句：

The valley was clothed in trees and shrubs.

"... with a dense and beautiful growth of trees"，（山峰）覆盖着茂密美丽的树木，说到树林时，英美作家常用"a growth of trees"这个说法。

2.［原文］望之蔚然而深秀者……

［译文］... the eye wanders...

［说明］原文里没有主语，译文补充了"the eye"作为主语，巧妙而自然地译了"望之"的主体。

译例 2

▶ **原文**　山行六七里，渐闻水声潺潺，而泻出于两峰之间者，酿泉也。峰回路转，有亭翼然临于泉上者，醉翁亭也。

▶ **译文**　A walk of two or three miles on those hills brings one within earshot of the sound of falling water which gushes forth from a ravine, known as the Wine-Fountain; while hard by in a nook at a bend of the road stands a kiosque, commonly spoken of as the Old Drunkard's Arbour.

［原文］山行六七里，渐闻水声潺潺……

［译文］A walk of two or three miles on those hills brings one within earshot of the sound of falling water...

翟氏译文不拘泥字面形式，更注重运用恰当的英语表达方式再现原文的意义和意境，这个句子译得好，好在用一个名词短语做主语，谓语用了一个成语"bring... within earshot of"，传译了"渐闻水声潺潺"之妙。一般译者可能会把这个句子译成主从复合句，翟氏只用一个简单句就译出了极具审美意味的英语句子，文字读来很有味道。译文的与众不同不仅在翻译技巧，技巧后面是深厚的文学底蕴和审美修养。

译例3

▶ **原文** 醉翁之意不在酒，在乎山水之间也。

▶ **译文** But it was not wine that attracted him to this spot. It was the charming scenery which wine enabled him to enjoy.

💡 **说明** 译者对这句话的理解是好的，作者来到这里不是为了饮酒，而是借酒欣赏山水美景，"It was the charming scenery which wine enabled him to enjoy"。这句译文把醉翁边饮酒边欣赏美景的意境很巧妙地表达出来，译者用先行主语"It"开始的强调句，符合原文语气。

译例4

▶ **原文** 若夫日出而林霏开，云归而岩穴暝，晦明变化者，山间之朝暮也。

▶ **译文** The sun's rays peeping at dawn through the trees, by-and-by to be obscured behind gathering clouds, leaving naught but gloom around, give to this spot the alternations of morning and night.

💡 **说明** 译文采取意译的叙述方式，表达了山间晨曦时而"林霏开"时而"岩穴暝"的变化情景，其变化之明显有如"朝暮"之别。译文意境之美可比肩原文，尤其是"give to this spot the alternations of morning and night"，以此译"山间之朝暮"，非一般译者能及也。

译例5

▶ **原文** 野芳发而幽香，佳木秀而繁阴，风霜高洁，水清而石出者，山间之四时也。

▶ **译文** The wild flowers exhaling their perfume from the darkness of some shady dell; the luxuriant foliage of the dense forest of beautiful trees; the clear frosty wind; and the naked boulders of the lessening torrent;—these are the indications of spring, summer, autumn, and winter.

1.［原文］幽香……

［译文］perfume from the darkness of some shady dell...

［说明］"幽香"中的"幽"字是一个难点，不知英语里有无对应词，但翟理斯另辟蹊径，"shady dell"，树荫笼罩的小山谷，即来自"僻静"处的芳香，准确译出了"幽香"的含义。

2.［原文］佳木秀而繁阴……

［译文］the luxuriant foliage of the dense forest of beautiful trees...

［说明］此译文中的几个细节处理得很好，其中"佳木""繁阴"和"秀"的含义用一个英语短语都译出来了，且行文顺畅。

3.［原文］风霜高洁……

［译文］the clear frosty wind...

［说明］用"clear"和"frosty"形容"wind"，符合"高洁"的含义。

译文前面四个小句，除第一个小句，皆用短语翻译，最后用一个完整句子指出这是一年四季的不同景象，概括前面的内容。

译例6

▶ 原文　朝而往，暮而归……

▶ 译文　Morning is the time to go thither, returning with the shades of night.

💡 说明　"朝而往，暮而归"，原文是排比句，他将"朝而往"译作"Morning is the time to go thither"，而将"暮而归"译作一个分词短语

"returning with the shades of night"，作为句子附属成分。

　　译者没有依据原文句式翻译，而是依据原文意思按照英语行文方式译，形式上未必要对应，意义的准确更重要，翻译中有创作。

译例 7

▶ **原文**　至于负者歌于途，行者休于树，前者呼，后者应……

▶ **译文**　Burden-carriers sing their way along the road, travelers rest awhile under the trees; shouts from one, responses from another...

💡 **说明**　"歌于途"，"sing their way along the road"，道尽"负者"一路边走边歌的情景，此句译文妙在"way"和"road"同时出现在一个句子里，地道的表达方式。

译例 8

▶ **原文**　苍颜白发，颓然乎其间者，太守醉也。已而夕阳在山，人影散乱，太守归而宾客从也。

▶ **译文**　Among them is an old man with white hair, bald at the top of his head. This is the drunken Governor, who when the evening sun kisses the tips of the hills, and the falling shadows are drawn out and blurred, bends his steps homewards in company with his friends.

1.［原文］已而夕阳在山……

　　［译文］... when the evening sun kisses the tips of the hills...

　　［说明］"夕阳在山"，夕阳照在山顶上，译者用了一个生动的动词"kisses"，英语词典有解释："to gently touch sth"（轻拂），并有例句："The sunlight kissed the warm stones."

2. ［原文］人影散乱……

［译文］and the falling shadows are drawn out and blurred...

［说明］"drawn out and blurred" 再现了 "散乱" 的景象。关于 "to draw sth out"，《新牛津英语词典》有一个解释："to make sth last longer"，夕阳西下，万物影子变长，相互交错而显得凌乱，译者的 "... are drawn out and blurred" 所指即这个景象。

译例 9

▶ **原文** 树林阴翳，鸣声上下，游人去而禽鸟乐也。

▶ **译文** Then in the growing darkness are heard sounds above and sounds below: the beasts of the field and the birds of the air are rejoicing at the departure of man.

📍 **说明** "游人去而禽鸟乐也"，"rejoicing" 后面的介词 "at" 表示原因，"因为" 或 "由于"，总是跟在形容词后面。英语里这个用法较多，词典里有例句：

1. They were impatient at the delay.

2. She was delighted at the result.

使用 "at" 比使用 "because" 简单，节约文字，使用 "at" 只构成一个短语，而使用 "because" 则需要一个从句。

二、翟里斯翻译《聊斋志异》

《聊斋志异》目前已经有三个译本：

1. Denis C. & Victor H. Mair: *Strange Tales from Make-do Studio*（Beijing: Foreign Languages Press, 1989）;

2. John Minford: *Strange Tales from a Chinese Studio*（London：Penguin，2006）;

3. Herbert A. Giles: *Strange Stories from a Chinese Studio*（London：Thos. de la Rue & Co.，1880）。

我们从翟理斯《劳山道士》译文中选取几个例句进行讨论。

译例 1

▶ **原文**　邑有王生，行七，故家子。少慕道，闻劳山多仙人，负笈往游。登一顶，有观宇，甚幽。一道士坐蒲团上，素发垂领，而神光爽迈。

▶ **译文**　THERE lived in our village a Mr. Wang, the seventh son in an old family. This gentleman had a *penchant* for the Taoist religion; and hearing that at Lao-shan there were plenty of Immortals, he shouldered his knapsack and went off for a tour thither. Ascending a peak of the mountain he reached a secluded monastery, where he found a priest sitting on a rush mat, with long hair flowing over his neck, and a pleasant expression on his face.

1. ［原文］少慕道……

　　［译文］This gentleman had a *penchant* for the Taoist religion...

　　［说明］这里的"慕道"译作"had a *penchant* for..."，意为"爱好""嗜好"。这个英语表达我们平时用得不多。关于"少"，可理解为"从年轻时起"，译者将其直接译作一个简单句，以"gentleman"做主语，或者也可以说，"This young gentleman"，以此避免复杂的主从复合句。

2. ［原文］……甚幽。

　　［译文］secluded...

　　［说明］此处的"幽"译作"secluded"，英语词典解释为"quiet and private"，意为"清静""僻静"，恰当的选词。

3.［原文］一道士坐蒲团上，素发垂领，而神光爽迈。

［译文］... he found a priest sitting on a rush mat, with long hair flowing over his neck, and a pleasant expression on his face.

［说明］译者将原文"一道士坐蒲团上"译为"he found a priest sitting on a rush mat"，句子以"he"为主语，以"a priest sitting on a rush mat"作为动词"found"的宾语，然后用一个"with"短语，译道士"素发垂领，而神光爽迈"神态。译文句子补充了主语，将其整合成一个完整的英语句子，这样的处理是好的。

译例 2

▶ **原文**　凌晨，道士呼王去，授以斧，使随众采樵。王谨受教。过月余，手足重茧，不堪其苦，阴有归志。

▶ **译文**　Very early next morning the priest summoned Wang, and giving him a hatchet sent him out with the others to cut firewood. Wang respectfully obeyed, continuing to work for over a month until his hands and feet were so swollen and blistered that he secretly meditated returning home.

📍 **说明**　青年王生来到劳山，道士不授业，只让他每日上山砍柴，王生不堪其苦，想回家。

译者为什么用"he secretly meditated returning home"译"阴有归志"？查词典得以下解释："to plan sth in your mind; to consider doing sth"，原来"meditate"有"暗自盘算""打算……"之意，这个词与"secretly"合用表达原文"阴有"的意思很恰当。

参看以下译文：

1. He decided he could bear it no longer and secretly began to long for home.（by John Minford）

2. Unable to bear the toil, he nursed secret intentions of returning home.

（by Denis C. & Victor H. Mair）

译例3

▶ **原文** 一夕归，见二人与师共酌，日已暮，尚无灯烛。师乃剪纸如镜，粘壁间。俄顷，月明辉室，光鉴毫芒。

▶ **译文** One evening when he came back he found two strangers sitting drinking with his master. It being already dark, and no lamp or candles having been brought in, the old priest took some scissors and cut out a circular piece of paper like a mirror, which he proceeded to stick against the wall. Immediately it became a dazzling moon, by the light of which you could have seen a hair or a beard of corn.

💡 **说明** 此段译文复合句多，句子较为复杂，但结构严密，衔接紧凑。生活在维多利亚时代（1837—1901）的翟理斯（1845—1935），其英语似带有那个时代文学语言的烙印。综观其英语译文，常能窥见其运用文学语言的自如。翻译《聊斋志异》这样的经典作品，似乎需要在语言上做些润色，以译出古典文学的意味。

译例4

▶ **原文** 又一月，苦不可忍，而道士并不传教一术。心不能待，辞曰："弟子数百里受业仙师，纵不能得长生术，或小有传习，亦可慰求教之心；今阅两三月，不过早樵而暮归。弟子在家，未谙此苦。"

▶ **译文** But after a time he could not stand it any longer; and as the priest taught him no magical arts he determined not to wait, but went to him and said, "Sir, I have travelled many long miles for the benefit of your instruction. If you will not teach me the secret of Immortality, let me at any rate learn some trifling trick, and thus soothe my cravings for a knowledge of your art. I have now been here two or three months, doing nothing but chop firewood, out in the morning and back at night, work to which I was never accustomed in my own home."

💡 **说明** 在这个段落里，王生直接引语的译文有几个地方处理得好，略作说明。

1. ［原文］受业……

［译文］... for the benefit of your instruction

［说明］此处"业"类似"学业"，跟随老师学习，此译文意为"受益于仙师的教导"，虽是介词短语做状语，但传达了"受业仙师"的意思。此句里的两个称呼，谦称"弟子"用"I"，尊称"仙师"为"Sir"，然后用"your"，足够好了。

2. ［原文］亦可慰求教之心……

［译文］"soothe my cravings for a knowledge of your art"，"慰藉我的求教之心"，好搭配，表达了原意。翟理斯理解原文好，译文也好。

3. ［原文］今阅两三月，不过早樵而暮归。

［译文］I have now been here two or three months, doing nothing but chop firewood, out in the morning and back at night...

［说明］译者用"nothing but"这个形式表达"不过"，意思和口气都到家，"早樵而暮归"用一个状语短语译了原意，简洁而有节奏美。

这个小段道尽了王生的怨气，译文每个句子处理得当，衔接又好，传达原文的效果是好的。

译例5

▶ **原文** 道士笑曰："我固谓不能作苦，今果然。明早当遣汝行。"

王曰："弟子操作多日，师略授小技，此来为不负也。"

▶ **译文**　"Did I not tell you," replied the priest, "that you would never support the fatigue? Tomorrow I will start you on your way home." "Sir," said Wang, "I have worked for you a long time. Teach me some small art, that my coming here may not have been wholly in vain."

📍 **说明**　王生所说，"师略授小技，此来为不负也"，意思是，也算没有白来一趟，译文 "my coming here may not have been wholly in vain"。

萧红有一个短篇小说《牛车上》，其中有一句话是这样的：

"五云倒还活着，我就想看看他，也算夫妇一回……"

葛浩文翻译如下：

"Wuyun was still alive, and I felt like going to see him; at least we could be together as husband and wife one last time..."

"也算夫妇一回……"，这句话，译者理解似乎有误。北方话也说"夫妻一场"，意思一样，大约相当于"总算是夫妻""毕竟是夫妻""怎么说也是夫妻"等。

《红楼梦》第十九回有一句语气类似的话，宝玉到袭人家看望她，袭人让他吃点东西，说：

"既来了，没有空回去的理，好歹尝一点儿，也是来我家一趟。"

霍克斯翻译如下：

"Since you've decided to come," she said to Bao-yu with a smile. "we can't let you go without having tasted *something* of ours. You'll have to try *something*, just to be able to say that you have been our guest!"

意思是，"总得吃点什么，也算是你没白来我家"。从霍克斯的译文看，他对这句话的理解和表达比较正确，但译文还有斟酌余地。

此文中的"此来为不负也"，和"也是来我家一趟""也算夫妇一回"表达方式相近，语气相似。翟理斯译文很符合原文语气，十分难得。

三、翟理斯翻译《桃花源记》

译例 1

▶ **原文** 晋太元中，武陵人捕鱼为业。缘溪行，忘路之远近。忽逢桃花林，夹岸数百步，中无杂树……

▶ **译文** Towards the close of the fourth century A. D., a certain fisherman of Wu-ling, who had followed up one of the river branches without taking note whither he was going, came suddenly upon a grove of peach-trees in full bloom, extending some distance on each bank, with not a tree of any other kind in sight.

💡 **说明** 句中的主要信息"武陵人……忽逢桃花林……"放在译文主句结构里"a certain fisherman of Wu-ling... came suddenly upon a grove of peach-trees..."，其余附带说明成分用从句（who had followed...）和动词分词结构（extending some distance...）表示，句子虽然较长，但内容主次清楚，形式轻重分明，因而叙事有序。

翻译英语句子，时常要有"主次"意识和"轻重"意识，即内容的主次和形式的轻重，于是，就有了句子结构上的主干部分和随附成分，这是一个需要注意的问题。否则，译出来的句子可能是另一种感觉。

译例 2

▶ **原文** 芳草鲜美，落英缤纷，渔人甚异之。复前行，欲穷其林。

▶ **译文** The beauty of the scene and the exquisite perfume of the flowers filled the heart of the fisherman with surprise, as he proceeded onward, anxious to reach the limit of this lovely grove.

💡 **说明** 1. "落英缤纷"这一景色，译文用"The beauty of the scene"表示，"芳草鲜美"译文着重表示花草之芳香，"the exquisite perfume of the flowers"，这个奇异景象让捕鱼人感到惊奇，"filled the heart of the fisherman with surprise"。这个句子将原文隐含的因果关系明确地表达出来，而且，译文语序与原文大体一致。

💡 **说明 2.** 译文使用 "surprise" 的名词形式，而未用它的动词或形容词形式，译者是有考虑的。

译例3

▶ **原文**　林尽水源，便得一山，山有小口，仿佛若有光。便舍船，从口入。初极狭，才通人。复行数十步，豁然开朗。

▶ **译文**　He found that the peach trees ended where the water began, at the foot of a hill; and there he espied what seemed to be a cave with light issuing from it. So he made fast his boat, and crept in through a narrow entrance, which shortly ushered him into a new world of level country.

💡 **说明 1.** 这个句子译文补上了 "He found that..."，在古汉语里，其逻辑主语常常隐去；在英语里，这个逻辑主语需要显示出来，同时，这也是行文的需要，否则句子会显得突兀。同样，《劳山道士》里的 "一道士坐蒲团上……"，译文也补上了 "... he found a priest sitting on a rush mat..."。

💡 **说明 2.** "林尽水源"，树林的尽头就是水，"the peach trees ended where the water began"。"sth ends where sth else begins"，英语里常用的一个表达方式。

译例4

▶ **原文**　土地平旷，屋舍俨然，有良田美池桑竹之属。阡陌交通，鸡犬相闻。

▶ **译文**　... a new world of level country, of fine houses, of rich fields, of fine pools, and luxuriance of mulberry and bamboo. Highways of traffic ran north and south; sounds of crowing cocks and barking dogs were heard around.

💡 **说明 1.** 译文句子前半部分一连用了四个 "of" 短语来形容 "a new world of level country"，这个处理方式很巧妙，而且充分表达了原文意思，且读起来语速快，与原文风格相近。

💡 **说明 2.** 句子后半部分的 "阡陌交通，鸡犬相闻"，译文不但意思准确，也将原文两个四字语的平衡感传达出来了。

译例 5

▶ **原文** 自云先世避秦时乱，率妻子邑人来此绝境，不复出焉，遂与外人间隔。

▶ **译文** ... and they informed him that their ancestors had sought refuge here, with their wives and families, from the troublous times of the house of Ch'in, adding that they had thus become finally cut off from the rest of the human race.

💡 **说明** 原文以桃花源人的 "自云" 开始，译文则补充了 "... they informed him that..."，这个补充很必要，结合后面的 "adding that..."，也是 "... they informed him that..." 的延续，这样就构建了一个完整的英语句子，叙事逻辑自然，效果是好的。

四、翟里斯翻译《庄周梦蝶》

［原文］昔者庄周梦为胡蝶，栩栩然蝴蝶也，自喻适志与，不知周也。俄然觉，则蘧蘧然周也。不知周之梦为胡蝶与，胡蝶之梦为周与？周与胡蝶，则必有分矣。此之谓物化。

［译文］Once upon a time, I, Chung Tzu, dreamt I was a butterfly, fluttering hither and thither, to all intents and purposes a butterfly. I was conscious only of following my fancies as a butterfly, and was unconscious of my individuality as a man. Suddenly, I awaked, and there I lay, myself again. Now I do not know whether I was then a man dreaming I was a butterfly, or whether I am now a butterfly dreaming I am a man. Between a man and a butterfly there is necessarily a barrier; and the transition is called *Metempsychosis*.

💡 说明 1. 原文里的"庄周"是第三人称，译文引进了人称代词"I"，"I, Chung Tzu"，为行文方便；后面出现的"周"，也用了代词。

💡 说明 2. 宾语从句的"that"省略，如，"dreamt I was a butterfly""dreaming I was a butterfly""dreaming I am a man"。这个"that"是可以省略的，以使行文更简沽。

💡 说明 3. "栩栩然蝴蝶也"，"fluttering hither and thither"，分词结构将蝴蝶描画得"栩栩然；"to all intents and purposes a butterfly"，全然一只蝴蝶。这个句子译得好，译了词、译了句，也译了形象。

💡 说明 4. 不知周之梦为胡蝶与，胡蝶之梦为周与？

Now I do not know whether I was then a man dreaming I was a butterfly, or whether I am now a butterfly dreaming I am a man.

这个句子的译文行文通畅，让人爱读，文中"whether I was then..."和"or whether I am now..."的处理，显示译者思维的周密。

💡 说明 5. "*Metempsychosis*"，译者用这个词翻译"物化"，即庄周与蝴蝶的转化。陆谷孙《英汉大词典》解释此词为"（不少古代宗教所信仰的）灵魂转生"。

阅读丽贝卡·韦尔斯（Rebecca Wells）:
Devine Secrets of the Ya-Ya Sisterhood

简介

> 丽贝卡·韦尔斯（Rebecca Wells），小说家、剧作家，她曾以她的小说获得"美国西部图书奖"（Western States Book Award）。她创作的剧本有 *Splittin'Hairs* 和 *Gloria Duplex*。

希达·沃克（Sidda Walker）是薇薇·沃克（Vivi Walker）的长女，戏剧导演。薇薇·沃克是路易斯安那一个由四人组成的姐妹会（Ya-Ya Sisterhood）的主角。希达曾导演轰动一时的话剧 *Women on the Cusp*，《纽约时报》（*The New York Times*）戏剧评论员罗伯塔·莱达尔（Roberta Lydell）采访了希达，然后在评论中把希达母亲薇薇说成是个"踢踏舞童虐待者"（"a tap-dancing child abuser"），薇薇一气之下断绝了与希达的联系，拒听她从外地打来的电话，甚至威胁与她断绝母女关系。

姐妹会的姐妹们为了修复她们的母女关系，坚持把记录她们友谊的剪贴簿寄给希达，以便让希达了解她们和薇薇的过去，使她们之间达成谅解。

我们从小说 *Divine Secrets of the Ya-Ya Sisterhood* 中选取一些例句学习讨论。

一般来说，学习做汉英翻译，可读翻译教科书，可读好的翻译作品，但更好的途径是阅读英语原著，从中学习英语表达方式：好的用词、好的搭配、好的句子、好的修辞等，特别要从语言审美角度审视，领悟语言的

"美"与"力"、"文"与"雅"，悟出英语语言行文的特征。阅读不仅提高语言修养，而且提高审美修养。

从阅读中学习英语，目的是在写作和翻译中运用。阅读时要有比较意识，从英语联想到相应的汉语，这种联想很重要。

记得有人问一个做汉英翻译的英国翻译家，翻译之前做哪些准备，他说每天动笔翻译之前都要读文学作品。这很有启发，这样做不仅能从阅读中汲取语言滋养，也能帮助译者进入一种语言状态、翻译状态。一个英国翻译家尚且如此，更何况正在学习英语的我们。

例句 1 There had been no sign the theater critic would go for blood. Roberta Lydell had been so chummy, so sisterly-seeming during the interview that Sidda had felt she'd made a new girlfriend. After all, in her earlier review, Roberta had already proclaimed the production of *Women on the Cusp*, which Sidda had conducted at Lincoln Center, to be "a miraculous event in American theater." With subtle finesse, the journalist had lulled Sidda into a cozy false sense of intimacy as she pumped her for personal information.（p. 1）

📍 **说明**　上面这段文字是故事开始时记者罗伯塔·莱达尔采访希达时的情景。

1. "go for blood"，词典里有"be after/out for sb's blood"，意为"to want to hurt or punish sb"（想伤害或惩罚某人），这里的"go for blood"，就是这个意思。"There had been no sign..."，意思是莱达尔在采访希达时，没有伤害薇薇的迹象。

2. With subtle finesse, the journalist had lulled Sidda into a cozy false sense of intimacy as she pumped her for personal information.

这个句子有好几个英语搭配，用得好。

A. "With subtle finesse"，英语词典这样解释"finesse"："great skill in dealing with people or situations, especially in a delicate way"，用巧妙的手

腕、手段；

B. ... lulled Sidda into a cozy false sense of intimacy...

用微妙的手段使希达产生一种错觉，制造一种温馨的亲密的假象，"lull sb into sth"是固定短语，意为"诱使，麻痹"。

英语词典里有例句："His friendly manner lulled her into a false sense of security"，这个例句和文章里的句子如出一辙，也和汉语口语里的"套近乎"相似，为了达到某种目的，故意表现特别亲密。

C. ... as she pumped her for personal information...

为了套出希达的私密，记者问了她很多问题，"pump sb for sth"是固定短语，"try to get information from sb by asking them a lot of questions"，巧用这个固定短语可以节省文字。

例句 2. "Siddalee Walker, articulate, brilliant director of the hit show *Women on the Cusp*, is no stranger to family cruelty. As the battered child of a tap-dancing child abuser of a mother, she brings to her directing the rare and touching equipoise between personal involvement and professional detachment that is the mark of theatrical genius."（pp. 2-3）

💡 说明　这是《纽约时报》记者所写关于导演希达的评论，希达念给母亲听，想让她对记者的评论有个全面了解，母亲听不进去。但这段文字写得好。

首先，"equipoise"这个词在我们的阅读中不常见，意思是"a state of balance"（平衡，一种均衡状态），即在"personal involvement"和"professional detachment"之间保持平衡，"detachment"和"involvement"意思正相反，前者是"the state of not being involved in sth in an emotional or personal way"，超然状态。作为戏剧导演，排除个人情绪、个人好恶，而以客观、超然的态度进行指导，这样能更真实地反映现实，作为戏剧评论家，记者很看重导演所遵循的这个原则。

这个句子的表述方式很好，特别是这两个搭配"personal involvement"和"professional detachment"。

> **例句** 3. At the age of forty, Sidda was eager to bask in the light of recognition.（p. 6）

💡 **说明**　四十岁的导演希达渴望被人承认，我们若将汉语的这个意思译成英语，可能会照着汉语的语序逐字翻译，但作者这个说法很有色彩，很有味道，她渴望沐浴在被观众承认的荣光之中。这是作家的文学语言，既文且雅，读者不但懂得它的意思，也欣赏其表达方式所产生的美感。

我们在富有美感的语言中享受阅读。

作为译文，同样要讲究语言，语言跟不上人家不读，白译。我们翻译中国文化，翻译中国文学，用英语讲中国故事，总是要从词、句上下功夫，总是要一句话一句话地译，而且，还要让译文有美感，要让英语读者认可甚至欣赏，对于以汉语为母语的译者，这比较困难，但也不是遥不可及，不过要下很深的功夫学习。学习汉英翻译的学生、从事汉英翻译的译者，请关注英语的词与句，英语词、句里有无尽的学问，学好用词、造句是永远的基本功；让英语译文有文学色彩，更是永远的追求。

> **例句** 4. You know *everything* about female friendship. You've been bosom buddies with Caro, Necie, and Teensy for over fifty years. You are the *expert*. And your innate sense of drama is unimpeachable. It would be enormously helpful if you could send me ideas, memories—anything about your life with the Ya-Yas.（p. 6）

💡 **说明**　希达要导演戏剧《女人》（*The Women*），从西雅图给母亲写信希望得到帮助；母亲与 Ya-Ya 姐妹们在一起已经五十多年，对女性的事情有深入的了解。"And your innate sense of drama is unimpeachable"，"你与生俱来的戏剧感（或对戏剧的感觉）不容置疑"，"unimpeachable"，意

为 "that you cannot doubt or question"，汉语说 "不容置疑"，日常口语里也说 "没的说"。有些英语单词意义含量大，用汉语表达往往需要一个词组或一个句子，这些词用好了能使文字精练。

例句 5. She had wanted to kiss him the first time she saw him. Something about his slow smile, the shape of his jaw, that long, lean body, that imagination. Something athletic and relaxed about the way he moved, something unhurried about his whole attitude.（p. 9）

💡 说明　这个小段里有三个以 "something" 起始的不完全句，其完整形式应该是以 "There was..." 起始，英语这种形式的排比句用得不少，行文速度快，表现力强，读者可感觉到希达对她的男朋友迷人魅力的直觉、敏感与激情。

为表达某种特别情感，以取得某种特定效果，不完全句具有很强的表现力。

可比照原文行文风格试着将这三个排比句译成汉语，看看效果如何。

美国作家罗伯特·沃勒（Robert Waller）写的 *The Bridges of Madison County* 里有写男主人公金凯德（Kincaid）的一句话，也是重复使用 "something"，也是不完全句：

But there was something, something about him. Something very old, something slightly battered by the years, not in the appearance, but in his eyes.

美国作家 E. B. 怀特的散文 "Once More to the Lake" 里有一段不完全句，写大雨来临时电闪雷鸣的气氛和大雨过后度假者心花怒放的情景，可参照。

Then the kettle drum, then the snare, then the bass drum and cymbals, then crackling light against the dark, and the gods grinning and licking their chops in the hills. Afterward the calm, the rain steadily rustling in the calm lake, the return of light and hope and spirits, and the campers running out in joy and relief to go swimming in the rain...

这个段落使用的都是不完全句，把风雨欲来雷电交加的紧张气氛写得让人感觉如临其境。

例句 6. At sixty-seven, she was still fit from playing tennis twice a week. She had put on five pounds since she'd tried to quit smoking, but she still could have passed for a much younger woman.（p. 10）

💡 说明

1. ... she was still fit from playing tennis...

此处的介词"from"表示原因，因为打网球，六十七岁了她还是很结实。

2. "pass for"，意为"be accepted as..."，看着（给人的印象）像一个年轻得多的女人；《牛津高阶英汉双解词典》里有一个例句：

He speaks the language so well he could easily pass for a German.

他德语讲得真好，人们很容易以为他是德国人。

这个英语固定短语很有用，可学着使用。

例句 7. Vivi turned her head to face Caro and began mouthing words with no sounds.（p. 13）

💡 说明　"to mouth words"，说话时只动嘴唇不出声音，很形象的用法。在本书的另外一处也使用了这个说法：

Mr. Hollywood himself must not have heard the actual poot. He's still on the other side of the stage, still examining girls. But when he hears us laughing, he looks over our way, and I can see his lips moving, mouthing the words, "Be quiet."（p. 54）

在 J. D. 塞林格的短篇小说 "For Esmé—with Love and Squalor" 里也出现了这个说法：

She went on to say that she wanted *all* her children to absorb the meaning of the words they sang, not just mouth them like silly-billy parrots.

例句 8. Caro and Necie both studied the photograph, then handed it to Teensy, who was snapping her fingers in a demand to have the image passed to her.（p. 14）

💡 说明　Ya-Ya 四姐妹出游，蒂恩西（Teensy）开车，薇薇拿出希达小时候的照片给大家看，卡罗（Caro）和奈希（Necie）看完传给蒂恩西，蒂恩西正啪啪打着手指，示意她们赶紧把照片递给她。她没说话，只一个动作便表示了，"in a demand to have the image passed to her"，透露她急着要看照片的心情。这个句子写得好，行文有节奏，形象鲜明，富有美感。

例句 9. At the creek, the women got out of the car. Necie carried the basket of food, and Teensy pulled a fresh thermos of Bloody Marys from the trunk. Without offering, Vivi helped Caro with her oxygen tank, and without acknowledgment Caro accepted her help. The four Ya-Yas walked down a short path, then slowly, carefully scrambled down to the creekbank...（p. 15）

💡 说明　Ya-Ya 四姐妹开车来到海湾游玩，这段文字描写她们卸车时的情景，薇薇帮卡罗搬氧气罐时并没有说"让我来帮你"之类的话，卡罗也没有对薇薇说"谢谢你"之类的话，因为她们之间的友谊深，免去了这些客套话。"Without offering"和"without acknowledgment"这两个用法是值得我们学习和借鉴的。

例句 10. From the bag she pulled a large brown leather scrapbook, stuffed fat with papers and various little items falling out. Its spine was cracked, and the leather was scratched and scarred. It appeared that the album had been taken apart and rebound after more pages had been added, and that those extra pages could barely be contained within the binding. The cover of the book was edged in gold, and in the lower right-hand corner, embossed in gold, was the name Vivi Walker.（p. 26）

💡 说明

1. ... scrapbook, stuffed fat with papers and various little items falling out

句中的"stuffed fat"写剪贴簿里塞了满满的东西，"falling out"写里面的东西哗啦哗啦往外掉，这两个附属于主句的分词短语描绘出一个可视的生动画面，作者的妙笔。

2. It appeared that the album had been taken apart and rebound after more pages had been added, and that those extra pages could barely be contained within the binding.

这个句子用不足 30 个词，说清了好几个细节：剪贴簿被拆开过；增加了更多的页数；然后又重新装订；重新装订的簿子几乎装不下增加的新页。把几件事情分在两个从句，"It appeared that... and that..."，将剪贴簿变化的微妙过程写得清清楚楚，一个词也加不进，一个词也减不掉；换个说法也难以把句子写得如此干净、精妙。用准确而少之又少的文字把复杂的事情说清楚是艺术。

3. "edged in gold"，封面是镶金边的。

4. "embossed in gold"，右下角作者的名字是凸印金色的。

例句 11. There was a photograph of an achingly handsome young man in a World War Ⅱ Army Air Corps uniform.（p. 29）

💡 说明　这个"achingly"是副词，可能是"extremely"的意思。

这个词偶尔能见到，但使用频率不是很高，《新牛津英语词典》是本大词典，也没有对其进行解释，只给了一个示例："a sound which was achingly familiar to me"（非常熟悉的声音）。

例句 12. The Ya-Ya who was on watch could only keep one foot in the conversation because she had to concentrate on how many heads were visible in the creek... Every half hour, the Ya-Ya in charge would stand up, look out at the water, and blow a whistle hanging from an old costume jewelry necklace. At the sound of the whistle, we immediately had to stop whatever we were doing and count off. (p. 34)

💡 **说明**　Ya-Ya 四姐妹经常带孩子们去郊游，有时是孩子们在海湾里游泳，大人在岸上聊天，此时就指定一个人边聊天边兼顾照看孩子，文中的 "keep one foot in the conversation" 所指就是这种情况。

大人一吹哨，孩子们就停下来，开始 "count off"，就是 "报数"，这样大人就知道水中的孩子是否全数都在。

例句 13. Basically, what you had to do was swim to the deep end and bob up and down in a panic, flailing your arms and screaming like you were about to take your last breath before sinking. (p. 34)

💡 **说明**　希达母亲薇薇很早就学习水上救生，经常带孩子们到海湾练习，孩子们都很愿意扮演溺水者。此段文字谈扮演溺水者在水中的动作。

1. "to bob up and down in a panic"，这是指在水中一会儿沉下去，一会儿浮上来，惊慌失措的样子，试比较下面这个句子：

As the tune wove in and out they bobbed up and sat down, puzzled and unsure of what to think and to do.

2. "flailing your arms"，指在水中用两只胳膊扑腾挣扎的样子。

以上两个句子中使用的动词 "to bob up and down" 和 "flailing" 都近乎专业用语，地道的英语用法。

例句 14. When she'd reach you, she'd shout, "Flail more! Dahlin! Flail more!" And you'd flap your arms harder and kick and scream with increased vigor. Then, with great assurance, Mama would hook her hand under your chin, lean your head back against her chest, and begin the rescue, using her mighty inverted scissors kick to propel the two of you through the water in short little bursts.（p. 35）

💡 **说明**　描写薇薇在水中救生时的动作：

1. flap your arms harder and kick...

此处的"flap"和"flail"意思相近，拍打或扑腾。

2. ... hook her hand under your chin, lean your head back against her chest.

她用手勾住你的下巴，把你的头贴在她胸上。

3. ... inverted scissors kick...

双腿（双脚）反剪式踢水动作。

以上是几个水中动作的英语说法，值得学习。

例句 15. Necie's hair was thick and brown and luxurious, and when she let it down, it was her crowning glory. On summer mornings at Spring Creek, when she had just awakened, Necie's hair tumbled down onto her shoulders and caught the early sun as she sat on the porch and drank coffee with the others.（p. 40）

💡 **说明**　在 Ya-Ya 四姐妹里，唯有奈希留长发。据小说作者说，在20世纪五六十年代的美国，已婚妇女或孩子妈妈留长发的不多。所以，希达对奈希的长发很好奇，有时便坐在她身后饶有兴趣地摆弄她的头发。

1. 用"luxurious"形容头发，指头发长得茂密、密实。

2. "crowning glory"："making sth perfect or complete"，词典里有例句：

The cathedral is the crowning glory of the city.

关于"glory"，词典有两个解释：一个是"great beauty"，另一个是

"a special cause for pride, respect or pleasure"。这两个意思用在这个上下文里似乎都说得通，可依据情况酌情而译。

3. "... tumbled down onto..."，奈希的头发散落在肩上，指女人的长发散落下来时多用"tumble"这个动词表示。

例句 16. "Shirley Temple represents what is best about America," he says. "Her innocence and smile are a ray of sunshine that beams across these forty-eight states. And when times look down and regular Joes have trouble buying a cup of coffee, Shirley's dimples can cheer up even the saddest Depression hobo. 'Little Miss Sunshine' has danced her way into the hearts of millions, lifting up our land with her unique brand of sweetness."（p. 53）

📍 说明　20世纪30年代，美国著名童星秀兰·邓波儿（Shirley Temple，1928—2014）六岁开始演电影，七岁获奥斯卡金像奖特别奖，她的表演给大萧条时期的美国人民带来了欢乐，提振了美国人的情绪。美国举行"Shirley Temple Look-Alike Contest"，主持人兰斯·莱西先生［Mr Lance Lacey，四姐妹中的卡罗称他为好莱坞先生（Mr. Hollywood）］四处奔走，寻找合适的参赛人选。他来到 Ya-Ya 四姐妹所在的小镇，向大家介绍秀兰·邓波儿时讲了上面的话。这段文字写得好，每一个句子都是好英语，表达方式很新颖，值得背诵，体会英语句子的"beauty and power"。

1. ... represents what is best about America...

秀兰·邓波儿代表了美国最好的精神，或，秀兰·邓波儿是美国精神的最好的象征，或，秀兰·邓波儿体现了美国最好的精神，这里的"represent"可解释为"代表"，或"体现"，或"是……的象征"。

2. Her innocence and smile are a ray of sunshine that beams across these forty-eight states.

她的天真和笑容如同一线阳光照亮了美国四十八州，这个说法符合当时的实际，并非过度的夸张。

3. ... when times look down...

根据上下文，这里的"look down"可理解为时代不景气，指当时的经济大萧条。

4. Shirley's dimples can cheer up even the saddest Depression hobo.

此处的"cheer up"是日常用语，但在这个上下文里，它有更多的含义，秀兰·邓波儿的笑容让因为大萧条而失业的沮丧的工人们高兴起来，振作起来。

5. "Little Miss Sunshine" has danced her way into the hearts of millions, lifting up our land...

她的舞蹈跳进了千百万人的心中，提振了全国人民的士气。

6. "Joes"，这里指普通人。

7. "Depression hobo"，指美国 20 世纪 30 年代因经济大萧条而失业的工人。

例句 17. She put on a Rickie Lee Jones CD of songs from the forties, poured herself a glass of brandy, sat down, and tried to make herself read a Jungian book on marriage. Three pages in, she closed the book.（p. 61）

💡 说明 短语"Three pages in"是独立主格结构，意思是读了三页便合上书，简洁的说法。

例句 18. It is around ten in the morning and things are already hot. You can smell the morning sun hitting the grass and bringing up smells like lemon. I lean my head back and smell things, wherever I am. To me, smells are like an invisible person that a lot of people forget is even there. I would rather lose my eyes than my sense of smell.（p. 66）

💡 说明 这是 Ya-Ya 四姐妹在野地里游玩时，野草经过太阳照晒后发出一种近乎柠檬的味道，薇薇喜欢这种味道，闻到这种味道时很有感慨，宁可失去眼睛，也不愿意失去她的嗅觉。

... the morning sun hitting the grass and bringing up smells like lemon.

这个表达方式把可闻而不可见的野草味道写得带有动感。

例句 19. Sleeping in the porch is the best thing in the world. You fall asleep with the sound of the crickets, and you wake up with the sound of birds chirping. When you're still half asleep, they sound like a waterfall.（p. 67）

💡 **说明** Ya-Ya 四姐妹经常在一起睡觉，特别享受一起在薇薇家的门廊里睡觉。入睡时听着蟋蟀的声音，醒来时听见鸟儿的鸣叫，半醒半睡时，她们听见的声音如同瀑布一样，写出了她们享受大自然、生活在大自然中感觉到的乐趣。

"with the sound of..."是一个既简单又普通的介词短语，像这个句子的写法，写好了能产生一种审美效果。

例句 20. We get quiet and just lie there for a moment, with our bundles of supplies stashed beneath the beds.（p. 69）

💡 **说明** 这里的"stashed"是个动词，意为"藏"或"隐藏"，这个动词很新颖；也可用作名词，指"藏起来的东西"，如下面的句子所示。

We pull out our stash from under the beds, lift up our nightgowns, and take turns rubbing a raw onion all over our bodies so the mosquitoes won't carry us away.（p. 69）

Ya-Ya 四姐妹计划当天夜里在树林里实行一个秘密行动，她们先是和薇薇母亲一起打牌，天晚了母亲说该睡觉了，母亲走了以后，她们假装保持安静，让母亲以为她们已经睡着了，于是她们便开始行动：把藏在床下的东西（stash）拿出来……

例句 21. I hear that Miss Mitchell has been staying inside her apartment ever since October because the swirl is just too much for her. She's just been having to rest and take aspirin every half hour. I can imagine how she feels after all she has been through to write the best book in the world, and then to have the movie opening and all. (p. 90)

💡 **说明**　薇薇给奈希写信汇报她在亚特兰大的所见所闻，谈到《飘》（*Gone with the Wind*）作者玛格丽特·米切尔（Margaret Mitchell）的状况，写完小说作者已经非常疲惫，又即将举行 *Gone with the Wind* 电影首映式。当时亚特兰大热闹非凡，到了天旋地转的地步。作者用 "swirl" 这个词描写亚特兰大的境况，这个词的基本意思是 "旋转"，在这个上下文里有修辞效果。

例句 22. "Let me tell you, girl, this whole city is on fire with excitement! You can feel it crackling through the air. There are movie displays in every single store window, and it's like all of Atlanta is one giant movie advertisement." (p. 90)

💡 **说明**　Ya-Ya 四姐妹中的三个人去亚特兰大参加电影 *Gone with the Wind* 首映式，只有奈希没有去，薇薇写信告诉她首映式前夕亚特兰大的气氛。

Gone with the Wind 是玛格丽特·米切尔于 1936 年创作的小说，1937 年获普利策文学奖，1939 年拍成电影。因为玛格丽特·米切尔是亚特兰大人，她在那里创作的这部小说，所以在那里举行电影首映式，汉语有 "热火朝天" 之说，"形容场面、情绪或气氛热烈高涨"。这个词如何译成英语呢？《新时代汉英大词典》有译文："reach the peak of enthusiasm" "be in full swing" "be bustling or buzzing with activity"，这几个说法结合上下文都可以选择使用。

但用 "this whole city is on fire with excitement! You can feel it crackling through the air" 来翻译汉语的 "热火朝天" 再好不过，生动、形象，而且与汉语意思十分契合。

例句 23. She did not doubt that the two of them were meant for each other. She had not questioned this since the afternoon she witnessed the two of them sitting in a swing together sometime late in 1938, holding hands, not speaking, swinging in an easy rhythm.（p. 125）

🔖 **说明** 1938 年下半年，吉纳维芙（Genevieve）看见她的儿子杰克（Jack）和薇薇一起打秋千，迅速拍下一张照片。一句 "swinging in an easy rhythm" 描绘出两个年轻男女轻松愉快、悠然自得、相互友爱的情景。

例句 24. Lizzie Mitchell stood in front of Sidda wearing a blue shirtwaist dress with a gray sweater draped over her shoulders. Painfully thin, with sad blue eyes, she had a frail kind of beauty. Her face, her whole body appeared tired. In her early twenties, she had beautiful skin, but her teeth were bad, and even Sidda could see she wore the wrong shade of lipstick. She carried a suitcase, and for a moment Sidda thought the woman was a traveler who had stopped to ask for directions.（p. 130）

利齐·米切尔（Lizzie Mitchell）是女推销员，来到希达家向她母亲薇薇推销妇女化妆品。希达通过自己的眼睛，透过自己的观察，为我们刻画了一个鲜活的形象，我们可以想象这个女推销员的长相、穿着以及她的家境和经济状况。

"she had a frail kind of beauty"，"frail" 通常用来描写身体虚弱，当它和 "beauty" 搭配时，汉语怎么表达，值得研究。

例句 25. Through her tears, Vivi gazed at the moon. A silent prayer for Jack issued from her body. Moonlight in the summer sky, look down on my love from up on high. Shine on him now while he is safe and shine on him when he flies through enemy skies. Let his journeys into the sky bring him closer to you, so that while he is away from me, he will be safe. Tell him I love him, tell him

I am longing for him, tell him I will always wait for him. Your milky brilliance can protect him from all enemies. He is a tender boy, do not let him suffer. Moonlight over the only town I know, bring my love back home so we can live and be happy.（p. 160）

💡 说明　薇薇的男朋友杰克应征入伍，当一名飞行员。薇薇想念在远方的恋人，希望他安然无恙。她对着月光为他祈祷。

在中国文化里，月亮是引发人们各种遐想、代表多种意象的象征；这段英语文字也把月亮当作"爱"的女神，祈祷月亮保护身在远方的恋人，寄托对杰克的思念。这段文字里两处用了"my love"，皆指薇薇的恋人杰克。文中有两个排比值得留意：连续两次出现"Shine on him"，连续三次出现"Tell him"。还有"milky brilliance"，形容月亮光辉的颜色，绝好的搭配。

这是一段抒情文字，对着月亮抒发对自己恋人的真挚的感情，写法值得学习。

例句 26. Crickets, she thought. They've serenaded me since the day I was born. Breathe in, breathe out. Right now I am sitting in the light of the moon. Right now my dog is beside me and we are taking a moon bath.（p. 164）

💡 说明　一天晚上，希达带着自己的爱犬来到湖边，在月光下听着湖边的蟋蟀鸣叫。"They've serenaded me since the day I was born"（好像是对我唱着小夜曲），"we are taking a moon bath"（我们正在享受月光浴），两个简单又富有诗意的表达方式。

例句 27. When she finished that, she moved on to "Shine On, Harvest Moon," accompanying her singing with light foot tapping when she came to the line, "I ain't had no lovin' since January, February, June, or July."（p. 164）

💡 说明　此时希达心情好，她开始轻声唱歌，她很久没有这样唱歌了，先唱 "Blue Moon"，然后唱 "Shine On, Harvest Moon"，边唱边用脚轻轻击打节拍，"accompanying her singing with light foot tapping"，这个表达方式足以衬托她的心情之好。

例句 28. Lightly thumping her tail against the wooden steps, Hueylene watched her mistress. Sidda might as well have been singing dog lullabies. In fact, Sidda was singing a sort of lullaby, songs to calm the baby girl who'd lived inside herself for forty years.（p. 164）

💡 **说明**　希达唱歌的时候，她的爱犬 Hueylene 用尾巴轻轻拍打木台阶，她唱歌好像是给她的狗唱催眠曲，实际上，她是在安慰她的内心世界，这里的 "the baby girl who'd lived inside herself for forty years" 是指她自己。

例句 29. This made the cocker spaniel lay her blonde furry head on Sidda's lap and give a great sigh. Sidda's chest was opened, her head felt tingly and good. The singing had given the inside of her body a little massage.（p. 165）

希达唱完最后一段歌词，她的西班牙猎犬把头依偎在她怀里，并叹了一口气，此时希达心里感觉很舒服，也有点激动，最后一句 "The singing had given the inside of her body a little massage"，和前面的 "to calm the baby girl who'd lived inside herself for forty years" 一样，以另一种方式表达唱歌使她的心灵得到慰藉，很新颖的表达方式。

例句 30. Often the music flowed from black people whose songs touched a sadness inside Vivi that she herself had no words for. In those days, it seemed, everybody sang.（p. 165）

💡 **说明**　作者说，在希达唱歌时，她不知道，在她妈妈薇薇成长的三四十年代，在路易斯安那州的桑顿（Thornton），你走在街道上总能听见有人在唱歌或吹口哨，家庭妇女出来晒衣服时唱歌，园丁除草时唱歌，甚至商人们出入银行时也吹口哨。那时，人们的会客室里都有钢琴，但他们唱歌并不表明他们幸福，尤其是黑人唱歌，"whose songs touched a sadness inside Vivi that she herself had no words for"，这些歌曲在薇薇的心灵里引起一种忧伤的情绪，然而，她却找不到合适的词语来描述这种情绪。很简单的表达方式，既自然，又巧妙，意思也清楚。

例句 31. While the guests sang to her, she smiled wide, eyes glistening, with her father on one side and Jack Whitman on the other.（p. 184）

💡 **说明** 在薇薇的生日晚会上，一边站着父亲，一边是她的男朋友杰克·惠特曼（Jack Whitman，他特意从空军请假回来为薇薇庆祝生日），当客人们对着她唱"祝你生日快乐"时，"she smiled wide, eyes glistening"，我们可以想象她当时的心情，但这个简单的英语句子如何用汉语表达出来，需要思考。

例句 32. In Jack's embrace, Vivi danced, floating, held safely in the frame of his arms. Her eyes half closed, a tiny smile on her slightly opened mouth, she felt royal.（p. 185）

💡 **说明** 薇薇和她的恋人杰克一起跳舞，"floating"一词，刻画出薇薇飘然起舞的优美姿态；"she felt royal"则表达了她幸福的心情，此处的"royal"指极好的心情、情绪等，陆谷孙《英汉大词典》里有一个例句："He is in royal spirits."译为"他情绪极好"。

例句 33. The Ya-Yas had planned for weeks to spend the night together at Vivi's the night of the dance. They'd looked forward to staying up late, munching ham sandwiches, downing tall glasses of cold milk, and rehashing the details of what everyone wore, said, did, and who danced with whom.（p. 187）

💡 **说明**　Ya-Ya 四姐妹早就计划在薇薇生日舞会之后一起在她家里过夜，第二个句子里有四个分词短语："staying" "munching..." "downing..." "rehashing"。关于 "rehash"，这是一个很新鲜的动词，《新牛津英语词典》有一个解释很好："consider or discuss（something）at length after it has happened"，陆谷孙《英汉大词典》解释为 "重复谈论"，两个解释意思相近。其实就是舞会之后，她们会谈论一番：在舞会上谁穿了什么服装，说过什么话，做了什么事，谁和谁跳了舞等。这些都是女孩们喜欢谈论的话题。

例句 34. When they first heard the yelling and screaming from down the hall, they assumed that it was Vivi's brother, Pete, roughhousing with buddies. They were surprised to hear such a ruckus this late at night, but Pete always had three or four pals sleeping over, and they were known to get rowdy. Taylor Abbott had a lot more tolerance for loud boys than for loud girls.（p. 188）

💡 **说明**　薇薇过十六岁生日，父亲泰勒·阿博特（Taylor Abbott）送给她一枚钻戒，她母亲巴吉（Buggy）很不高兴，认为丈夫应该给自己的妻子买钻戒。在薇薇和她的姐妹们已经躺下准备睡觉时，巴吉来到她们卧室，强行从薇薇手上把钻戒摘下来拿走了。没过多久，她们便听见楼下厅里传来大喊大叫的声音，以为是薇薇的哥哥皮特（Pete）和他的朋友们在打闹。实际上是泰勒·阿博特和巴吉因为薇薇的钻戒之事在吵架，吵得很厉害，泰勒·阿博特逼着巴吉回到薇薇房间把钻戒重新给薇薇戴在手上。

关于动词 "roughhouse"，英语词典解释："fight sb or play with sb roughly"（打闹）。"ruckus" 和 "rowdy" 也出现在文章里，同属于一个意义范畴的词汇。

例句 35. "Viviane needs to learn self-sacrifice, she needs to be near others who are chaste and pure in body and soul. She needs the discipline only the nuns of Saint Augustine's can give her."（p. 196）

💡 **说明** 薇薇的母亲巴吉认为 Ya-Ya 姐妹的行为方式离经叛道、违背传统，她决定送薇薇去女修会学校（a convent school），她给女修院院长（Mother Superior）写信说了上面的话。

1. "learn self-sacrifice"，她的女儿需要学习自我牺牲。

2. "chaste and pure in body and soul"，巴吉认为，她的女儿不能和 Ya-Ya 姐妹一起鬼混，她应该和身心贞洁的人们在一起，而这样的人只有在女修院里才有。

3. "She needs the discipline only the nuns of Saint Augustine's can give her"，指薇薇必须到女修院里接受修女们的管教。

> **例句** 36. She is a flower made by God, but she is wilting. And if I do not remove her from the temptations of the world, she will die before she has had the chance to bloom in the spirit.（p. 196）

💡 **说明** 这是巴吉给女修院院长信中的另一段话，说她的女儿是上帝培育的一朵鲜花，但是这朵鲜花已经开始凋谢，"but she is wilting"，留意 "wilting" 和 "flower" 的搭配，还有后面的 "bloom"。"the temptations of the world" 是指来自社会各方面的对薇薇的诱惑，包括现代的公立学校，更包括薇薇所在的 Ya-Ya 姐妹会，她要把薇薇送进女修院，使之与社会隔离。

> **例句** 37. Pete checked his wristwatch, then went around to get in on the driver's side. He looked serious, his usual athletic swagger replaced by a heaviness.（p. 206）

💡 **说明** 皮特是薇薇的哥哥，薇薇去女修院，他开车送妹妹到火车站，此时他的心情很不好，原来走路神气十足的样子，现在脚步变得沉重了。

关于"swagger", 词典有解释:"a way of walking or behaving that seems too confident", 神气十足, 大摇大摆, 一种非常自信的姿态; 这里的"athletic"是指身体健壮, 这两个词的搭配为我们刻画出身体强壮的皮特自信的形象。

例句 38. Rushing to her side, Teensy and Genevieve enveloped Vivi in hugs. The suddenness of it disoriented Vivi, and she could not respond. She felt as though they were onlookers and she was a wreck on the side of the road. (p. 229)

💡 说明　薇薇在女修院里没有了自由, 被严加管教, 院长对她很严厉, 曾经打过她的耳光, 但女修院里有一个叫索兰斯的修女 (Sister Solange) 对她特别同情, 处处关照她, 主动提出帮她联系外面的人把她接出去。薇薇告诉她可以给吉纳维芙·惠特曼 (Genevieve Whitman) 打电话, 这位吉纳维芙就是她的恋人杰克的母亲, 也是 Ya-Ya 姐妹会中蒂恩西的母亲。当她们母女俩突然出现在她面前时, 她觉得自己好像是一辆停在路边被撞坏的汽车, 而她们则像站在旁边看热闹的过路人, 她因为吃惊而感到不知所措, "disoriented"这个词的意思和"confused"类似。

阅读塞林格（J. D. Salinger）：
"For Esmé—with Love and Squalor"

简介

　　J. D. 塞林格是美国著名作家，1951 年出版长篇小说《麦田里的守望者》（*The Catcher in the Rye*），受到读者欢迎，特别是受到青年学生的追捧，成为美国文学的经典作品。此外还有《弗兰妮与祖伊》（*Franny and Zooey*，1961）、《抬高房梁，木匠们》（*Raise High the Roof Beam, Carpenters*）等，以及短篇小说集《九个故事》（*Nine Stories*，1953）。现取 *Nine Stories* 中的 "For Esmé—with Love and Squalor" 学习、讨论。

　　"For Esmé—with Love and Squalor" 初载于《纽约客》（*The New Yorker*，1950 年 4 月 8 日），在学者中和读书界引起反响。这是一篇以"二战"为背景的很好的小说，堪称短篇杰作。研究塞林格的学者对这篇小说很重视。学习翻译的人不妨读一读，领略塞林格的英语风采。

　　小说前半部分，即 "Love" 部分，有美军中士（Sergeant），即叙事者 "I"，英国十三岁女孩艾斯美（Esmé），和她五岁的弟弟查尔斯（Charles）；后半部分，即 "Squalor" 部分，有 Sergeant X（即前半部分的 "I"）和他的伙伴 Z 下士（Corporal Z. Clay）。

　　诺曼底登陆（1944 年 4 月 6 日）前夕，中士和他所在部队正在英国德文郡为登陆战进行情报工作培训；后半部分发生在 VE Day（即 1945 年 5 月 8 日，第二次世界大战欧洲胜利日，德国投降日，VE 指 Victory in

Europe）之后，背景在德国巴伐利亚。

这篇小说可多读几遍，争取读懂其中的"曲笔""含蓄"与"幽默"。

现选取其中部分句、段，看塞林格如何叙事、如何描写、如何塑造人物，从中汲取滋养，提高我们汉英翻译的实践能力。

例句 1. I walked down the long, wet cobblestone hill into town. I ignored the flashes of lightning all around me. They either had your number on them or they didn't.

说明　情报工作培训在一个下雨天结束，小说主人公美军中士百无聊赖，披上雨衣离开军营到小镇上转一转，这时正在下雨，电闪雷鸣不断。"They either had your number on them or they didn't."这个英语句子是一个固定表达，"they"指闪电，意思是闪电随时可以击中你。陆谷孙《英汉大词典》里有一个类似的例句：

It seemed that the flashes of lightening had his number on them.

例句 2. At the moment, their choir coach, an enormous woman in tweeds, was advising them to open their mouths wider when they sang. Had anyone, she asked, ever heard of a little dicky-bird that dared to sing his charming song without first opening his little beak wide, wide, wide? Apparently nobody ever had. She was given a steady, opaque look.

说明　美军中士信步来到教堂前，得知里面有唱诗班在排练，进去后，见到上面所描述的这个情景。

"Had anyone, she asked, ever heard of a little dicky-bird that dared to sing his charming song without first opening his little beak wide, wide, wide?"这个句子值得注意的地方是，用间接引语形式表达直接问话内容，不但意思清楚，而且语言简洁、自然，这一叙事方式值得借鉴。

好的文学作品善用修辞，这里的唱诗班指挥用小鸟做比喻，如童话一般。好的比喻能使语言活泼、形象生动。

例句 3. Her voice was distinctly separate from the other children's voices, and not just because she was seated nearest to me. It had the best upper register, the sweetest-sounding, the surest, and it automatically led the way.

💡 说明　中士注意到一个十三岁上下的女孩，即小说的主人公之一艾斯美，此处的"register"描写乐器或嗓音，她的声音与众不同，属于最好的高声区，或女高音，声音甜美、稳健，实际上她是在领唱，"automatically led the way"。

例句 4. I said I certainly had been, and that I had heard her voice singing separately from the others. I said I thought she had a very fine voice.

💡 说明　注意前面例句 3 的这句话："Her voice was distinctly separate from the other children's voices"，而此例句是这样说的："I had heard her voice singing separately from the others"。

两个句子都是描写艾斯美的声音，作者用了同一个词的两种形式，一个是形容词"separate"，因为句子系动词"was"的缘故；一个是副词"separately"，因为动词"singing"的缘故。

例句 5. Their voices were melodious and unsentimental, almost to the point where a somewhat more denominational man than myself might, without straining, have experienced levitation.

💡 说明　这是描写孩子们唱歌声音的几个词语，"melodious"，"好听，悦耳"；"unsentimental"，"不带很明显的感情色彩"，教堂里唱诗班的孩子们唱歌时不像一般唱歌那样表现出强烈的感情；"denominational"，"教派的"，这个词我们用得不多，"a somewhat more denominational man"，意思是宗教信仰比较强的人；"levitation"，一种飘浮或升空的感觉，宗教信仰比较强的人听孩子们唱歌时会有这种感觉。这些词汇都是用来赞美孩子们唱得好。

例句 6. The instant the hymn ended, the choir coach began to give her lengthy opinion of people who can't keep their feet still and their lips sealed tight during the minister's sermon. I gathered that the singing part of the rehearsal was over, and before the coach's dissonant speaking voice could entirely break the spell the children's singing had cast, I got up and left the church.

💡 说明 "the spell the children's singing had cast"，此处"spell"相当于"charm"，注意，与之搭配的动词用的是"cast"。"我"陶醉于孩子们美妙的歌声之中，但对唱诗班老师的发言，却做了另一番描述："her lengthy opinion""the coach's dissonant speaking voice""break the spell"，"我"不喜欢听，所以站起来走了。作者没有在叙述中直书褒贬，对歌声和唱诗班老师的两种不同反应都在客观描述里。

例句 7. I crossed the street and entered a civilian tea-room, which was empty except for a middle-aged waitress, who looked as if she would have preferred a customer with a dry raincoat.

💡 说明 作者没有直接描述茶馆女招待的表情，但她不欢迎这个浑身被雨浇得湿漉漉的顾客，读者可以想象她的表情。这是作家描写人物的一种手法。

例句 8. It was the first time all day that I'd spoken to anyone. I then looked through all my pockets, including my raincoat, and finally found a couple of stale letters to re-read. One from my wife, telling me how the service at Schrafft's Eighty-eight Street had fallen off, and one from my mother-in-law, asking me to please send her some cashmere yarn first chance I got away from "camp".

> 🔎 **说明**　中士进了茶馆，要了一杯茶和一杯饮料，这是一天之内他第一次和人说话，可见军营生活的无聊与孤独。等待茶和饮料之际，他从衣服口袋里翻出两封旧信，已经读过几遍了，信中所写都与中士所关心的事情格格不入：妻子来信告诉他，第八十八大道的施拉夫连锁店买卖萧条，岳母来信说，他有空离开军营时为她买点开司米羊毛线，在中士心中都是很无聊的事情。这些都在暗示人们的麻木、对于战争的残酷如此无知，甚至对于亲人的安危也毫不关心。

> 例句 9. The small boy, who was about five, wasn't ready to sit down yet. He slid out and discarded his reefer; then, with the deaden expression of a born heller, he methodically went about annoying his governess by pushing in and pulling out his chair several times, watching her face.

> 🔎 **说明**　艾斯美的弟弟查尔斯很淘气，来到茶馆不安分，一会儿把椅子推到桌子底下，一会儿又拉出来，眼睛盯着她们的家庭教师，故意气她。文中的 "methodically went about..."，传神的词汇，一个淘气小男孩的形象跃然纸上。

> 例句 10. He immediately picked up his napkin and put it on his head. His sister removed it, opened it, and spread it out on his lap.

> 🔎 **说明**　作者只用了三个简单的动词，写了姐姐的三个动作："removed it, opened it, and spread it"，在公共场合姐姐看见弟弟的这种表现，没有发脾气，没有训斥弟弟，以这种方式描写了姐姐的耐心。

> 例句 11. I got up and drew a chair for her, the one opposite me, and she sat down on the forward quarter of it, keeping her spine easily and beautifully straight.

💡 **说明** 中士先到了茶馆，过了一会儿，唱诗班活动结束了，艾斯美和她弟弟，还有她们的家庭教师也来到茶馆，中士赶紧站起来为艾斯美拉出一把椅子让她坐下。这段文字描绘了艾斯美的坐姿，她坐在椅座靠前的位置，腰板挺直，坐姿很放松也很优雅。先说她坐的位置，然后用一个分词短语描写她的坐姿，很简单的结构，很简单的用词，创造了一个优雅的形象。

例句 12. Her governess was now urgently signalling her to return to her own table—in effect, to stop bothering the man. My guest, however, calmly moved her chair an inch or two so that her back broke all possible further communication with the home table.

💡 **说明** 艾斯美和一个不认识的美国大兵坐在一起说话，家庭教师不放心，让她赶紧回到自己的座位。但她不好喊她回来或者过去把她拉回来，只好冲她做手势催她回来，而且脸上一副很着急的样子。这里的"urgently signalling her"很形象，给人留下深刻印象。再有，艾斯美稍微挪动了一下椅子，背朝家庭教师，让她无法继续干扰她和中士的谈话，"broke all possible further communication"，准确而巧妙的表达方式。

例句 13. One of them threw an empty whisky bottle through my aunt's window. *Fortunately*, the window was open. But does that sound very intelligent to you?

💡 **说明** 艾斯美不喜欢美国兵，对中士说了上面的话。下面是中士的回答，解释了为什么美国兵会有这种鲁莽行为。

It didn't especially, but I didn't say so. I said that many soldiers, all over the world, were a long way from home, and that few of them had had many real advantages in life. I said I'd thought that most people could figure that out for themselves.

💡 **说明** 开头一句 "It didn't especially" 是中士回答艾斯美的问话 "But does that sound very intelligent to you?" 然后他说，很多士兵因参战而远离故土，不能享受正常生活所带来的好处，这对他们不公。最后他说，这个道理多数人懂得。这说明他的理性思维很清楚，这一细节影射第二次世界大战欧洲胜利日之后中士的变化，战争中他身心受到摧残，变成另外一个人，几乎让人认不出来。

例句 14. Just then, I felt someone's warm breath on the back of my neck. I turned around and just missed brushing noses with Esmé's small brother. Ignoring me, he addressed his sister in a piercing treble: "Miss Megley said you must come and finish your tea!" His message delivered, he retired to the chair between his sister and me, on my right.

💡 **说明** 这个小段描写查尔斯，他过来告诉姐姐家庭教师让她回到自己的座位去喝茶。他先是来到中士的身后，距离很近，中士的脖子感觉到他呼出的热气，"I felt someone's warm breath on the back of my neck"，当他回头看时，两个人的鼻子差点碰上，"just missed brushing noses"。

"Ignoring me, he..."，但查尔斯却不理睬他，这几个文字把调皮而又可爱的查尔斯写得活灵活现。

"His message delivered"，传达完了家庭教师的话以后，查尔斯便坐在他的椅子上。

以上两个独立主格结构的使用更显简单的文字，巧妙地搭配，体现文学作品描写的形象性，值得揣摩。

例句 15. "Father said I have no sense of humor at all. He said I was unequipped to meet life because I have no sense of humor."

💡 **说明** 艾斯美与中士讨论关于幽默问题，父亲说，她因为没有幽默感而无法面对生活。中士对幽默感问题有不同的理解，他这样说：

Watching her, I lit a cigarette and said I didn't think a sense of humor was of any use in a real pinch.

他所说的"in a real pinch",是说在一些具体情况下,或在紧急情况下,幽默感没什么意义。这是他自己的切身体会,在战争面前,在生死未卜的情况下,谁还在乎有没有幽默感,然后他接着说:

This was a statement of faith, not a contradiction, and I quickly switched horse. I nodded and said her father had probably taken the long view, while I was taking the short(whatever *that* meant).

1. This was a statement of faith, not a contradiction...

这两种说法并不矛盾,是处于不同环境下人们的不同信仰。

2. switched horse

这是个固定短语,英语有"change horse"之说,二者意思相近,在这个上下文里,意思是赶紧改变口风。

3. "the long view",她父亲是指在通常情况下,在和平时期,"幽默感"确实重要;但在战争时期,在大决战的前夜,他所面临的是生与死,此时"幽默感"对他没有什么意义,这就是他所说的"while I was taking the short(view)"。

在战场上拼搏的人与生活在和平环境里的人对人生有不同感受,主人公的这番话有谴责战争的内涵。

例句 16. At that point, I felt an importunate tap, almost a punch, on my upper arm, from Charles's direction.

说明 中士和艾斯美正在说话,查尔斯用力地拍他的胳膊,要给中士说一个谜语,他认为这个谜语很难猜中,他很得意,急着要考一下中士,所以他使劲拍中士胳膊。这里的"importunate"是个很好的词。

《牛津高阶英汉双解词典》这样解释:"asking for things many times in a way that is annoying"(纠缠不休的)。由此我们可以想象查尔斯拍打中士胳膊的样子，很形象。

> **例句** 17. "I shall write to you first," she said... "so that you don't feel compromised in any way."

> 💡 **说明**　艾斯美和中士一起谈了一段时间，临别时，艾斯美提议给中士写信，而且是她先写；若是中士先给艾斯美写，可能会遭到非议，人们会怀疑他在战争期间给英国女孩写信，这对他的声誉会造成不好的影响。所以女孩说，"you don't feel compromised"。这里 "compromised" 的用法，对多数学习英语的人可能比较陌生，弄清它的意思，研究它的用法，很值得。《牛津高阶英汉双解词典》里有很好的解释："to bring sb/yourself under suspicion by acting in a way that is not very sensible"，因行为不当而受到怀疑，并有例句：

She had already compromised herself by accepting his invitation. 她因为接受了他的邀请而引起别人的怀疑。

由此可见，艾斯美考虑事情很周到，一方面希望和中士通信，一方面又不想给他造成不好的影响。

在 *The Making of a Royal Romance* 里，有一个描写威廉王子的句子是这样说的：

Even though there were no paparazzi lurking outside nightclubs, William was wary and didn't want to be caught in any compromising situations.（p. 132）

这里的 "compromising" 和前面的 "compromised" 意思相似。《牛津高阶英汉双解词典》这样解释："if sth is compromising, it shows or tells people sth that you want to keep secret, because it is wrong or embarrassing"（有失体面的，不宜泄露的）。

"compromising situations" 也是一个很好的搭配。

> **例句** 18. "He's furious," Esmé said. "He has a violent temper. My mother

had a propensity to spoil him. My father was the only one who didn't spoil him."

💡 **说明**　艾斯美谈到她弟弟的脾气，说他脾气暴躁，这里的"propensity"相当于"tendency"，而"My mother had a propensity to spoil him"，汉语则习惯说，"母亲总是惯着他"。从字面上看，两个表达方式不同，但所表达的意思是一样的。做汉英翻译不追求字面的对应，而要尽量找到英语的习惯说法把汉语的意思表达出来。

> **例句** 19. "Good-bye," Esmé said. "I hope you return from the war with all your faculties intact."

💡 **说明**　告别时，艾斯美对中士说了上面的话。此处的"faculties"用复数，指身心功能，即指身体和心理方面的健康，她说这句话的意思是，"我希望你身心健康，安全归来"。但中士从战场归来时，他的状况完全不是艾斯美所希望的那样，身心受到严重摧残。

艾斯美的这句话在小说里占有重要位置，小说接近尾声时，艾斯美给中士寄来了信，还寄来她父亲的手表，中士读完了信，看着在运输过程中被打碎的表蒙子，突然间他感到困了。

小说最后有这样一句话，有深意：

"You take a really sleepy man, Esmé, and he always stands a chance of again becoming a man with all his fac—with all his f-a-c-u-l-t-i-e-s intact."

以下例句摘自小说的后半部分。

诺曼底登陆之后，前半部分里的中士发生了很大的变化。小说主要描写中士在心理和精神上的变化，他从一个身体健康、思维敏捷并具有幽默感的年轻中士变成难以辨认的另外一个人。战役结束，他仍然驻扎在德国，下面的文字描写他在自己房间里的状况。

> **例句** 20. He quickly picked up something else from the table, a letter from

his older brother in Albany. It had been on his table even before he had checked into the hospital. He opened the envelope, loosely resolved to read the letter straight through, but read only the top half of the first page.

💡 **说明**　他的桌子上凌乱地堆放着包裹、信件等，但他没有心思拆开看。此时他从桌子上拿起一封信，是他哥哥从美国奥尔巴尼写来的，这封信放在桌子上已经有一段时间了。他拆开信封，想读，但又不是很想读。作者用了一个副词"loosely"来描写这种没有心思读信的心态，这个副词用得准确、恰当，值得学习。

试与"firmly resolved"相比较。

例句 21. But he was a young man who had not come through the war with all his faculties intact, and for more than an hour he had been triple-reading paragraphs, and now he was doing it in sentences.

💡 **说明**　在这个句子里又重复了"he had not come through the war with all his faculties intact"。中士现在在看书，每个段落都要反复读三遍，进而恶化到每个句子都要读三遍，因为他头疼，精神不能集中。这对一个曾经充满智慧、思维敏捷又有幽默感的年轻中士是非常痛苦的。

例句 22. Then, abruptly, familiarly, and, as usual, with no warning, he thought he felt his mind dislodge itself and teeter, like insecure luggage on an overhead rack.

💡 **说明**　中士拿出一支烟，但点烟时手指发抖，香烟一点味道也没有，但他还是继续抽。忽然间，他有一种感觉，觉得他的脑子要崩塌了，好像头顶上方架子上的行李开始晃动，要掉下来似的。通过这个比喻，我们可以想象此时中士的心理已经处于崩溃的边缘。

可查查词典，看看动词"dislodge"的用法。

例句 23. He put his arms on the table and rested his head on them. He ached from head to foot, all zones of pain seemingly interdependent. He was rather like a Christmas tree whose lights, wired in series, must all go out if even one bulb is defective.

💡 **说明** 他浑身疼，而且各处的痛点是相互联系的，只要一个地方疼，就引起全身疼痛。作者用了一个比喻描写这种状况，好像圣诞树上用电线串在一起的灯泡，有一个出了毛病，所有的灯泡都会熄灭。文学作品中修辞的作用就是把抽象的概念写得可知可感，让读者更深切地、更具体地读懂作者要传达的意思。

例句 24. He opened the package without any interest, without even looking at the return address. He opened it by burning the string with a lighted match. He was more interested in watching the string burn all the way down than in opening the package, but he opened it, finally.

💡 **说明** 中士收到一个包裹，对包裹里有什么东西、是谁寄来的，此时他都没有了兴趣。他点燃一根火柴，烧断系着包裹的线绳，他对线绳燃烧时冒出的火苗更有兴趣。战争给他造成的创伤使他的心理扭曲，作者的这些描写都有很深的内涵。最后，他在包裹里发现了艾斯美给他写来的信。信的内容是这样的，我们不妨读一读，体会艾斯美对中士的关切心情：

June 7, 1944

DEAR SERGEANT X,

I hoped you will forgive me for having taken 38 days to begin our correspondence but, I have been extremely busy as my aunt has undergone streptococcus of the throat and nearly perished and I have been justifiably saddled with one responsibility after another. However I have thought of you frequently and of the extremely pleasant afternoon we spent in each other's company on April 30, 1944 between 3.45 and 4.15 p.m. in case it slipped your mind.

We are all tremendously excited and overawed about D-Day and only hope that it will bring about the swift termination of the war and a method of existence that is ridiculous to say the least. Charles and I are both quite concerned about you; we hope you were not among those who made the first initial assault upon the Cotentin Peninsula. Were you? Please reply as speedily as possible. My warmest regards to your wife.

阅读罗布·汉弗莱斯（Rob Humphreys）：
London（片段）

简介

这段文字取自一本介绍英国伦敦的导游书籍《伦敦》（*London*）。

介绍城市的文章所叙内容大体相似，不外是人口、面积、气候、政治、经济、文化等。所不同者在文字，文字一般化和文字引人入胜所得效果则不同。当我们作为英语学习者将其作为一篇文章来读，我们会发现这是一篇优美的散文。其词语的选择、短语的搭配、句子的组织，都是纯正的英语，都能在我们眼前碰出闪亮的火花。假如我们在阅读过程中注意感受英语语言之美，这段文字会让我们激动不已。

［原文］Considering the temperateness of the English climate, it's amazing how much mileage the locals get out of the subject—a two-day cold snap is discussed as if it were the onset of a new Ice Age, and a week in the upper 70s starts rumours of drought. The fact is that English summers rarely get hot（though the last couple of years have had July heat waves）and the winters don't get very cold, though they're often wet. The bottom line is that it's impossible to say with any degree of certainty that the weather will be pleasant in any given month. May might be wet and grey one year and gloriously sunny the next, and the same goes for the autumnal months—November stands an equal chance of being crisp and clear or foggy and grim.

例句 1. ... it's amazing how much mileage the locals get out of the subject...

说明　这个句子中的 "mileage" 是一个含义新鲜的名词，《牛津高阶英汉双解词典》这样解释："the amount of advantage or use that you can get from a particular event or situation"（好处），并有例句：

I don't think the press can get any more mileage out of that story.

例句 2. a two-day cold snap... and a week in the upper 70s...

说明　以名词词组作为句子开头是简洁文字的高明手段，否则需要一个完整句子来表达同样的内容，那样就复杂了，这两个词组都是以主语身份出现在句子里。

例句 3. The bottom line is that...

说明　这个词组用得比较广，其基本意思是 "the most important thing" 或 "the essential thing"。

例句 4. ... and the same goes for...

说明　句子前半部分说五月有时潮湿灰暗，有时阳光灿烂，而秋季的几个月里情况也是一样，有时潮湿灰暗，有时阳光灿烂，这个说法避免重复，也省略文字，值得学习。

例句 5. November stands an equal chance of being crisp and clear or foggy and grim.

说明　关于 "stand a chance of..."，陆谷孙《英汉大词典》说 "有……希望" "有……可能"，这个解释符合这句话的意思，十一月的天气有可能是清新爽朗，也有可能是有雾阴冷。

Symbols of China（《符号中国》）英文鉴赏

简 介

英文版本 *Symbols of China* 由译林出版社和英国 Compendium Publishing 合作出版，是一部用英语介绍中国文化的新书，英语写得好，很值得学习和借鉴。

译林出版社对外合作部主管王玉强介绍本书形成过程时说：

为了更符合英文的行文方式和文章架构，英文版的文字不是由中文版翻译而成，而是完全根据外国专家的指导意见重新以英文直接写成，更请到母语为英语的哈佛大学东亚系高才生逐字逐句地润色推敲，确定英文地道流畅。

本书由联合国教科文组织的文化专家、《国际博物馆》的主编伊莎贝尔·万松女士作序，由牛津国际出版研究中心首位主任——保罗·理查德森先生撰写了介绍引言。

现介绍书中一些具有文化内涵的汉语名称的汉语说法。

一、汉字

例句 1. Chinese characters—Han Zi—are the basic units of the Chinese language. Each character has a single syllable and can denote a variety of meanings, and characters are combined to form words and sentences. Chinese characters are distinctive for their combination of image, sound and meaning.（p. 42）

💡 **说明** "汉字"一般译作"Chinese characters"，在 *Symbols of China* 中的译文里加了拼音"Han Zi"。汉字是汉语的基本单位。汉字是单音节词，有的是多义的。汉字合起来构成词汇和句子。它将形象、声音和意义结合在一起，这是它的特点。

例句 2. Chinese characters are distinctive for their composition. Many characters are pictograms, which depict the objects referred to, or ideograms, which illustrate meaning in an iconic fashion.（p. 42）

💡 **说明**　汉字的构成与众不同，很多汉字是象形字，描写相关事物的形态，很多汉字是表意字，以符的形式说明意义。

这里的"pictograms"指"象形字"，如，"the earliest form of the 'sun' character is a circle with a dot in the middle"，最早的"日"字是一个圆圈中间加一个"点"，发展成现在的"日"；"the earliest form of the 'moon' character resembles the shape of a crescent"，最早的"月"是一个"月牙形"，演变成现在的"月"。

这里的"ideograms"指"表意字"，如，"when the characters for 'sun' and 'moon' are combined the compound character refers to 'light'"，"日"和"月"结合起来便成了现在的"明"。"When the character for 'tree' is doubled, it becomes 'forest'"，双木为"林"；"If the character for 'person' is tripled, it becomes 'people'"，三人为"众"。

而"iconic"指代表事物的符号、图像等，就是构成汉字的偏旁。

例句 3. 各种形式汉字的英语说法：

1. 甲骨文，Oracle Bone Script

2. 大篆，Greater Seal Script

3. 小篆，Lesser Seal Script，或 Xiaozhuan

4. 隶书，Lishu，或 the Clerkly Script

5. 楷书，the regular script，或 the standard script

6. 行书，the semi-cursive script，或 the running script

7. 草体，the cursive script

例句 4. "活字印刷"的三种英语说法：

1. mobile character printing

2. printing with moveable type

3. moveable type printing

二、书法

例句 1. Before Wang Xizhi, calligraphy was simply used for information. It was Wang who transformed calligraphy into a transcendent art form, which aims at capturing aesthetic beauty through representing a higher order. He focused on variation of line and form and, above all, on the dynamic and rhythmic flow of energy.（p. 28）

💡 **说明** 这个段落有两个句子，第一句谈书法功能的变迁，在王羲之之前，书写是为了传达信息，但自王羲之开始，书写的功能改变了，不再是单纯地传达信息，他把书写变成了书法艺术。

1. a transcendent art form

这里的"transcendent"意为"extremely great"。

2. representing a higher order

这里"order"的意思和用法需要弄清楚，指书法的审美特征比单纯地传达信息更高级。陆谷孙《英汉大词典》有一个解释——"种类"，并给了一个例子："Her singing talent is of the highest order."（"她的歌唱天才超群"，也可以说"她的唱歌天赋一流"。）从这个例句中的"order"看，将其理解为"级别""等级"也未尝不可。

3. the dynamic and rhythmic flow of energy

这句话所依据的原文概念是什么，我们不得而知，但根据字面看，相当于汉语的"动态的有节奏的气势"，这有待进一步探讨。有专家说，书法有"体势"一说，所谓"'体势'是指一个字所呈现出的动态，以及由于点画的排叠汇集而展现出来的态势"，还有专家谈到王羲之时说，他"精研体势"。也许英译文所表达的是这个概念，这也有待进一步探讨。

┌ **例句** 2. 关于王羲之具有划时代意义的《兰亭序》和《快雪时晴帖》，*Symbols of China* 给了英译文：

1.《兰亭序》，"Preface to the Poems at the Orchid Pavillon"
2.《快雪时晴帖》，"Greeting Letter after Snow"

这两个英语译名可作参考。

三、梅、兰、竹、菊"四君子"

Symbols of China 有一段介绍梅、兰、竹、菊"四君子"（"Four Gentlemen"）或"四友"（"Four Noble Friends"）的文字，我们可参考学习。

┌ **例句** 1. When studying Chinese culture you may come across the terms "Four Gentlemen" or "Four Noble Friends". They refer to the plum blossom, orchid, bamboo and chrysanthemum.（p. 35）

💡 **说明** 第一个句子是主从复合句，第二个句子是简单句，结构和意思都比较简单。

┌ **例句** 2. In Confucianism "gentleman" indicates a lofty personality and upright character, of which these four plants are conceived to be the best embodiment.（p. 35）

💡 **说明** 这是一个主从复合句，形式比较复杂，但句子组织得很紧凑，主句带一个 "of" 引导的从句，"of..." 之前的部分可以独立存在，其后的从句是说，梅、兰、竹、菊最能体现君子品质，这个从句的功能是使君子品质的内涵更加丰满。而且，因为 "of which" 的关系，"embodiment" 被放在了句尾，这个位置强调了它的重要性。

另外，这句话这样安排也产生了明显的节奏感。语言本质上是有声的，阅读时只是用眼睛过一遍往往不会感觉到它的节奏，但朗读一下就会发现，其实语言和音乐一样有节奏。音乐是通过旋律（主要指节奏）表达思想感情，语言也一样，也是通过节奏（当然也有其他因素）来表达思想感情及其变化，节奏给了语言以美感。

例句 3. Their botanical features are interpreted as virtues expected of the ideal man, drawing admiration from the Chinese, who therefore often use the Four Gentlemen as the theme of paintings and poems to proclaim moral integrity.（p. 35）

💡 **说明** 这是一个主从复合句，包含多层意思，传达多层信息。在主句部分，梅、兰、竹、菊的植物学特征被喻为中国人所崇敬的君子之风，中国人又将 "四君子" 用作书画和诗词的主题，以此来宣示高尚的道德和正直的品格。

如此丰富的内容仅用一个句子表达出来，而且句子形式并不十分复杂，主句带一个分词短语，然后是一个 "who" 引导的从句，写作者用一个很容易理清的句式将如此纷繁的内容表达得这么清晰，是写作技巧，也是语言艺术。

例句 4. 梅 the plum blossom

Despite the chilling weather the plum blossom displays its beauty at a time when other flowers are still hiding from the cold. Its petals are soft and delicate, but its spirit is tough. Its pride prevents it from flowering together with others—

it cannot bear that kind of degradation.（p. 35）

💡 **说明**　这段文字用梅花的诸多特征比喻君子的高尚品格，当众花在严寒的天气里躲藏起来时，唯有梅花在绽放，展示它的美；虽然它的花瓣柔软脆弱，但它具有顽强不屈的精神；它的自尊让它花不与众，因为它不容忍自己堕落。

文中使用了一系列拟人的修辞方式，梅花有精神（spirit），有自尊（pride）等，用梅花的这些品格比喻君子之风。

其对比写法也值得注意，比如第一句，一方面是梅花不惧严寒，另一方面是众花躲避严寒；第二句，一方面写它的花瓣柔软脆弱，另一方面写它的精神顽强不屈。两个句子的对比效果明显，都是为了凸显梅花的坚强性格。

例句 5. In the Song Dynasty (960-1279), a famous poet named Lin Bu led a hermit's life on a hill near the West Lake in Hangzhou, Zhejiang Province, raising cranes and planting plum trees. He had no family, but took care of the plum trees as his wife and the cranes as his sons, making friends with nature. Since then, the plum blossom is often associated with hermit life.（p. 35）

💡 **说明**　文中提到的 Lin Bu，即林逋（967—1028），人称和靖先生，北宋隐逸诗人，性孤高，喜恬淡。林逋隐居西湖孤山，终生未娶，喜植梅养鹤，自谓"以梅为妻，以鹤为子"，人称"梅妻鹤子"，由此，梅花和隐居联系起来。

例句 6. 兰 the orchid

The Chinese celebrate the orchid as a symbol of moral purity and refinement, for it often grows in ravines far away from worldly noise and bustle. It is alone but not lonely, because it has achieved full realization of its beauty in its aloofness. As a "gentleman", it keeps its independence without being seduced by fame or wealth. It is quite natural that it easily arouses sympathy from people with the same attitude to life.（p. 36）

💡 **说明**　这里有几个赞美君子的词语搭配和表达方式，如，"moral purity and refinement"，道德上的纯洁和教养；"far away from worldly noise and bustle"，远离尘嚣；"alone but not lonely"，独处但不孤独；"without being seduced by fame or wealth"，拒绝名利的诱惑。

这些都是表达汉语文化概念的很好的方式，对我们做汉英翻译都有启示。

这段文字里有一个动词值得注意，"The Chinese celebrate the orchid..."，此处的"celebrate"意为"to praise"，赞美；当我们表达汉语的"赞美"时，"celebrate"和"praise"是同义词。

还有一个词组，"arouses sympathy"，这里的"sympathy"未必是通常意义上的"同情"，不妨将其理解为"同感"，唤起一种"意气相投"的感觉。

全段共有四个句子，每个句子的意思表达得都很准确，而且巧妙，读起来感觉轻松而明快。

例句 7. Evidently, the orchid has always been appealing to an innermost dream of the Chinese literati—being free from vulgar minds and secular troubles.（p. 36）

💡 **说明**　这句话赞美兰花，实则赞美中国文人学士，这个句子写得好。

这里的"to appeal to sb"，意为"to attract or interest sb"，对某人有吸引力、引起兴趣等；"an innermost dream"，可以理解为"内心的追求"；"the Chinese literati"，中国文人学士。但短语"vulgar minds"中的"minds"指什么，怎么译为好，值得思考。

当此文作者写"vulgar minds"时，其所依据的原文是怎样表述的，这个英语是对应的直译还是灵活的意译，我们不得而知，只好依据上下文做判断，给出一个合理的解释。

首先，在这个上下文里，"minds"指"persons"的可能性不大，《牛津高阶英汉双解词典》说，当"mind"作为"person"讲时，是指"intelligent person"，即智者、有才智的人。

但该词典对"mind"的另一个解释可作参考，即"thoughts""interest"（思想，兴趣）。

美国实用主义哲学家霍勒斯·卡伦（Horace M. Kallen，1882—1974）有一篇文章"Style and Meaning"，文中出现了"minds"这个词，他说：

Rhetoric books, editors' minds and writers' dispositions are full of rules about how and what and when and where to choose among words. But I have not noticed that these rules ever helped an aspiring writer...

此处的"editors' minds"显然是指思想、意识之类，这和我们讨论的"minds"用法相同，都是指"思想"。

鉴于此，不妨将"being free from vulgar minds and secular troubles"译作"摈弃低俗的思想，摆脱世俗的烦扰"。

例句 8. 竹 the bamboo

Though not blessed with dainty blossoms, it has won its unique place in Chinese culture with its straightness and integrity. As an evergreen plant, bamboo fully exemplifies the qualities of modesty and strength. More importantly, the Chinese interpret straightness as honesty and hardness as strength.（p. 36）

💡 **说明** 这段文字有几处需要略加说明：

1. 关于"be blessed with"，《牛津高阶英汉双解词典》有一个解释："to have sth good such as ability, great happiness, etc."，这个句子是说，虽然竹子不开花，但它以其"诚实正直"的品格在中国文化中赢得独特的地位。

2. "straightness and integrity"，这两个英语词汇意思一致，重叠使用

是为了加重分量。

3. 后面两个句子进一步解释 "straightness"，中国人将 "正直"（"straightness"）视为 "诚实"（"honesty"），将 "坚强"（"hardness"）视为有 "力量"（"strength"）。

例句 9. Su Dongpo, a famous poet in the Song Dynasty, sighed that "For gentlemen, a meal without meat is still enjoyable, but a garden without bamboo is unbearable."（pp. 36-37）

💡 说明　苏东坡曾说过："可使食无肉，不可居无竹。无肉令人瘦，无竹令人俗。"

清代紫砂艺人陈介溪曾制一把小壶，上有题词 "宁可食无肉，不可居无竹"。明清篆刻家也有治 "不可居无竹" 印章者。

例句 10. 菊 the chrysanthemum

Its perseverance in the face of frost and cold won it the reputation as a gentleman of distinguished virtue. It especially echoes to the melancholy of those who refuse to compromise with secular mediocrity and who find no place to bring their talents into full play.（p. 37）

💡 说明　这是书中赞美菊花的一段文字，共两个句子。第一句，"Its perseverance in the face of frost and cold"，可译为 "不惧寒霜的品格" 或 "在寒霜面前表现出不屈不挠的精神"。第二句比较长，但结构清晰，一个主句带两个从句："It especially echoes to the melancholy of..."，此处的 "melancholy" 可以理解为一种 "忧郁情绪"，两个从句，一个是 "who refuse to compromise with secular mediocrity"，那些拒绝向世俗平庸之辈妥协的人们；另一个是 "who find no place to bring their talents into full play"，那些怀才不遇的人们。

试将第二句翻译如下，供参考：

"对于那些拒绝向世俗的平庸之辈妥协和那些怀才不遇的人们，菊花不惧寒霜的品格尤其与他们的忧郁情绪产生共鸣。"

这里需要澄清一个问题：为什么菊花会引起他们的"忧郁情绪"？

这两类人里一类是不肯随附尘俗者，另一类是怀才不遇者。在文中的另一处还特别提到屈原和陶潜，说他们都视菊花为精神之友。屈原政治上遭陷害，自沉于汨罗江，陶潜不屑官场，宁归田园。

在严寒中绽放的菊花与忧国忧民的仁人志士有一个共同特征——孤傲，因此，这些人心中产生忧郁情绪，应该不难理解。

例句　11. Many top literati in Chinese history, for instance, Qu Yuan (340-278 BC) and Tao Qian (365-427) took the chrysanthemum as their spiritual friend and paid tribute to it in their works.（p. 37）

💡 说明　屈原《离骚》中有"朝饮木兰之坠露兮，夕餐秋菊之落英"著名诗句。

陶渊明《饮酒》诗（其五）有"采菊东篱下，悠然见南山"诗句。

四、围棋

例句　1. Go chess, also known as "weiqi", is a board game for two players. With a history of more than two thousand years, it is one of the oldest games in China. In traditional Chinese culture, mastery of weiqi is vital for any cultivated person. The seemingly simple game in fact involves great stratagems and a grasp of China's rich philosophical traditions.

💡 说明　围棋一般英译为"Go chess"，也可音译为"weiqi"。

"vital"在此表示必不可少，"cultivated person"指有文化、有修养的人，"mastery of weiqi is vital for any cultivated person"是说，有文化、有修养的人都必须会下围棋。

例句 2. In ancient China, mastery of weiqi was considered one of the four essential skills of the cultivated man or woman, the other three being mastery of music, calligraphy and painting. During the Tang Dynasty（618-907）, weiqi became increasingly popular among both the literati and the populace, and it was introduced to Japan and Korea where it acquired great popularity.（p. 40）

💡 说明　这里的"essential"和上文的"vital"意思相近，都是"必不可少"，或者"非常重要"。古代有文化、有修养的人"琴、棋、书、画"样样行。唐朝时，围棋在文人和普通百姓当中都很流行，后来传到日本和朝鲜（特别是现在的韩国），在那里围棋传播很广。

这里将"琴、棋、书、画"这四个方面的修养译作"the four essential skills"，我们不妨将"skills"理解为"技艺"或"技能"。

例句 3. Unlike Western chess, with its hierarchy of pieces, all the stones of weiqi are the same, in either black or white. The two colours symbolize the two elementary forces of the universe, yin and yang. The continuously changing configurations symbolize their dynamic interplay, representing the infinite possibilities of transformation and the varied entities of the world, changing moment by moment, stone by stone.（pp. 40-41）

💡 说明　国际象棋中的各个棋子有等级之分，其地位不同，功能不同，走法也不同，所以才有"hierarchy"之说。

第二句中的"symbolize"意为"象征"，中国围棋棋子只有黑白二色，象征阴阳；英语词典有一个"symbolize"的例句：

The use of light and dark symbolizes good and evil. 明暗的运用象征善良和邪恶。

第三句中的"configurations"指围棋的布局，布局的不断变化则象征双方的互动，表示世上的事物每时每刻都在变化，每移动一个棋子都会引起变化，这就是变化的无限可能性和世界每时每刻都在变化的存在形式。

┌─────┐
│例句│ 4. Perhaps the most remarkable thing about weiqi is its seamless marriage of simplicity and sophistication, in which an almost infinite number of possibilities are conjured up with a limited number of stones.

这句话是说，围棋最神奇的地方是简单与复杂的自然结合（"seamless marriage" 的字面意思是 "无缝结合"），即，有限的棋子包含无限的可能性，此处的 "conjured up" 可以理解为 "使……出现"，或 "引起"。

五、风水

┌─────┐
│例句│ 1. The term "fengshui" literally refers to wind and water, which are crucial features to take into consideration when evaluating a geographic location.（p. 28）

📍 说明 "风水" 用拼音音译，然后用直译说明它的意思。

┌─────┐
│例句│ 2. Fengshui seeks the fit between one's inner being and the external world.（p. 28）

📍 说明 英语词典这样解释作为名词的 "fit"："the way that two things match each other or are suitable for each other"。风水追求两个事物的和谐状态，句中的 "one's inner being" 意为人的 "内心世界"，"the external world" 意为 "客观世界"，风水寻求二者的和谐。

┌─────┐
│例句│ 3. In the various theoretical frameworks of fengshui, it is usually stressed that a person living in a particular place should match his or her external environment, including the land, the river, and even the entire universe.（p. 28）

📍 说明 风水强调人和外部环境相和谐的理念，这里用了动词 "match"。

例句 4. It is assumed that heavenly power influences earthly lives, and that human beings should adjust themselves to the power, invisible and intangible as it may appear.

说明 此处的 "adjust" 指人类应该调整自己以适应大自然，以上三个词的连用，"fit" 作为名词，"match" 和 "adjust" 作为动词，其本身就含有 "协调" 的意思。

例句 5. The practice of fengshui, which originated in the Taoist tradition in ancient China, also held the belief that there are correlations between humans and the universe.（p. 28）

说明 风水学相信人和宇宙之间有联系；此处的 "相信" 不是用 "believed" 表示，而是用了一个词组 "held the belief that..." 来表示。

例句 6. For instance, following the Taoist tradition, the practitioners of fengshui study the energy flow within a person's body, and attempt to find out whether it goes with the wind or water flow in his or her surroundings.

说明 这里的 "energy flow" 所表达的是汉语 "气" 的概念，《新时代汉英大辞典》和林语堂的《当代汉英词典》在解释汉语这个概念的 "气" 时，都用了 "energy" 这个词。

阅读威廉·麦克斯韦尔（William Maxwell）：
So Long, See You Tomorrow

简介

威廉·麦克斯韦尔（William Maxwell, 1908—2000），美国杰出作家，著有六部长篇小说、三部短篇小说集、一部文学评论集等。曾获多个奖项，长篇小说《再见，明天见》（*So Long, See You Tomorrow*）便是六部长篇小说中的一部，获美国图书奖（the American Book Award）。

1936年，麦克斯韦尔来到纽约，在《纽约客》杂志做编辑，直到1976年，长达四十年，此时正是该杂志发展最好的时期。他在《纽约客》的四十年编辑生涯中帮助成就了一些著名的美国作家，如，J. D. 塞林格（J. D. Salinger）、约翰·厄普代克（John Updike）、约翰·契弗（John Cheever）、尤多拉·韦尔蒂（Eudora Welty）等。

So Long, See You Tomorrow 故事以20世纪20年代伊利诺伊州的林肯小镇为背景。一个冬天的早晨，佃农劳埃德·威尔逊（Lloyd Wilson）在他工作的农场被杀害，杀害他的正是他的朋友克拉伦斯·史密斯（Clarence Smith），原因是劳埃德·威尔逊与克拉伦斯·史密斯妻子有婚外情。五十年后，小说的叙事者开始追述这起凶杀案的来龙去脉，这便是这部经典作品的由来。

关于 *So Long, See You Tomorrow*，有评论说：

This is one of the great books of our age. It is the subtlest of miniatures that contains our deepest sorrows and truths and love—all caught in a clear, simple style in perfect brushstrokes.

麦克斯韦尔的文字简淡并富美感，文风含蓄有深意。鉴赏他的行文风格，研究他的词、句功夫，对学习英语和汉英翻译大有裨益。

例句 1. Lloyd Wilson got up at five thirty as usual, dressed, and built two fires. While he was waiting for the one in the kitchen range to catch, he stood talking and joking with her. He was in a cheerful mood and left the house whistling.（p. 4）

💡 说明　佃农劳埃德·威尔逊早晨很早起床，先是生两个火炉，然后去牛舍干活，这段文字描写他离家之前的情景。这里的 "kitchen range" 是指厨房里的炉灶，"to catch" 意为 "to begin to burn"，威尔逊生了两个火炉，其中一个在厨房，他在等着火炉着起来时，和她说笑。

"He was in a cheerful mood and left the house whistling"，这句话刻画了威尔逊的心情。

人心情不好或悲愤时一般不吹口哨，只有闲哉悠哉、心情好或得意时才吹口哨。句中 "left the house whistling" 只用一个词就写活了威尔逊出门时轻松愉快的样子。英语里谓语或谓语动词后面常用这种分词结构，对前面所叙之事做补充或进一步说明。简练文字的手段，一个分词有一个完整句子的功能。另一句 "he stood talking and joking with her"，其分词结构有类似功能。

例句 2. In those days—I am talking about the early nineteen twenties—people in Lincoln mostly didn't lock their doors at night, and if they did it was against the idea of a burglar.（p. 5）

💡 说明　英语单词 "idea" 是常用词，在这个句子里有特定含义，与常用的意思略有区别。《牛津高阶英汉双解词典》有一个解释："a feeling that sth is possible"。例句：

I have a pretty good idea where I left it—I hope I'm right.

这个解释和例句可帮助理解句中的"idea"。

关于介词"against"，陆谷孙《英汉大词典》说，"为……做准备"，例句：

My house is insured against fire.

"it was against the idea of a burglar"，意思应为，夜里锁门"是为了提防小偷"，或"以防被盗"等。

例句 3. When my father was getting along in years and the past began to figure more in his conversation, I asked him one day what my mother was like. I knew what she was like as my mother but I thought it was time somebody told me what she was like as a person. To my surprise he said, "That's water over the dam," shutting me up but also leaving me in doubt, because of his abrupt tone of voice, whether he didn't after all this time have any feeling about her much, or did have but didn't think he ought to. In any case he didn't feel like talking about her to me.（p. 6）

💡 说明　这是小说的叙事者与他父亲的对话，"I"指书中的叙事者。

1. getting along in years

也说"getting on in years"，"getting old"的另一种说法，上了年纪。

2. That's water over the dam

意为"那是过去的事了"。陆谷孙《英汉大词典》说，"water over the dam"和"water under the bridge"通用；《牛津高阶英汉双解词典》对"water under the bridge"有解释："used to say that sth happened in the past and is now forgotten or no longer important"。简单而有余味的表达。

3. ... leaving me in doubt... whether he didn't after all this time have any feeling about her much, or did have but didn't think he ought to.

意思是，让"我"弄不明白，他是说，过了这么长时间，对母亲已经没有多少感情呢，或是说，还有些感情但他认为不应该有呢。

这个句子用词简单，句子形式和所表达的内容微妙；如果安排不好，句子可能冗长，意思也可能说不清楚。

例句 4. Very few families escape disasters of one kind or another, but in the years between 1909 and 1919 my mother's family had more than its share of them...（p. 6）

💡 说明

1. Very few families escape disasters...

这个"escape"及其搭配"escape disasters"值得留意，《新牛津英语词典》解释"escape"时这样说："succeed in avoiding or eluding something dangerous, unpleasant, or undesirable"，解释中强调"succeed"，意为"成功避开……""成功躲过……"，翻译"escape"时应把这层意思译出来。词典有一个例句："a baby boy narrowly escaped death"，意为"小男孩险些丧命"，或"小男孩捡了一条命"。

2. my mother's family had more than its share of them...

这句话和前面的"Very few families escape disasters..."联系着，1909至1919年期间，几乎家家都有过灾难，可"我"母亲家遇到的灾难比一般的家庭多。别的作家未必这样写，若我们将汉语的这个意思译成英语，也不一定这样说，但这是作者的表达方式和行文风格。

文有简文，画有简画。中国写意国画善简笔，清初画家朱耷，号"八大山人"，多有简笔画，寥寥几笔，勾勒传神。文与画在艺术表现形式上有相同之处。

例句 5. My younger brother was born on New Year's Day, at the height of the influenza epidemic of 1918. My mother died two days later of double pneumonia. After that, there were no more disasters. The worst that could happen had happened, and the shine went out of everything.（p. 7）

💡 说明

1. "The worst that could happen had happened"，有可能发生的最坏的事情都发生了。

2. ... and the shine went out of everything.

关于作为名词的 "shine"，陆谷孙《英汉大词典》有固定短语："take the shine out of..."，或 "take the shine off..."，意为 "没有了欢乐"。此处的 "shine" 喻指生活中的 "欢乐" 或 "乐趣"，"... and the shine went out of everything"，"一切都变得暗淡无光"，或 "生活没有了乐趣"，英语里这类比喻用法比较多。

例句 6. He left on Tuesday morning, carrying a grip that was heavy with printed forms, and came home Friday afternoon to a household that was seething with problems he was not accustomed to dealing with. His sadness was of the kind that is patient and without hope.（p. 10）

💡 说明

1. "... seething with problems he was not accustomed to dealing with"，"seething with..." 意为 "full of"，星期五他回家时正赶上家里出现了一大堆问题，这些问题如何处理，他不知所措。英语有几种限定名词的方式，用前置的形容词和后置的定语从句等，此句属于后置的定语从句。

2. His sadness was of the kind that is patient and without hope.

文中出现在从句里的形容词 "patient"，是用来说明 "sadness" 的性质，指忍受 "悲伤" 时的态度。陆谷孙《英汉大词典》有解释："显示出忍耐的；（长期）忍受苦难的"。这里指这种 "悲哀" 是要 "默默忍受" 的。至于 "without hope"，直译是 "没有希望"，意思是没有尽头，难以解脱。

这句话如何翻译才好，不论就这一个句子孤立地直译，还是结合上下文做意译，译成通畅的汉语，都需要做变通，变通出来的句子可能会随译者而不同。

例句 7. One night—I don't know how old I was, five or six, maybe—bedtime came and I kissed my mother good night as usual and then went over to my father and as I leaned toward him he said I was too old for that any more. By the standards of that time and that place I expect I was, but I had wanted to anyway. And how was I to express the feeling I had for him? He didn't say, then or ever. In that moment my feeling for him changed and became wary and unconfident.（p. 11）

💡 说明　儿子睡觉前去亲吻父亲，遭到拒绝，五六岁的年龄已经有了自尊心，孩子的心理因此受到伤害，对父亲的感情产生变化。这段文字展示孩子性格的转变过程，不论是凭借想象，还是有这方面的亲身经历，作者对这一细节把握准确，文字也实在。"In that moment my feeling for him changed"，当时"我"对他的感情就变了；"and became wary and unconfident"，孩子从此变得小心翼翼、不自信。

例句 8. Ninth Street was an extension of home, and perfectly safe. Nobody ever picked on me there. When I passed beyond Ninth Street, it could be rough going. The boys in the eighth grade dominated the school yard before school and at recess time. They were, by turns, good-natured in a patronizing way, or mean, or foulmouthed about girls, or single-mindedly bent on improving their proficiency in some sport.（p. 28）

💡 说明

1. an extension of home

"extension" 一般指扩展、延伸等，多指实体或实际事物的扩展、延伸或传播，如，"the extension of the subway""the extension of new technology into developing countries"；文中的"an extension of home"指故事叙述者对第九大街的感觉，在这条街道上和在家里一样，感觉安全。我们用英语表达这个意思时，会想到一些不同说法，麦克斯韦尔只用一个名词词组来表达这个意思。

2. "They were, by turns, good-natured... or mean, or foulmouthed..., or single-mindedly bent on..."，这里的"by turns"省略了好几个"sometimes"，这个词用多了有时是修辞的需要，有时也难免显得重复。麦克斯韦尔有简洁、含蓄的意识。

3. rough going

关于"rough"，词典有解释："violent，where there is a lot of violence or crime"。

例句 9. All this took place in plain sight of everybody, all the boys I had grown up with, and no hand was ever raised in my defense, nobody ever came to my rescue—I expect partly because they had their own vulnerabilities and did not want to be singled out for attack, but obviously there was something about me that invited it. Since I did not know what it was, I couldn't do anything to change it, and any emotion I felt—physical inadequacy, fear, humiliation, the whole repertoire of the adolescent—showed in my face. I was such easy game that I wonder that their pleasure in tormenting me lasted as long as it did.（p. 29）

💡 说明

1. All this took place in plain sight of everybody...

"All this"指"我"在学校受欺侮，大家就眼睁睁地看着。这个意思也有别的说法，"All this took place in front of everybody"，或"All this took place before the eyes of all the boys I had grown up with"。麦克斯韦尔常与众不同，其文字读着感觉新鲜；同样，"and no hand was ever raised in my defense", 简洁而新颖。

2. 关于 "vulnerable",《牛津高阶英汉双解词典》说: "weak and easily hurt physically or emotionally"; 文中的 "vulnerabilities", 从词典的解释看, 可能指 "physically weak", 也可能是 "easily hurt, emotionally", 含义比较多, 翻译时可酌情处理。

3. "the whole repertoire of the adolescent", 其中的 "repertoire" 一般指艺术家的全部剧目、曲目、节目, 或作家、作曲家的全部作品等。《新牛津英语词典》还有一个解释: "a stock of skills or type of behaviour that a person habitually uses", 这个解释接近文中这个词的意思, 指青少年时期所有弱点都写在脸上, 属 "behaviour" 之类。

4. I was such easy game that...

弱势者经常受到强势者的欺负, 汉语里有 "某某好欺负" 的说法, 这个意思用英语如何表达? 关于 "game", 陆谷孙《英汉大词典》有一个解释很好, "被嘲弄、攻击、凌辱的目标", 正好符合作者所指。

例句 10. Kept warm by the coat and some lap robes, Clarence Smith had spent the night before the murder on his own farm and in the morning concealed himself behind a haystack and waited for Lloyd Wilson's lantern to come bobbing across the pasture. (p. 39)

💡 说明 英语有一部分动词后面可以跟着分词 "ing" 的形式, 文中的 "come bobbing" 就是一例, 写想象中的威尔逊提着灯笼经过牧场时灯笼来回晃动的情形, 一幅有动感的画面。

例句 11. I don't know what she looked like. Most farm women of her age were reduced by hard work and frequent childbearing to a common denominator of plainness. (p. 37)

💡 **说明**　这里写的 "she" 指劳埃德·威尔逊的妻子，与丈夫分居后，一个人带四个孩子艰难度日。

1. 关于 "reduce"，有一个特定词义，词典说: "to force sb/sth into a particular state, usually a worse one"，表达这个意思时常用被动式 "be reduced"。

曾有一篇报道伊拉克战争的文章，写因为美国侵略者的狂轰滥炸，"Iraq was reduced to nakedness"，一个句子写尽了美国发动的野蛮战争给伊拉克造成的惨状。

2. 形容词 "plain" 描写女人时，指相貌平常，少有姿色。

3. 关于 "denominator"，陆谷孙《英汉大词典》说，意为 "共同特性，共同特色"。"Most farm women... plainness"，这句话可试译一下。

例句 11. Roaming the courthouse square on a Saturday night, the tenant farmers and their families were unmistakable. You could see that they were not at ease in town and that they clung together for support. The women's clothes were not meant to be becoming but to wear well... The back of the men's necks was a mahogany color, and deeply wrinkled. Their hands were large and looked swollen or misshapen and sometimes they were short a finger or two.（p. 55）

💡 **说明**

1. "unmistakable"，农民进城，从模样、举止、装束一看就知道是庄稼人。

2. "not at ease"，在城里，人、地生疏，感觉不自在，不像在家里或农场上那样随便、自如，因此，他们常聚在一起，"clung together for support"，心理上相互支持，避免一个人难堪；这种情况既真实又典型，不仅在美国是这样，各国的佃农差不多都是如此。

3. The women's clothes were not meant to be becoming but to wear well...

作为佃农的妇女穿衣服没有条件讲究，不求合身、得体，只求结实、禁穿。我们做汉英翻译时，表达这个意思可能倾向于寻找形容词表示，但作者用的是一个谓语动词结构，"to wear well"。

例句 12. With their heads almost touching, his father and Mr. Wilson study the difficulty. Wrenches and pliers pass back and forth between them with as much familiarity as if they owned their four hands in common.（p. 60）

💡 说明　克莱特斯（Cletus）父亲和威尔逊干活的农场相邻，如果克莱特斯父亲的农机出了问题，不启动，远处的威尔逊就会过来帮忙。

Wrenches and pliers pass back and forth between them with as much familiarity as if they owned their four hands in common.

这个部分写得好，两个人一起修理机器，手里的工具熟练地递过来递过去，好像他们共享四只手。作者以这样的方式表现他们配合默契。

这句话不以"They"而是以"Wrenches and pliers"做主语，意在行文简洁，也在突出扳、钳；还有"four hands in common"，读者看见的是扳、钳和四只手，一幅处于动态的画面，形象、生动。

例句 13. A gentleman doesn't have one set of manners for the house of a poor man and another for the house of someone with an income comparable to his own. He never enters the farmhouse without knocking. Even though it is legally his. And he remembers to wipe the spring mud off his shoes.（p. 62）

💡 说明　作家描写人物，少用抽象观念，多通过具体情节和鲜明形象来塑造，好作家都是这样。《红楼梦》人物多是通过情节塑造的，对人物的结论性概念多是研究者和理论家得出的。这段文字意在告诉读者"A gentleman"不势利，作者没有这样说，而是用事例说明之。这里的每句话都是叙说"A gentleman"如何地"不势利"，对待穷人和有钱人的态度没有厚薄之分。

作者第一句话的写法似乎与众不同，一般有可能说，他对待穷人和富人态度一样，或者说，他对待穷人和富人态度没有两样。作者一上来就说"A gentleman doesn't have..."，一个有个性的叙述方式。

例句 14. As Aunt Jenny is drawn toward the farm, so the hired man, Victor Jensen, feels the pull of town.（p. 67）

💡 说明 这是故事一个情节中的一句话，珍妮大婶（Aunt Jenny）要回农场，"is drawn toward the farm"，而维克多·詹森（Victor Jensen）则要进城，"feels the pull of town"。一个要回农场，一个要进城，在汉语，字面上的差异不大，英语用了两个完全不同的动词搭配，而又有相同的重读音节和相同的节奏，读起来好听。

例句 15. Though he had brothers he was on good terms with, the person he turned to for companionship or when he had something weighing on his mind was the overserious man on the neighboring farm. After twelve years he found it hard to believe there had ever been a time when he and Clarence weren't friends.（p. 72）

💡 说明 这两个句子较长，主句之外，有让步从句、定语从句和时间从句，较为复杂，但用词简单，行文自然，读来轻松，没有沉重、拗口之感。"Though he had brothers he was on good terms with"，这是一个带定语从句的让步从句，定语从句修饰"brothers"，连接紧密，犹如句子的自然延续。第二句 "... he found it hard to..."，这种句式在英语里常有，结合后面的成分翻译时，汉语也许另有表述方法。

作者的语言修养好，文字技巧高，能感受到这种写法从容不迫的语气。

翻译这段文字，可遵循原文语序，或做适当变通。将意思说清楚不是很难，但说得和原文一样轻松、自然，一气呵成，不是很容易。有兴趣者可试着将其译成轻松、自然、不拗口的汉语。

例句 16. Between these crises they lived like any other married couple. You could not have told from her voice as she said, "I'm about to put things on the table, Lloyd," or his voice as he said, "Pass the salt and pepper, please," that there was anything wrong. (p.76)

💡 **说明** 劳埃德·威尔逊和妻子之间感情有问题，但从日常言谈上听不出来。

英语句子有时谓语动词与宾语距离较远，但不论多远，英语句法结构总能显示句子各成分之间的关系。

这个句子谓语动词是 "told"，宾语是 "that" 引导的从句，其间有两个由介词 "from" 引导的较长状语结构，其中又有两个直接引语，也较复杂，但作者以其沉静的笔法把事情说得清清楚楚。

例句 17. She loved to stand and talk, and one listener was as good as another. "Stop me if I've told you this before, I don't want to repeat myself," she said, but there was no stopping her, or even getting a word in edgewise. (p. 90)

💡 **说明**

1. ... and one listener was as good as another...

老太太爱说话，对谁都爱说，不挑人。英语和汉语表达这个意思时可能各有不同说法，作者的这个说法好，词、句简单，意思清楚，听着感觉好。

2. ... or even getting a word in edgewise

《牛津高阶英汉双解词典》里有例，"(not) get a word in edgewise"，这似乎是个固定说法，意为说话太多而让别人插不上嘴，家常聊天时很有这样的人。这个 "edgewise" 很形象。原有 "侧身" 之意，指动作时也说 "edgeways"。

例句 18. To an outsider it seemed that Aunt Jenny was relegated to the position of waiting on them. Waiting on them was her whole pleasure, and she did not ask herself whether they valued her sufficiently. Or at all. Innocence is defined in dictionaries as freedom from guilt or sin, especially through lack of knowledge; purity of heart; blamelessness; guilelessness; artlessness; simplicity, etc. There is no aspect of the word that does not apply to her. (p. 96)

💡 **说明** 作者对"innocence"做了全面定义，不论是取自词典，或是作者的总结，意在用来形容珍妮大婶。最后的"There is no aspect of the word that does not apply to her"，概括了珍妮大婶的单纯，表现在各个方面的单纯。如果分别用这些词或短语来正面描写珍妮，文字就多了，而且啰嗦，作者很懂得文字的"简洁"之美。

翻译这个句子，或正说，或反说，都可以，译好了都好。

阅读威廉·麦克斯韦尔（William Maxwell）："Billie Dyer"

简介

　　麦克斯韦尔的散文《比利·戴尔》（"Billie Dyer"）发表于《纽约客》（*The New Yorker*，1989 年 5 月 15 日），后来收在他的小说集《比利·戴尔和其他故事》（*Billie Dyer and Other Stories*）里，有人这样评论麦克斯韦尔这本书的文字风格："William Maxwell's superb book of carefully honed stories, *Billie Dyer and Other Stories*, is a slim volume told in the same calm, wise voice as that of his novel, *So Long, See You Tomorrow*... I guess the best way to describe Maxwell's writing in this volume is quiet restraint, gently guiding the reader back and forth between past and present."

　　这篇文章回忆一个黑人男孩的童年、成长、学医，以及后来成为一位受人尊敬的医生的经历。

　　通过阅读这篇散文，我们感觉麦克斯韦尔是一个文学修养很深、语言功底很厚的作家，他的文笔给人留下难以磨灭的印象。

　　现选择其中一些片段供阅读，请留心他的叙事文字，阅读他的文字是一个语言赏鉴和审美的过程。

　　例句 1. If you were to draw a diagonal line down the state of Illinois from Chicago to St. Louis, the halfway point would be somewhere in Logan County.

The county seat is Lincoln, which prides itself on being the only place named for the Great Emancipator before he became President. Until the elm blight reduced it in a few months to nakedness, it was a pretty late-Victorian and turn-of-the-century town of twelve thousand inhabitants.

💡 **说明**　文章起始处，是作者用心比较多的地方。海明威说写小说要写好第一个句子。《白鲸》（*Moby Dick*）这本大书开头也很特殊，只用了三个词："Call me Ishmael"。这个句子却成了一个名句，引来学者对它进行研究。英国作家简·奥斯汀（Jane Austen）的《傲慢与偏见》（*Pride and Prejudice*）开头也是一个广为人知的句子"It is a truth universally acknowledged, that a single man in possession of a good fortune must be in want of a wife"。

此文的起始句也是一个好的开头，作者似乎是在地图上面向读者指点小城林肯（Lincoln）的位置，顺便说了两句话描述它的过去和现在，清楚且具吸引力。

其中有两个表达值得注意：

1. "which prides itself on..."，意思是"值得它自豪的是……"。

2. "reduced it... to nakedness"，"把……变得一片荒凉"，意思是说在短短几个月里因为树木的枯萎这个小城变得一片荒凉。

例句 2. The town of Lincoln was laid out in 1853, and for more than a decade only white people lived there. The first Negroes were brought from the South by soldiers returning from the Civil War. They were carried into town rolled in a blanket so they would not be seen. They stayed indoors during the daytime and waited until dark for a breath of fresh air.

💡 **说明**　美国南北战争结束后，返乡的士兵从南方带来黑人做奴隶。开始时，他们白天不许出屋，到了晚上才能出来透口气。

1. "The first..."，译成汉语可以说"第一批"（"第一批"有时指人或指货物）；北方常说"第一拨"，在这个上下文里，说"第一拨"比较自然。英语可以说"batch"或"group"，但这里的"The first"已经很好了。

2. 文中有几处以分词结构代替从句的地方，行文简洁，语义浓缩，有节奏感，如"by soldiers returning from the Civil War""They were carried into town rolled in a blanket"。

> **例句** 3. The men cleaned out stables and chicken houses, kept furnaces going in the wintertime, mowed lawns and raked leaves and did odd jobs. The women took in washing or cooked for some white family and from time to time carried home a bundle of clothes that had become shabby from wear or that the children of the family had outgrown.

💡 说明 这个段落里作者用了十来个动词，都是与相关动作最贴切、最简单的常用动词，未用一个副词来修饰，近乎白描。这和 E. B. 怀特所主张的"Avoid fancy words""Write with nouns and verbs"相一致。

1. "that had become shabby from wear"，这里的介词"from"表示"因为"或"由于"，"wear"是名词，这句话可以说，"把一捆穿旧的衣服抱回家"。

2. "that the children of the family had outgrown"，孩子长大了，衣服小了，不能穿了，这个意思用一个"outgrow"表达得这样清楚。《牛津高阶英汉双解词典》里有例句：

She's already outgrown her school uniform.　她长得连校服都不能穿了。

用简单方式表达复杂概念，这本身就是一种"美"，值得学习。

> **例句** 4. In 1853, Lincoln celebrated the hundredth anniversary of its founding with a pageant and a parade that outdid all other parades within living memory. The *Evening Courier* brought out a special edition largely devoted to old photographs and sketches of local figures, past and present, and the

recollections of elderly people. A committee came up with a list of the ten most distinguished men that the town had produced. One was a Negro, William Holmes Dyer... He was invited to attend the celebration, and did.

💡 **说明** 中国古典文论有"淡"之说，苏轼说："所贵乎枯淡者，谓其外枯而中膏，似淡而实美。"明代学者袁宏道说："凡物酿之得甘，灸之得苦，唯淡也不可造；不可造，是文之真性灵也。"以"淡"之观念阅读"Billie Dyer"，可以感受到作者写作时选词、造句讲究"简"，语气平和，但爱憎分明。看看此段文字里的"outdid"，意为"did better"；"largely devoted to"，在这个上下文里，意思是用很多版面登载老照片等；"past and present"，意思是当地人的素描（"sketches of local figures"）有在世的，也有过世的；特别是"He was invited to attend the celebration, and did"，这里的"and did"指"and he attended the celebration"。

他的这种写法可谓"简"，可谓"淡"，"似淡而实美"。

例句 5. I have been looking at an old photograph of six boys playing soldier. They are somewhere between ten and twelve years old. There are trees behind them and grass; it is somebody's back yard. Judging by their clothes... the photography was taken around 1900.

💡 **说明**

1. I have been looking at an old photograph of six boys playing soldier.

关于此处的动词"play"，英语词典说"to pretend to be or do sth for fun"（假装），并给出例句："Let's play pirates."（我们玩扮海盗）；"playing soldier"，分词短语做定语，相当于一个定语从句。

2. They are somewhere between ten and twelve years old.

此处的"somewhere"是副词，常和"around"或"between"连用，意思相当于"approximately"，这是这个词的一种常见用法，很有英语味道。

3. There are trees behind them and grass...

作者为什么这样说，而不是说"There are trees and grass behind them..."？也许这是作者在修辞上的考究。若将这两句话翻译出来，能感觉语气上的差别。

试比较："在我的后园，可以看见墙外有两株树，一株是枣树，还有一株也是枣树。"（鲁迅：《秋夜》）

鲁迅为什么这样说，而不是"在我的后园，可以看见墙外有两株枣树"？

作家的这种具有个性的表达方式，也是一种修辞方式，能在读者心中产生一种不同一般的效果。

例句 6. In Springfield, the feeling against slavery was strong; a runaway slave would be hidden sometimes for weeks until the owner who had traced him that far gave up and went home.

说明 比利·戴尔（Billie Dyer）的祖父阿伦·戴尔（Aaron Dyer）生来就是奴隶，直到 21 岁时才获得自由，然后他就来到斯普林菲尔德（Springfield）。这段文字说在斯普林菲尔德反抗奴隶制的情绪很强烈，所以成了奴隶们的逃亡之地。但逃亡到这里的奴隶仍然要隐藏几个星期的时间，直到追踪他们的奴隶主放弃为止。

作者多是平铺直叙地描述，少用习语，行文自然，看其字词的搭配、句子的结构与衔接，都写得好。如：

1. the feeling against slavery was strong

这个介词"against"表示"opposing"，用于表达某种社会情绪，例如"the feeling against hegemony""the fight against terrorism"等。

2. until the owner who had traced him that far gave up and went home

句中的"that far"指奴隶主追到斯普林菲尔德以后就放弃了，这个写法可仿效。

作家的语言与他们的信仰，即他们的审美倾向有关，好的作家都相信语言之"自然"美。

例句 7. Then Aaron Dyer would hitch up the horse and wagon he had been provided with, and at night the fugitive, covered with gunnysacks or an old horse blanket, would be driven along some winding wagon trail that led through the prairie. Clop, clop, clopty clop... Sometimes Aaron Dyer sang softly to himself. Uppermost in his mind, who can doubt, was the thought of a hand pulling back those gunnysacks to see what was under them.

说明　这段文字描写阿伦·戴尔帮助隐藏逃亡的奴隶时的心情。虽然有时嘴里哼着小调，但心里却是提心吊胆，生怕有人掀开遮盖逃亡奴隶的麻袋片，不但奴隶会被抓回，他也会没命了。

1. "hitch up the horse and wagon"，套上马车。

2. "Clop, clop, clopty clop"，马车在草原小路上行驶时发出的声音，这个描写能让我们感觉到马车的速度。描写声音的词汇比较麻烦，可通过阅读积累。

3. "Uppermost in his mind"，这个"Uppermost"可以做副词用，也可以做形容词用，在这个上下文里可译作"心里最害怕的是……"，一般情况下可译作"心中想得最多的是……"。

例句 8. Sitting in the window seat in the library I would look out and see Mr. Dyer coming up the driveway to the cellar door. If he saw me playing outside he would say "Evening," in a voice much lower than any white man's. His walk was slow, as if he were dragging an invisible heaviness after him. It did not occur to me that the heaviness was simply that he was old and tired.

说明　这里的"I"是指作者自己。

1. "Sitting ... I would look out and see..."，这个"look out and see"很自然，学习这个说法。

2. 第三句里的"dragging an invisible heaviness",戴尔(这里是指戴尔的父亲艾尔弗雷德·戴尔)老了累了,走路很吃力,用一个抽象名词"heaviness"写出一个形象,我们几乎能看见戴尔老人走路的样子。

例句 9. Like all old houses, it gave off sounds. The stairs creaked when there was no one on them, the fireplace chimneys sighed when the wind was from the east, and the sound, coming through the living-room floor, of coal being shoveled meant that Alfred Dyer was minding the furnace.

说明 这里描写的是作者自家的一栋老房子,处处漏风,处处作响。注意这里使用的几个动词,房子常常发出声响("it gave off sounds"),楼梯的响声("The stairs creaked"),火苗冲向壁炉烟囱发出的声音("the fireplace chimneys sighed")等,都是用最简单的方式来表达,作者不担心说得不充分、不透彻。相反,这样写更有想象的空间、玩味的余地,这种叙事风格体现在细节的描写上,如:

1. when there was no one on them

楼梯上没有人的时候,这里只用一个具有动词功能的"on"。

2. when the wind was from the east

刮东风的时候,也只是用了一个具有动词功能的"from"。

例句 10. Whoever it was that tried to worship where he wasn't wanted, it was not Alfred Dyer. He was for decades the superintendent of the African Methodist Episcopal Sunday school and led the choir. He knew the Bible so well, his daughter said, that on hearing any scriptural quotation he could instantly tell where it came from.

说明 Whoever it was that tried to worship where he wasn't wanted, it was not Alfred Dyer.

这是一种强调说法,若有谁要去不欢迎他的教堂做礼拜,是谁也不会是艾尔弗雷德·戴尔。

原文句子讽刺美国种族隔离，当时林肯地区的白人只在三个方面愿意和黑人共享：医生（因为那时没有黑人医生）、自来水和墓地。黑人不能到白人教堂去做礼拜，既然如此，艾尔弗雷德·戴尔是不会去的，他有这样的志气。

例句 11. Billie Dyer's mother was born in Sedalia, Missouri, the legal property of the wife of a general in the Union Army. Her father and mother ran away and were caught and returned, and General Smith put her father on the block and he was sold to someone in the South and never heard of again. When her children asked what the place where she was born was like, she told them she couldn't remember.

💡 说明　这段话值得注意的是作者连用了五个 "and"，使我们对他的叙事语气产生了一种感觉。他在批判美国奴隶制时，没有使用激烈的言辞，没有表现出激愤的情绪，而是用一种沉静的有节制的（"quiet restraint"）的文字慢慢道来，我们却可以感受到他对美国奴隶制的血泪控诉。

提到文中的连接词 "and"，我们想起金岳霖在他的《论翻译》中说过这样的话：

得一语言文字所表示的意义是比较容易的事，得一语言文字所表示的味是比较困难的事。洋人之中也许有很好的汉学家，然而得到中国文字底意味的，恐怕是非常之少。在中国学习英语的人非常之多，然而得到英文意味的人恐怕并不很多。有一位英国文学家说 "And the Lord said" 这几个字神妙到不可言状，可是，就我个人说，我就得不到这神妙的味。这还是就一种语言文字底味说。如果我们要译味，我们不但要得到一种语言文字底味，而且要得第二种语言文字底味才行。最简单的说法也许是说，要译味非习于双方最丰富的生活不行。习于双方最丰富生活的人也许不能译味，能译味的人一定是习于双方非常丰富的生活的人。

金岳霖在这段文字中说了两件事，一是"译味"不容易；二是译者需要生活体验。缺乏生活体验者说话往往带学生腔，有生活体验者说的话有味道。

麦克斯韦尔在文中使用的"and"值得咀嚼，他所使用的是沉静的文字，但他所抒发的是对奴隶制的愤懑之情，这是一种极高的文字境界。

这虽然只有几十个字，却写了一部黑人奴隶的血泪史，一部人间悲剧。几个平常动词再现无情的事实，没有形容词，没有副词，可能也没有任何形容词或副词能表现历史的残酷和作者的愤怒，这些都隐在文字的背后。麦克斯韦尔的这种写法帮助我们认识语言的"力量"和"美感"从哪里来。

例句 12. As I sorted out the conversation of the grown people in my effort to get a clearer idea of the way things were, I could not help picking up how they felt, along with how they said they felt.

💡 说明　这个句子稍长，叙述方式委婉，大概意思是这样的：

我尽力通过大人的谈话了解那时的情况是怎样的，我也不禁想弄清楚他们是怎样感觉的，以及他们说他们是怎样感觉的。

朗读一下，能体会到句中轻、重音节形成的起伏和节奏，行文如诗，颇具美感。

例句 13. For things that are not known—at least not anymore—and that there is now no way of finding out about, one has to fall back on imagination. This is not the same thing as the truth, but neither is it necessarily a falsehood.

💡 说明　对于那些不为人知的事情，至少不再为人所知，而且有些事情现在已经无法了解，人们只好依靠想象。想象毕竟不等于事实，然而，想象出来的事情未必就是虚假的。

作者思想深邃，其表达技巧颇含辨证与逻辑，虽只有两句话，但意思完整，不带片面性。很朴素的思维方式，有说服力，有感染力。

例句 14. He ran all the way home, to keep from getting wet. He threw open the front door and fought his way through drying laundry to get to the kitchen, where his mother was, and said, "Mama, I'm starving," and she gave him a piece of bread and butter to tide him over.

💡 说明　这段文字描写比利·戴尔小时候上学的情景，放学时正赶上下雨，别人家的孩子有雨衣雨鞋，比利只能冒雨往家里跑，直奔厨房跑去，因为他的母亲在那里。见了母亲第一句话是"妈妈，我饿死了"。

"she gave him a piece of bread and butter to tide him over"这句话理解起来没有困难，但如何译成恰当的汉语，值得思索。

例句 15. Saturday night his mother took the washtub down from its nail in the kitchen and made him stand in it while she poured soapy water over his head and scrubbed his back and arms. When she said, "Now that's what I call one clean boy!" he stepped out of the tub, his eyes still shut tight, and she threw a towel around him, and then it was Clarence's turn to have the inside of his ears dug at with a washrag.

💡 说明　母亲在厨房里给孩子洗澡，把穷人家孩子洗澡的情节写成真实的场面，这里的动词发挥了重要作用。"she poured soapy water over his head"，把肥皂水从头顶浇下去；"scrubbed his back and arms"，然后搓他的胳膊和后背；"she threw a towel around him"，洗完了扔一条毛巾披在他身上，这里用了一个"threw"。轮到克拉伦斯时，母亲用浴巾给他挖耳朵。作者把这个洗澡的情景写得生动活泼，这些情景主要是用生活中几个常用的动词创造出来的。学习过程中应多关注英语动词，这对文学作品的汉英翻译很重要。我们做翻译，单是句法正确远远不够，只有语言灵活、形象生动的作品读者才爱读。而"灵活"的语言和"生动"的形象是一个长期培养的功夫。

在非英语环境里学习英语，主要靠阅读，在阅读中体验英语表达方式的奥妙，读多了，自然会有所感悟。

例句 16. "You'll be bending over a washtub soon enough. Go to school and show that white woman you aren't the stupid person she takes you for."

说明　女儿玛丽不愿意上学，因为老师不喜欢黑人孩子，经常取笑她，说一些难听的话。她问母亲："为什么我不能留在家里帮你洗衣服熨衣服呢？"然后母亲说了上面的话。

母亲对自己的女儿说，孩子，别着急，你很快就会趴在木盆上给人家洗衣服的，而且要洗一辈子，悲惨的命运在等着你。此时我们能体会母亲的辛酸与愤怒。同时，她也在告诉孩子要跟这个白人老师抗争，反抗她的种族歧视。

我们能体会到作者对他描写的黑人具有同情心和同理心，他所组织的语言具有多么强大的力量。

例句 17. He fell asleep to the sound of his father's voice in the next room reading from the Bible... One night when he went to bed it was December 31, 1899, and when he woke up he was living in a new century.

说明　世纪交替之夜是一个不寻常的时刻，年轻人、年轻学子会欢呼跳跃，今夜无眠；但这个日子对于黑人孩子比利·戴尔而言，和往日一样，没有什么特别的意义。作者的笔触是那样的平淡、那样的冷静，没有感情色彩，但却含义深刻。

"He fell asleep to the sound of his father's voice in the next room reading from the Bible..."比利听着父亲在隔壁房间里读《圣经》的声音进入了梦乡，这个句子只有十几个词，但传达的信息很多，简洁的写法值得推敲。

例句 18. He had fought in the Civil War on the Union side, and been mustered out of the Army with the rank of Captain. Though he had no further military service, he was always spoken of as Captain Harts.

说明

1. "mustered out of the Army"，此处指退役，"muster out" 是一个固定说法，还有 "muster in"，表示应征入伍。

2. ... he was always spoken of as Captain Harts.

退役之后，人们总是称他哈茨上尉，这里的 "spoken of" 的用法值得学习。

例句 19. He was a member of the local bar association but applied himself energetically to many other things besides the practice of law.

说明　句中的 "He" 系指比利·戴尔的同学约翰·哈茨（John Harts）的父亲哈茨上尉（Captain Harts），他后来资助比利·戴尔学医。

这里的 "bar" 和 "law"，皆指哈茨上尉从军队退役后以律师为业。此句妙在前面有 "a member of the local bar association"，后面有 "besides the practice of law"。其实，没有后面这个部分，句子仍然完整，有了它，不但完整，而且完美。二者前后照应，不论意义或形式，都有平衡感。同一意思用两个不同方式表达，不觉重复，意在凸显 "他还做了很多其他事情"，且读起来节奏明快、爽朗。

例句 20. He said, "Mama, I don't feel good," and her hand flew to his forehead. Then she went and got the bottle of castor oil and a big spoon, and said, "Don't argue with me, just open your mouth." Lying in bed with a fever, he listened to the old mahogany wall clock. Tick... and then tock... and then tick... and then tock...

说明　"Tick... and then tock... and then tick... and then tock..."，写钟表

走动时的象声词，这个写法让我们感觉到它比正常速度慢了许多，慢速是由省略号 "..." 和重复使用的 "then" 表达出来的。写嘀嗒声的慢速实是表现比利·戴尔的心情，小孩子没有耐心躺在床上养病，感觉时间过得太慢。

此文中另一处描写马车拉奴隶逃跑时的声音，"Clop, clop, clopty clop"，这个声音听起来速度就很快，暗示奴隶逃跑时的心情。

作者在他的一部长篇小说 *So Long，See You Tomorrow* 里使用了同样的象声词表示钟表的声音：

The wall clock says seventeen minutes after two（tick/tock tick/tock）and the odor of bay rum lingers on the air.（p. 86）

通过声音表现心理，作者的写作技巧。

例句 21. The French people were friendly when he went into a shop or attempted to converse with them. He sat down on a park bench and children congregated around him. Soon they were sitting on his knees and, pointing, told him the French words for his eyes, nose, ears, and neat mustache.

📍 **说明** "一战"期间，比利·戴尔作为军医随美军驻扎在法国。这段文字写法国小孩在公园里与他亲近的情景。他们坐在他的膝上，用手指着告诉他，眼睛、鼻子、耳朵、胡子等用法语怎么说。

这段文字写出了孩子们的天真与活泼，他们对于一个美国黑人没有戒心，和他在一起感到开心。作者用平淡的文字写平常事，写出来的东西耐读，这是一种文字功夫。对一个文风成熟的作家这也许驾轻就熟、自然而然，但对我们英语学习者可能不是轻而易举的事情。多读一些这样的文字，仔细观察这种现象，并有所感悟。

麦克斯韦尔不论写什么事情，也不论怎么写，读者读起来都没有障碍；他总能用轻巧而自然的表达方式把事情写得很有趣味，很有魅力。

阅读布拉姆·斯托克（Bram Stoker）：
Dracula（片段）

[原文] Beyond the green swelling hills of the Mittel Land rose mighty slopes of forest up to the lofty steeps of the Carpathians themselves. Right and left of us they towered, with the afternoon sun falling upon them and bringing out all the glorious colours of this beautiful range, deep blue and purple in the shadows of the peaks, green and brown where grass and rock mingled, and an endless perspective of jagged rock and pointed crags, till these were themselves lost in the distance where the snowy peaks rose grandly. Here and there seemed mighty rifts in the mountains, through which, as the sun began to sink, we saw now and again the white gleam of falling water. One of my companions touched my arm as we swept round the base of a hill and opened up the lofty, snow-covered peak of a mountain, which seemed, as we wound on our serpentine way, to be right before us.（p. 14）

例句 1. Beyond the green swelling hills of the Mittel Land rose mighty slopes of forest up to the lofty steeps of the Carpathians themselves.

💡 说明　这句话描写了三个层次或三个高度的山景：首先是中部地区的小山丘，山丘后面是布满森林的山坡，森林一直延伸到高高耸起的陡峭的喀尔巴阡山脉，而这样一个具有多层次含义的句子只用了一个谓语动词 "rose" 搭配一个介词短语 "up to" 就把句子组织得严丝合缝，令人惊叹。这句话是一个以状语开头的倒装句，谓语动词 "rose" 之后是主语 "mighty slopes of forest"，"up to" 是接续 "rose" 的介词，将后面的 "the lofty steeps..." 联系起来形成一个完整的句子。

例句 2. Right and left of us they towered, with the afternoon sun falling upon them and bringing out all the glorious colours of this beautiful range, deep blue and purple in the shadows of the peaks, green and brown where grass and rock mingled...

💡 说明　这也是一个以状语开头的倒装句，主语 "they" 指山脉，"with" 短语引出两个分词结构，一个是 "afternoon sun falling upon them"，另一个是 "bringing out all the glorious colours"，紧接着便是描述颜色："deep blue and purple in the shadows of the peaks" "green and brown where grass and rock mingled..." 我们可以想象山峰阴影里的深蓝和紫色、草石丛中的绿色和褐色，而且这两个词组都各有五个重读音节，读起来能感觉到明显的节奏。

例句 3. Here and there seemed mighty rifts in the mountains...

这也是一个以状语开头的倒装句。

在英语写景的文字里，以状语开头的倒装句似乎很有表现力。

葛浩文（Howard Goldblatt）翻译《王阿嫂的死》："The Death of Wang Asao"

简介

　　葛浩文在印第安纳大学随柳无忌（20世纪30年代初任南开大学外文系主任）读博士期间研究萧红，所以，他翻译萧红作品比较早。他翻译的第一本小说是萧红的《呼兰河传》，后又相继翻译了她的短篇小说。萧红的语言有特色，她的叙事方式与众不同，感情真挚、催人泪下。我们选取葛浩文翻译的《王阿嫂的死》，研究他再现原文、处理句子的技巧，作为我们学习汉英翻译的借鉴。

译例1

▶ **原文**　秋天一来到，王阿嫂和别的村妇们都坐在茅檐下用麻绳把茄子穿成长串长串的，一直穿着。

▶ **译文**　Now that autumn had arrived she sat with the other village women under the overhanging rush roofs using lengths of hemp cord to make string after long string of egg-plants.

译例 2

▶ **原文** 她只是穿啊，穿啊，两只手像纺纱车一样，在旋转着穿……

▶ **译文** They were preoccupied with threading the fruit, their hands weaving back and forth like looms, making one string after another.

📍 **说明** 这两个句子都有循环往复的动作，第一句，"用麻绳把茄子穿成长串长串的，一直穿着"，第二句，"她只是穿啊，穿啊，两只手像纺纱车一样，在旋转着穿……"汉语的这种句式如何翻译是好，葛浩文这样处理：第一句，"... using lengths of hemp cord to make string after long string of egg-plants"；第二句，"... their hands weaving back and forth like looms, making one string after another"。

译文两个部分都采用英语分词结构，句子形式简洁，意义明了，与原文情景吻合，效果好。

美国作家麦克斯韦尔的长篇小说 *So Long, See You Tomorrow* 中也有一个类似的句子：

Cletus carried load after load of junk up the outside cellar stairs and on out to the alley.

译例 3

▶ **原文** 雾气像云烟一样蒙蔽了野花、小河、草屋，蒙蔽了一切声息，蒙蔽了远近的山冈。

▶ **译文** The wildflowers, tiny stream, and grass huts were obscured by a cloud-like layer of fog which obliterated all sound and even blotted out the surrounding hills, far and near.

📍 **说明** 原文连用三个"蒙蔽"，译文则用三个近义词，"obscured""obliterated""blotted out"。原文重复是为了强调，译文不重复

是为了 "diversity" "variety"，显示不同语言的不同修辞方式、不同文化里作者和译者对自己语言的不同感觉。

此外，原文一连用三个排比小句；译文用一个被动结构和一个从句，语义结构有了变化，但准确表达了原意。

译例 4

▶ **原文**　草叶和菜叶都蒙盖上灰白色的霜。山上黄了叶子的树，在等候太阳。太阳出来了，又走进朝霞去。野甸上的花花草草，在飘送着秋天零落凄迷的香气。

▶ **译文**　The grass and the leaves of plants were covered with a layer of gray-white frost. The yellow-leaved trees on the mountain were waiting for the morning sun, and when it appeared over the horizon, it gave rise to a rosy dawn. Flowers and grass in the wild pastureland gave off an aroma that was filled with the chill and desolation of autumn.

💡 **说明**　"太阳出来了，又走进朝霞去"，作者这样说，译者说 "it gave rise to a rosy dawn"，"to give rise to" 是固定短语，用 "a rosy dawn" 译 "朝霞" 是创造性翻译，译文属规范英语。这句译文的启示：翻译萧红作品中特殊表达方式，葛浩文使用规范英语，这与 E. B. 怀特要用规范英语写作的主张一致，值得借鉴。

最后一句 "……秋天零落凄迷的香气"，"香气" 的修饰成分都放在前面，译文则用一个后置的定语从句描述 "aroma"，读来自然天成。这种后置的定语从句使用很广泛，学会使这种表达方式是写好、译好英语句子的一个重要技巧。

译例 5

▶ **原文**　王阿嫂拉着小环，每天在太阳将出来的时候，到前村广场上给地主们流着汗；小环虽是七岁，她也学着给地主们流着小孩子的汗。

▶ **译文**　Just before sunrise each morning Wang Asao went out with Little Huan to the square of the front village to slave away for the landlord. Little Huan may have been seven years old, but she was already learning how to serve the landlord as a slave-child.

💡 **说明**　"给地主们流着汗"，译者没有选择"to work hard for the landlord"，或"to sweat for the landlord"，这两个说法不足以表达作者的情绪，而"to slave away for the landlord"更能表现作者对王阿嫂母女的同情心，后面的"as a slave-child"也照应了前面的说法。原文重复了"流着汗"，译文也重复了"slave"，译者考虑周到。

译例 6

▶ **原文**　山上的虫子在憔悴的野花间，叫着憔悴的声音啊。

▶ **译文**　The insects making their homes in the withered wildflowers set up a din that had a withered quality to it.

💡 **说明**　汉语"憔悴"主要描写人的面容；英语"withered"既可修饰植物，也可修饰人的面容，以及身体某个部位的状态。《新牛津英语词典》有另外解释：A. to cease to flourish or decline，如，programmes would wither away if they did not command local support; B. to wither away 也可形容（某种理论）cease to exist because no longer necessary; C. 作为及物动词使用时，也有使人难堪、难为情之类含义，如，his clipped tone withered Sylvester。但"withered"是否可用来修饰声音，是否可将"憔悴的声音"译成"withered din"？葛浩文没有这样译，而是将其译作"The insects...

set up a din that had a withered quality to it"，这个"withered quality"是一个好搭配，不仅符合英语表达习惯，也巧妙地表达了原文意思。而且，像原文重复"憔悴"一样，译文也相应重复了"withered"，内容与形式都和原文契合。

译例 7

▶ **原文**　现在春天过了，夏天过了……王阿嫂什么活计都做过，拔苗，插秧。

▶ **译文**　Spring had come and gone, summer had come and gone... Wang Asao had performed every type of work imaginable, including weeding the fields and planting rice shoots.

💡 **说明**　"春天过了，夏天过了"，在汉语，在萧红，都是很自然的表述方式；葛浩文译文用了"had come and gone"，"Spring had come and gone, summer had come and gone"，在英语，"come and go"习惯连用，这里也有时间"来"与"去"的轮回。其排比句式与汉语相同，朗读时可感觉到反复的"come and gone"的节奏，一种乐感。一些乐曲主题句有类似重复。

译例 8

▶ **原文**　太阳在东边放射着劳工的眼睛。满山的雾气退去，男人女人，在田庄上忙碌着。羊群和牛群在野甸子间，在山坡间，践踏并且寻食着秋天半憔悴的野花。

▶ **译文**　The eastern sun slanted directly into the workers' eyes. As the fog burned off, gradually exposing the surrounding hills, the men and women in the fields increased their work pace. Clusters of goats and oxen foraged among the wild grasses that were beginning to wither in the autumn frost in the pastureland and on the hillsides.

💡 **说明** "满山的雾气退去"，"As the fog burned off, gradually exposing the surrounding hills"，译者用一个分词结构变通原文句式，把"满山的"译成一个动态景象，译活了。第二句的"在野甸子间，在山坡间"，指"羊群""牛群"所在位置；译文里，"in the pastureland and on the hillsides"指"the wild grasses"所在位置，同时暗示了"羊群""牛群"的位置，这是用简洁手段所做的合理变通。

以上两个变通不仅合理，而且行文有美感。

译例9

▶ **原文** 五岁的小环，开始做个小流浪者了。从她贫苦的姑家，又转到更贫苦的姨家。

▶ **译文** So Little Huan had become a homeless waif at the age of five. She had lived for a while with some impoverished paternal relatives, then had been bundled off to some maternal relatives who were, if anything, even worse off.

💡 **说明** 原文的"转"，作者没有说是小环自己"转"，还是被"转"，无论如何，其意可能近似"换"，又"换"到更贫苦的姨家。译者将其译为"bundled off"，英语词典说，"to send sb somewhere quickly and not carefully"，或"to send sb away hurriedly or unceremoniously"。在这个语境下，这大约相当于汉语的"打发"，暗含实在无能为力的意思，只好让她离开。若从这个角度解读"转"字，译文"bundled off"是一个好选择。

关于"if anything"，《牛津高阶英汉双解词典》解释说，"used to express an opinion about sth"，或者是"shows a tentative opinion"，这个短语在英语里用得比较多，对事物表达一种不十分肯定的意见，但可使叙事语气连贯并缓和。

译例 10

▶ **原文**　王妹子坐在王阿嫂的身边，炕里蹲着小环，三个人寂寞着。

▶ **译文**　Sister Wang sat at Wang Asao's side while Little Huan squatted on the *kang*; a sense of loneliness gripped all three of them.

💡 **说明**　"寂寞着"，这里可以说是三人当时的一种状态，译文用了动宾结构，"a sense of loneliness gripped all three of them"，"寂寞"译作"a sense of loneliness"，意为一种孤寂感，孤独无助；而"gripped"使名词或形容词的"寂寞"产生了动词的功能。

别人也可能另有译法，但葛浩文要这样译。他是个强势译者；原文理解好，译文表达"无不及"。

阅读阿瑟·鲁宾逊（Arthur Robinson）："The Boy on the Train"

简介

这篇文章发表在《纽约客》（*The New Yorker*，1988 年 4 月 11 日），文章以幽默的语言和情节讲述父子关系和子女教育问题，此文语句的表达方式很新颖，很好的英语学习材料。

例句 1. In 1891, at the age of five, Lewis Barber Fletcher travelled alone from Jacksonville, Florida, to the little town Camden, thirty-one miles northwest of Utica, in upstate New York. Fifty years later, his wife, children, and friends heard about his trip for the first time when this item appeared on the editorial page of the *Utica Daily Press* under a standing head, "50 Years Ago Today in the Press": "Lewis B. Fletcher, 5, arrived in Utica yesterday on a New York Central train on his way to join his mother in Camden. He was travelling alone from Jacksonville, Florida."

💡 **说明** 这是故事开头的一段文字，两句话，传达了很多信息。文字平淡，行文平稳，却把事情发生的时间、地点、人物、情节等有序地交代得清清楚楚。

1891 年，5 岁的刘易斯·巴伯·弗莱彻（Lewis Barber Fletcher）从佛罗里达的杰克逊维尔（Jacksonville）独自坐火车来到纽约州北部位于尤蒂卡（Utica）西北方向 31 英里（约 50 千米）的卡姆登小镇（Camden）。

50 年后，《尤蒂卡日报》（*Utica Daily Press*）在社论版面上的保留栏目"50 年前今天的趣闻"重登了这一信息，弗莱彻的家人和朋友才知道有这回事。

信息的传递以及各种信息在文中位置的精心安排都体现了作者熟练的写作技巧。

例句 2. Edward went over the trip from time to time, adding details, trying to get inside the boy to experience his anxiety and despair and very likely his distrust of people on the train, whose brief, unctuous kindnesses betrayed their fear of ending up with him on their hands

💡 说明　弗莱彻的孩子们听到这个消息后经常以此为话题调侃他们的父亲，上面的文字是他的小儿子爱德华（Edward）想象他父亲小时候乘坐火车时的内心活动。

这是一段神奇的文字，不足 50 个词叙述了这么多思想活动，让我们见识了英语的奥妙和魅力。

1. ... to get inside the boy to experience his anxiety and despair...

深入这个孩子的内心感受他的焦虑和绝望。

2. ... whose brief, unctuous kindnesses betrayed their fear of ending up with him on their hands.

他们用简短语言所表达的并非真诚的善意暴露了他们的担心，担心最终可能摆脱不掉这个孩子。

第二个句子，把车上人们的微妙心理活动说透彻了。

例句 3. Dinnertime was lecture time. The speeches flowed right past both boys in a meaningless litany they knew by heart. Conversation at the table was on two levels: one, loud, between their parents, who were both slightly hard of hearing and left their hearing aids turned off to save the batteries, and the other among the children, who could carry on a protracted quarrel without their parents' knowledge until Sarah—it was usually Sarah, raised her voice to alert her parents that she was being picked on.

📍 **说明** 饭桌上乱象丛生，大家说话的声音在两个层次进行（"on two levels"），老人因为耳聋而大声喊，孩子们乘机在争吵，萨拉（Sarah）因为感到委屈大声向父母告状。作者把这个乱作一团的景象用通顺的文字梳理得井井有条，让人爱读。写作技巧展现文字魅力，值得揣摩。

1. "litany"，指父亲在饭桌上的说教，像念祷文一样的老生常谈。

2. "a protracted quarrel"，没完没了的争吵。

3. "without their parents' knowledge"，指父母因耳聋而听不见。

例句 4. Their father's attitude toward Howard grew harsher and he often predicted Howard would amount to nothing unless he changed. Howard, near tears, would fight back and was sometimes sent away from the table. Their mother, tears streaming down her face, would say their father was always picking on Howard. "I don't see why you can't leave him alone," she'd say.

"He thinks life's a joke. Well, it isn't, and it's time he learned it isn't. Believe me, I know what I'm talking about."

📍 **说明** 这是父亲在教育霍华德，说他以为生活是玩笑，他不小了，应该懂得生活不是玩笑。

1. Howard would amount to nothing...

"amount to" 相当于 "equal to"，"amount to nothing" 意思是 "没出息"，或 "一事无成"。

2. 一般宾语从句都用连接词 "that"，文中有几处没有用，连接词 "that" 有时可以不出现。

例句 5. Howard had a bagful of tricks with which to annoy his father.

At the table he'd pour himself milk, starting with the pitcher close to the glass, then moving it higher and higher until it was a couple of feet in the air, all the time being careful not to spill. His expression was one of intense concentration, as though he was performing some difficult but necessary task. It was a performance that Edward loved, partly because they both knew what was coming.

Their father would strike the table with the flat of his hand. "We're not going to have such goings on at our table," he'd say.

💡 **说明**　英美作家擅长描写动作，写得细致、准确而又生动，读起来如同欣赏真人表演一般。值得学习。

1. Howard had a bagful of tricks with which to annoy his father.

这个句子里的"with which..."引导的是一个带有不定式"to annoy..."的从句，这个形式实际上是一个短语，其功能相当于一个完整的从句"with which he could annoy his father"，简洁的表达方式，节奏也好。

2. His expression was one of intense concentration...

他的神情高度集中，似乎是在执行一件难度很大但又必须完成的任务。

3. ... partly because they both knew what was coming.

此句是说他们知道他们的父亲会大发雷霆，这是他们所期待的。

例句 6. Their mother was self-conscious about having to wear a hearing aid and did her hair so as to conceal it; one had to look closely to see the cord that emerged from her hair at the back of her head and disappeared into her dress. She didn't want anyone to know about the embarrassing gear she wore under her clothes.

💡 **说明**　母亲戴助听器觉得不自在，她用头发把它盖上，电线在脑后从头发里出来再用衣裳遮住，不想让人知道。

这种心理和这种动作本身并不复杂，但用英语写清楚不是很容易；正因为作家用简单行文写得清楚，所以读起来舒服，文字变成了艺术。

1. "self-conscious"，不自在，不自然，局促不安，后面多跟 "about"。

2. "gear"，这里指她所戴的助听器具。

例句 7. Edward—thin and small-boned—had more passive ways than Howard's of resisting his father. He was rarely hungry, and at dinner, invariably became nauseated half way through the meal. The nausea always came suddenly, usually when he had food in his mouth. He'd park it（a family expression）in a cheek and wait for the nausea to pass, meanwhile dangling his fork between two fingers and batting it between thumb and little finger, day-deaming.

💡 说明 有的文学作品强调趣味性和幽默感，表现在作家用语言创作的情节和形象。文中爱德华用两根手指夹住叉子，在拇指和小指之间晃来晃去，脸上一副 "day-dreaming" 的表情。作者用简单的表达方式创造的形象，读来有趣。

Edward... had more passive ways... of resisting his father.

爱德华对付他父亲的办法不是直面对抗，而是消极反抗，汉语有时也说 "蔫儿坏"，和 "passive ways" 的意思相近。

例句 8. ... and when there was nothing else to do he'd make notes for the lectures he'd someday give his sons on How to Get Ahead and Be Somebody. "You don't get anything in this life without working... You'd never get anywhere until you learn to apply yourselves... How do you suppose we got this nice home? Nobody handed it to us. I worked hard for everything we've got... If you don't develop some get-up-and-go, you'll never amount to anything or have anything."

💡 说明 这是父亲教育儿子们说的话，具有传统观念的父母教育孩子时总爱这样说，但孩子们年轻时听不进去，长大以后他们明白了，也晚了。

1. How to Get Ahead and Be Somebody

陆谷孙《英汉大词典》将"get ahead"解释为"获得成功"，将"somebody"解释为"重要人物，有名气的人"，并举例："the desire to be somebody，出人头地的欲望"。这个标题式的句子虽然很简单，但如何译成汉语，需要琢磨。

2. You'd never get anywhere until you learn to apply yourselves...

"get anywhere"，取得成功；"apply yourselves"，努力。这句话的意思是，除非你们努力奋斗，你们是不会成功的。

3. If you don't develop some get-up-and-go, you'll never amount to anything or have anything.

如果你们不努力进取，你们是不会有出息的。

这几个表达方式和用词虽然都很简单，但所表达的意思都很清楚，读者也可以感受到父母鼓励、鞭策儿女上进的恳切心情。

阅读吉尔伯特·海厄特（Gilbert Highet）: "The Mystery of Zen"

简介

吉尔伯特·海厄特（Gilbert Highet, 1906-1978），苏格兰人，古典文学家、文学评论家、诗人、作家，后赴美执教希腊文和拉丁文。这篇文章是他为德国青年哲学家奥根·赫尔利格（Eugen Herrigel）的《箭术中的禅》(*Zen in the Art of Archery*) 写的书评。奥根·赫尔利格"二战"前在日本东京大学任教，受当地文化影响，他对神秘主义（mysticism）产生兴趣，决定研究神秘的日本禅宗（Zen Buddhism）。赫尔利格在日本禅师指导下，经过六年亲身体验，不懈习练，终于学成，为总结他的经验，写了这本小册子。

这篇书评写得好，英语搭配之新颖、句子之清晰、行文之流畅皆达到很高境界，从中选几个段落学习、研究，意在提高我们的英语写作与翻译。

例句 1. It is well written, and translated into good English. It was delightfully short, and implied much more than it said.

💡 **说明** 这是书评作者对 *Zen in the Art of Archery* 文字的评价。

句中的 "delightfully short"，因为书的篇幅短小而内容丰富，读来让人感觉愉悦。"delightfully short" 是副词与形容词的搭配，在我们几十年的英语写作或翻译经验里，可能很少这样写过或这样译过。这两个词的搭配，英语作家写起来很随意，但若在现代汉语中找出相应的搭配比较困难，可能需要一个句子来表达。

词典里有一例，"a delightful book"，一本读起来让人感觉心情愉快的书，这是一个形容词和名词的搭配。

关于"and implied much more than it said"，书的含义比字面所说丰富得多，表达方式却如此简单。

例句 2. One day I took it off the shelf and read it again; this time it seemed even stranger than before and even more unforgettable. Now it began to cohere with other interests of mine.

说明　关于"cohere"，英语词典这样解释："to have a clear logical connection so that together they make a whole"，连贯起来，一致起来，使完整。

例句 3. Something I had read of the Japanese art of flower arrangement seemed to connect with it; and then, when I wrote an essay on the peculiar Japanese poems called *haiku*, other links began to grow.

说明　这里的"connect with it"是说插花和禅有联系，"grow"是说当作者写关于日本俳句的论文时，也和别的事情产生联想，这两个动词和前面提到的"cohere"，有内在联系。

例句 4. Herrigel knew that there were scarcely any books which did more than skirt the edge of the subject, and that the best of all books on Zen constantly emphasize that Zen can never be learned from books, can never be studied as we can study other disciplines such as logic or mathematics.

说明　作者赫尔利格知道，禅不能通过课本学到，也不能像学习逻辑、数学等科目那样学到。关于动词"skirt"，英语词典解释："to be or go around the edge of sth"。根据这个定义，"which did more than skirt the edge of the subject"是说，在所有写关于禅宗的书中，几乎没有一本能够深入探讨它的实质，所论不过都是禅宗的皮毛。

动词搭配"skirt the edge of..."用得好，可效仿。

例句 5. At once he met with confused refusals. His Japanese friends explained that he would gain nothing from trying to discuss Zen as a philosopher, that its theories could not be spread out for analysis by a detached mind, and in fact that the normal relationship of teacher and pupil simply did not exist within the sect, because the Zen master felt it useless to explain things stage by stage and to argue about the various possible interpretations of their doctrine.

💡 **说明** 当作者开始寻找禅宗老师时，他遭到拒绝。朋友们告诉他，以哲学家的身份讨论禅没有用处；局外人不能把禅的理论展开来进行分析；实际上，在禅宗里不存在那种常规的师生关系，因为禅宗老师认为有步骤地对其进行解释、对它的含义进行争论都是没有意义的。

读这段文字，下面几点值得关注：

1. 为什么他屡屡遭拒，日本朋友说出三个理由，用三个"that"引导的从句表示，"that... that... and in fact that..."，然后，又用"because..."进一步说明，这个框架决定了这段文字的连贯性（coherence）；第三个"that"之前加了"in fact"短语，作者说，在禅宗的活动里，实际上不存在师生关系，"in fact"的插入是为了强调这种特殊现象。至于它的位置，放在"that"之前最合适。这里有作者的感觉；或因"that"连续出现三次需要一点变化，声响上的一点变化，节奏上的一点缓冲，等等，读来似能感受到这种效果。

2. 文中有两个搭配，"confused refusals"和"detached mind"，前者包含因屡屡遭拒而迷惑不解。后者的意思比较微妙，翻译起来需斟酌；所谓

"detached mind"，指非寄身其中者，无法与之讨论禅的理论。英语是一个词组，汉译时可能需要做解释。

例句 6. He was not even allowed to aim at a target for the first four years. He had to begin by learning how to hold the bow and arrow, and then how to release the arrow; this took ages.

💡 说明　日本朋友告诉这位德国哲学家，研究日本禅宗最好的办法，也是唯一的途径，是通过学习一门能够体现禅宗的艺术。因为他自己善射击，于是他选择了一个教授射箭的禅宗大师做他的老师，这位老师同意接受他做自己的学生。但课程需要六年时间，开始老师只允许他学习如何拉弓持箭，甚至不允许他瞄准，拉弓这一个动作持续了四年之久。

例句 7. The Japanese hold the bow above the head, and then pull the hands apart to left and right until the left hand comes down to eye level and the right hand comes to rest above the right shoulder; then there is a pause, during which the bow is held at full stretch, with the tip of the three-foot arrow projecting only a few inches beyond the bow; after that, the bow is loosed.

💡 说明　日本人拉弓的姿势和西方的方式不同，这个段落里有不少关于日本箭术的术语，如：

1. "and then pull the hands apart to left and right"，向左右拉开两只手。

2. "the left hand comes down to eye level and the right hand comes to rest above the right shoulder"，左手降到眼睛高度，右手停在右肩上方，两个句子用了"comes"，一个是"comes down"，另一个是"comes to rest"，表示出手的下降过程。

3. "the bow is held at full stretch"，把弓拉满。

4. "with the tip of the three-foot arrow projecting only a few inches beyond the bow"，箭头露出弓弦只有几英寸。

例句 8. When Herrigel tried this, even without aiming, he found it was almost impossible. His hands trembled. His legs stiffened and grew cramped. His breathing became labored.

💡 说明　当这位德国人照着老师的要求去做时，才知道太困难了，于是他跟老师说，他学不了，想放弃。

1. "His hands trembled"，手发抖。

2. "His legs stiffened and grew cramped"，腿僵硬，甚至痉挛（抽筋）。

3. "His breathing became labored"，呼吸急促。

例句 9. It is because you are not breathing correctly. You must learn to breathe in a steady rhythm, keeping your lungs full most of the time, and drawing in one rapid inspiration with each stage of the process, as you grasp the bow, fit the arrow, raise the bow, draw, pause, and loose the shot.

💡 说明　他要放弃，老师指出，他的手抖腿抽筋，是因为呼吸不对，老师告诉他，呼吸时，节奏要稳、要匀，保持稳定的节奏，"a steady rhythm"，让肺里的空气充足，"keeping your lungs full"；这里的"inspiration"是指吸气，整个过程，每一个步骤都要快速吸一口气，比如握弓、上箭、举弓、拉箭、停顿、放箭等。

例句 10. "You must hold the drawn bowstring like a child holding a grown-up's finger. You know how firmly a child grips; and yet when it lets go, there is not the slightest jerk—because the child does not think of itself, it is not self-conscious, it does not say 'I will now let go and do something else,' it merely acts instinctively."

💡 说明　当赫尔利格进入射箭阶段时，日本禅师还告诉他手如何握弓，就像小孩抓着大人手指那样。当他松开手时，他并没有意识到什么，他不会说，"我现在要松开手去做别的事情啦"。他只是出于本能在做动作。

例句 11. That night, after a cup of tea and long meditation, he went into the archery hall, put on the lights at one end and left the target dark, with only a thin taper burning in front of it. Then, with habitual grace and precision, and that strange, almost sleepwalking, selfless confidence that is the heart of Zen, he shot two arrows into the darkness. Herrigel went out to collect them.

He found that the first had gone to the heart of the bull's eye, and that the second had actually hit the first arrow and splintered it. The Master showed no pride. He said, "Perhaps, with unconscious memory of the position of the target, I shot the first arrow; but the second arrow? *It* shot the second arrow, and *it* brought it to the center of the target."

💡 **说明**　赫尔利格只练持箭姿势就练了四年。现在禅师允许他开始练习射箭，但不允许他看靶子，因为禅师射箭时是不看靶子的，有时甚至是闭着眼睛。赫尔利格故意挑战说："你能把眼睛蒙上吗？"禅师接受挑战。

禅师射了两箭，第一支箭射中靶心，第二支箭射中第一支箭，而且将其劈开。禅师并没有因此而得意，他说，"我射中了第一箭"（"I shot the first arrow"），但关于第二箭，他说 "*It* shot the second arrow, and it brought it to the center of the target"，他没有说 "我" 射中了第二箭，他强调说是 "*It*"，这个 "*It*" 指什么，值得考虑。他也许是说，这是 "禅" 在起作用，功夫到了，射箭便有如神助。

这是一个让人难以置信的故事，这也许就是艺术领域的所谓 "出神入化"。赫尔利格用了六年时间修成正果。禅师的这种境界更是非一日之功。

这个故事的启示：有信仰，下真功夫，对艺术的追求可以达到一个境界；有信仰，下真功夫，读书、翻译也可以达到一个境界。

例句 12. The Zen artist sits down very calmly; examines his brush carefully; prepares his own ink; smooths out the paper on which he will work; falls into a profound silent ecstasy of contemplation—during which he does not think anxiously of various details, composition, brushwork, shades of tone, but rather attempts to become the vehicle through which the subject can express itself in painting; and then, very quickly and almost unconsciously, with sure effortless strokes, draws a picture containing the fewest and most effective lines. Most of the paper is left blank; only the essential is depicted, and that not completely. One long curving line will be enough to show a mountainside; seven streaks will become bamboos bending in the wind; and yet, though technically incomplete, such pictures are unforgettably clear. They show the heart of reality.

💡 **说明** 这是吉尔伯特·海厄特在为 *Zen in the Art of Archery* 写的书评 "The Mystery of Zen" 中的一段关于日本禅宗艺术家作画的描述，这段文字描写画家作画前如何进入状态的情景。"sits down very calmly" "falls into a profound silent ecstasy of contemplation"，作画前的准备；"examines his brush carefully; prepares his own ink; smoothes out the paper on which he will work" "Most of the paper is left blank" "One long curving line will be enough to show a mountainside; seven streaks will become bamboos bending in the wind..."，画家用最少的线条勾勒出山的边缘和几棵竹子，画面上有大面积的留白；"They show the heart of reality"，句中的"heart"指"the most important part of sth"（实质、要害），画以最简洁的方式显示现实的"实质"，这和我们传统国画的简笔画相似。

禅宗为具有中国特色的佛教宗派，传说于南北朝时期由菩提达摩传入中国，在中国得到发展，后传入日本，禅宗文化也影响了日本绘画风格。

版权声明

　　本书为学习英语和中英翻译的师生编写，经典例句撷取自原版英文著作及刊物，在此郑重声明对原作者和出版人的尊重和感谢。特在此提供南开大学出版社业务电话：022-23502505，原作者、出版人或其代理人可据此联系我社协商版权付费事宜。